LINCOLN CHRISTIAN COLLEGE AND SEMINARY

What some leaders are saying about *Hunkering Down:*

"I could hardly put this book down until I had finished reading it! Tom Summers, who has devoted his whole career to pastoral care teaching and ministry in the public mental health context, has written a unique combination of an autobiography and some of the historical efforts of clinical pastoral education (CPE). The story of CPE in such places as New York and Boston often has been told, but his informal writing style opens up a vivid southeastern narrative to add to CPE's story. Anyone who has been through CPE or who is contemplating entering it will find *Hunkering Down* both exciting and informing. For that matter, anyone involved in education more generally will find this book enlightening."

—Wayne E. Oates, Ph.D.*
Professor of Psychiatry Emeritus
University of Louisville

*Deceased (21 October 1999)

"The author has woven an intricate and fascinating story. It is a tapestry that brings together the threads of his own personal and professional life journey and a person-centered history of the most important innovation in pastoral care training in the twentieth century—the CPE movement. Like Anton Boisen, its grandfather, Tom Summers shares his struggles and crises, his learnings and growing from continually exploring his inner world—a world that causes him to identify with the image of the wounded healer. But this writer's inward journey is interwoven with his turning outward in courageous prophetic application of CPE principles to address social oppression, including homeless and severely mentally ill persons, racial minorities, gay and lesbian persons, Central America's poor, and oppression by the powerful war forces in our society. He affirms by his action and advocacy the conviction that the action-reflection model of CPE should include active justice ministry. His historical remembrances are particularly rich concerning the Southeast Region of the Association for Clinical Pastoral Education. But this is linked throughout with the continuing evolution of the national movement over four decades and the leading thinkers who influenced these developments. This is communicated by his right-brain use of images—like hunkering down, the Edisto River near his boyhood home, and the chicken egg business that he and his father generated. Readers will come away from this book enriched by countless insights from an insider in what he appropriately calls a 'priceless educational approach.' "

—Howard Clinebell, Ph.D.
Professor Emeritus
School of Theology at Claremont

"In reading *Hunkering Down*, I found Tom Summers sharing his strong pilgrimage from southern youth to ordained minister integrating themes of pastoral care in state mental hospitals to public ministry in the streets. I felt that I 'hunkered down' with him as he played in a river in childhood while later protesting its potential destruction; or walked as chaplain in a large state hospital while marching in the streets to support mentally ill individuals and their families living in the communities."

—Duane Parker, Ph.D.
Former Executive Director
Association for Clinical Pastoral Education

HUNKERING DOWN

HUNKERING DOWN
My Story in Four Decades of Clinical Pastoral Education

THOMAS A. SUMMERS

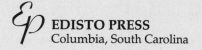

EDISTO PRESS
Columbia, South Carolina

HUNKERING DOWN

Copyright © 2000 by Thomas A. Summers
All rights reserved

No part of this book may be reproduced or transmitted in any form or by any means, electronical or mechanical, including photocopying, recording or by any information storage and retrieval system without written permission by the author, except in the case of brief quotations embodied in critical articles or reviews.

The opinions expressed in the book are solely those of the author and do not represent any particular agency or organization.

Library of Congress Catalog Number: 98-93130
ISBN: 0-9664713-0-X
First Printing

Grateful acknowledgment is made for permission to reproduce the following material: Excerpt from "Starting Over: New Beginning Points for Theology" by Robert McAfee Brown. Copyright © 1980 by Christian Century Foundation. Reprinted by permission from the 14 May 1980, issue of the *Christian Century*. Excerpt from *Harry Emerson Fosdick: Preacher, Pastor, Prophet* by Robert Moats Miller. Copyright © 1985 by Robert Moats Miller. Reprinted by permission of Oxford University Press. Excerpt from *A History of Psychiatry: From the Era of the Asylum to the Age of Prozac* by Edward Shorter. Copyright © 1997 by Edward Shorter. Reprinted by permission of John Wiley & Sons, Inc. Excerpt from "Little Gidding" in *FOUR QUARTETS*. Copyright © 1943 by T. S. Eliot and renewed 1971 by Esme Valerie Eliot. Reprinted by permission of Harcourt Brace & Company.

Scripture quotation is taken from the HOLY BIBLE, NEW INTERNATIONAL VERSION. Copyright ©1973, 1978, 1984 by International Bible Society.

Printed in the United States of America

This book is printed on recycled paper.

Publisher's Cataloging-in-Publication
(Provided by Quality Books, Inc.)

Summers, Thomas A.
    Hunkering down : my story in four decades of clinical pastoral education / Thomas A. Summers.
–1st Ed.
p. cm.
Includes bibliographical references and index.
LCCN : 98-93130
ISBN : 0-9664713-0-X

1. Summers, Thomas A. 2. Clinical pastoral education (Movement)—Biography. 3. Mental health clergy—United States—Biography.
4. Church work with the mentally ill—United States.
5. United Methodist Church (U.S.)—Clergy—Biography.
I. Title.

BV4012.3.S86 2000   259/42/092
[B]   QB199-1861

Published by: Edisto Press, 3017 Kilkee Circle, Columbia, SC 29223
Printed by: Wentworth Printing Corporation, West Columbia, SC

TO

Marilyn Boyd Summers

Whose natural beauty and honesty brightens
up the world around her

Rives Chalmers

A therapeutic guide who has walked with
others through stirring times

The Memory of Obert Kempson

A cherished mentor and remarkable representative
of the clinical pastoral movement

97509

Contents

Photograph sections begin following pages 42, 90, 138 and 186.

Acknowledgments

In developing this book over the past four years, I owe a profound debt of gratitude for many persons and resources. Without them, my writing efforts would have been in vain.

For instance, I am very appreciative for the more than thirty-five years that I had the good fortune of ministering and teaching within the context of the South Carolina Department of Mental Health. The opportunities afforded me by its officials and staff were both generous and enlivening.

My writing endeavor received much inspiration from the companionship with my wife—Marilyn Boyd Summers. Her interest and encouragement helped me to continue on with this particular project amidst the realities of many interruptions. I am grateful for her support in my using some evening, weekend, and holiday time to help bring the dream for this book finally to fruition.

As I developed the opening chapters related to my personal origins, I was visited time and again by a deep gratitude for the guiding hand and love so faithfully given to me long ago by my parents—Anabel and Carroll Summers—in those early, formative days. The past history of this nurturance has played its part in the present birthing of *Hunkering Down*. I have felt also the usual constancy in my brother Carroll's support and interest in my writing attempts over these recent years.

I would not have had the opportunity to make this kind of personalized exploration into the history of these four decades without the rich learning moments experienced throughout the years with clinical pastoral education students. Unforgettable are the hundreds of these persons with whom I have been privileged to journey as their pastoral supervisor. Their intentionality in learning and growing has enhanced both the personal and vocational sides of my life.

Gratefulness further is felt for some clinical pastoral colleagues and others in their providing helpful comments after reading some of my drafts. These readers included the following persons: Jerry Alexander, Howard Clinebell, Russell Davis, George Fitchett, Charles Hall, Jasper Keith, Wayne Oates, Duane Parker, Orlo Strunk, and Jo Clare Wilson.

Much time and interest were given to me by various persons in the locating of some of the photographs shown in the book. These persons, whose coordination with their archives and files offered invaluable assistance, are mentioned in a section at the back of the book. That portion also contains the acronyms, or codes, that are used as citations for the sources of various photographs.

Comforting guidance about the world of computers was given at some critical times by my sons, Mason and Boyd Summers. Without their rescues, I may not have been able to wade through some of the unclear technological waters.

Profound thankfulness is held for those many consumers of public mental health services and their families from whom I have further learned about the nature of courage. Through witnessing their sufferings and hopes, they have been the primary teachers in my seeking more awareness about the social justice dimensions of the mental illnesses.

I am grateful for receiving permission from these following sources for the utilization of further copyrighted materials in the book: HarperCollins Publishers for allowing me to use Thomas Moore's quotation from his 1992 *Care of the Soul* and the excerpt from Mary Catherine Bateson's *Peripheral Visions: Learning Along the Way* (1994); Judson Press for its 1971 book *In Human Presence— Hope* by James B. Ashbrook; Association of Professional Chaplains for *Cura Animarum's* 1992 article "Anton Boisen—A Memoir" by John L. Cedarleaf and *AMHC Forum's* 1979 article "Response to an Experience of Severe Stress in the Light of Ideas of Anton T. Boisen" by Carroll A. Wise; Myron C. Madden for the excerpt from his *The Power to Bless* that was published by Abingdon Press in

ACKNOWLEDGMENTS

1970; Spring Publications for its 1997 copyright of James Hillman's *Insearch: Psychology and Religion*; and Raymond J. Lawrence for my article "A Parable: The Land of Long Ago and Its Light" that appeared in *Underground Report* (1991).

Early discussions with Rhett Jackson, Orlo Strunk, Bert Goolsby, and Dean Dubois about publishing issues provided me with great assistance. Stephen Steiger, Joy Kirven, Sherrie Joyner, Jim Little, and others on the Wentworth Printing Corporation staff worked with me very helpfully in getting this book produced. Jason Williamson of Conterra Communications paved the way for putting information about *Hunkering Down* on the Internet. The book would not have come to life without the interest and skills of such persons.

Some of the proceeds of *Hunkering Down* will be contributed to the annual statewide Mental Illness Awareness Walk that is conducted in South Carolina. Also, a portion of the proceeds will be given to the Southeast Region of the Association for Clinical Pastoral Education for a mission project devoted to severely mentally ill persons and their families.

Preface

John* sat silently for three or four minutes in my office. The eyes of the pastoral student soon moistened, and his expressive face displayed warmly the dawning of a slight smile. I asked curiously, "John, what's going on with you?" He and I were in the opening phases of a final pastoral supervision conference. This terminal time represented his successful completion of an eleven-week, intensive program of clinical pastoral education (CPE) in a hospital setting. I had served as his CPE supervisor at this state mental hospital.

"I was just thinking about how scared I was on that first day you took me to my assigned ward," the second-year seminarian replied. "A lot's gone on with me since that day, hasn't it?"

"Indeed, it has," I remarked. "And how would you describe what's happened with you over these past several months, John?"

The former banker proceeded then to review with me various features of his pastoral learning experience in this hospital parish. As he discussed his new understandings, he lifted up especially the thread of how he had grown from an initial stance of much reticence with patients, student peers, staff members, and me. During these full-time weeks, he had traveled toward a newly discovered sense of risking himself more with other persons in the total setting.

"What was that transition like for you?" I asked.

"At first I didn't know how to give up my fear in approaching patients. For awhile I just remained on the sidelines," the slightly graying student said.

"I would imagine that you felt life a young kid who might have

*Fictitious names for pastoral students are used in the book. In most instances a designated name represents a blended composite of different students.

been frightened about getting out on a big playground for the first time," I pondered.

John asserted, "You've got it."

"How did all of that change for you?" I inquired.

"When I began to hang in there more closely with what's going on inside of me and with the feelings of the patients," he responded. "I started finding out that I could go ahead and get out there and not get hurt. I began to know—almost for the first time in my life—that I had what it took in me to be close to other folks."

"I believe you've begun to understand what can rest powerfully at the heart of your pastoral care for others," I suggested.

At this last weekly conference, other summarizing explorations were made about this CPE pilgrimage that we had had together. The dialogue moved us into various overlapping areas. They included the following matters: his greater grasp on listening skills, some blind spots that he yet struggled with in creating relationships, a fresh understanding about the nature of the mental illnesses, the theological theme of grace, and his growing comfortableness around authority figures. He mentioned also that an awareness about some of his own personal anxieties had brought to him a deepened appreciation for the more exaggerated suffering known by the patients.

"Do you remember in that first orientation week," he said eventually as a parting comment, "when one of the chaplaincy staff members mentioned that a 'study of the living human document' is what CPE is built on? Well, I think I've started opening up some old and new chapters in my own document." John then walked away and into the future of his ongoing pastoral evolution.

This above vignette represents but one small snapshot of pastoral learning among a countless and diverse number in clinical pastoral education's rich history. CPE, which was once known as "clinical training" or "clinical pastoral training" in earlier days, began seventy-five years ago in the United States as a reform movement in theological education. This person-centered venture in pastoral learning has possessed an amazing theological vitality. The enterprise values for the student the aspects of overall supervision, peer group life, behavioral science, the generating of writ-

ten materials, pastoral and personal formation, reading assignments, pastoral care relationships, and pastoral supervision of that
pastoral care. Reflection about the student's clinical experience is
the key ingredient in this pastoral growth model.

The contextual bases for CPE programming have been aligned
more prominently with hospitals and other health care systems.
However, some current interests also include community-based
programs and other site arrangements. Clergy, seminary students,
and other religious or lay representatives are the primary enrollees
in these accredited settings.

The Association for Clinical Pastoral Education (ACPE), the
nation's major certifying and accrediting organization in the field,
now includes more than 360 such centers in the United States, 130
seminary members, and 680 certified CPE supervisors. Program
models in the centers include both full-time and extended offerings. Some are yearlong in length while others are more abbreviated (see website: www.acpe.edu).

The organizational focus of my book deals mainly with ACPE.
However, the overall clinical pastoral education interests in the
United States include other professional associations that are
devoted to CPE, for example, the National Association of Catholic
Chaplains and the College of Pastoral Supervision and Psychotherapy. Additional CPE organizations and emphases are present
in some other countries throughout the world.

Much of CPE has transpired historically at an intersection in the
learning process where *integration* is sought. This interweaving
dynamic rests at the very core of the movement.

For instance, Anton Boisen attempted to break an opening in the
wall between the two areas of religion and medicine by founding
CPE in the middle part of the 1920s. Also, the two words in the
main title of Charles Hall's book *Head and Heart* symbolize an
enduring CPE devotion to the meshing of both the conceptual and
the pastoral. Furthermore, pastoral supervision with students,
similar to my educational relationship as described with John,
intends to make joined connections between such poles as person
and role, theory and practice, or theology and behavioral science.

In abiding with this CPE tradition of integration, my book has interest in exploring both my own personal story in four decades as a CPE participant and also various developments of history in CPE. Hence, this project places the two at a junction point. It is there that my personal narrative crisscrosses with the history of CPE's ongoing saga. *Hunkering Down* attempts to offer an anatomy of those years.

This method of examining CPE's history is buttressed by my own subjective process. For instance, I share some of what I have done, witnessed, read, heard, and written about on this forty-year vocational trip. Other persons undertaking a similar recounting of their own stories naturally would report on some very different scenes and individuals. After all, it was once said that there is properly no history, only biography. (Ralph Waldo Emerson). Because of its informal tones, I have chosen to use in the book the more familiar first names of many persons rather than their more formal first names.

Furthermore, a strong motif in the book is shown in the gradual evolvement of the relationship between my CPE activities and social justice. The early roots of this particular thread can be found in chapter 1, but a fuller flowering is located in the final two chapters.

A characteristic of the writing style in the project is influenced by my favorite metaphor *hunkering down*. As can be seen, this particular symbol is used as the main title of the book. My earliest discovery of the term was during a moment in my initial years of ministry, and this event is described in chapter 4.

A literal meaning of hunkering down infers a crouching stance close to the ground. I am not encouraging the reader to view ministry as being offered primarily from a squatting position! Instead, I make metaphorical use of the imagery to suggest that interpersonal nurture can be derived from close moments of restful, informal, and natural conversation. In a pastoral sense, I utilize hunkering down's supportive and relational qualities. This is in stark contrast to the way that the expression occasionally is employed in today's culture indicating a defensive posture in warfare or sports.

My desire is that the reader might sense my figuratively hunkering down as I describe my journey through these CPE years. In knitting my own personal chronicle with that of various CPE developments, there are seven major themes that broadly shape the selection of my material and remembrances. They represent the central passageways through which the narrative flows.

For instance, I prize the effects of one's early origins on a progressing personal development throughout life. Likewise, one's vocation of ministry is impacted strongly by these early absorbed influences. Due to the importance of the formative years, the book spends considerable time in chapter 1 exploring some of these features. Hence, I delve into some of the background from which I oozed out of South Carolina life—not far from the coastal Lowcountry. Since the CPE tradition highly regards a person's daybreaking years, I feel assured also that my ancestral and cultural roots have provided profound contributions to the ways that I have experienced CPE and its other participants. Viewing late adolescence and young adulthood as having pivotal moments for ongoing personal/pastoral unfoldment, chapter 2 takes a considerable look at my college years. Readers are encouraged to meander through their own unique developmental stages at the same time as mine emerge throughout the entire book.

Another overall consideration is that of my positioning a certain amount of my CPE memoirs within the context of regional matters. The earliest regional gateway to my clinical pastoral career was a southeastern one, and it initially was located in the older Council for Clinical Training. The Council later was merged with other training groups into a newly organized Association for Clinical Pastoral Education in 1967.

Although the Southeast Region of ACPE has continued to be a cornerstone for me, I have cherished the opportunities of participating in many other venues of clinical pastoral education and pastoral activity. This combination of the regional and other much broader reaches shows up in my writing.

A further widely threaded characteristic of the material is represented by its interest in an ambience of various time periods. I have fondness for mentioning sundry dates and events, but an equal thrust points toward the ordinary atmosphere surrounding history.

Therefore, the reader is warned that there will be an encountering of various earthshaking descriptions that are directed to an environmental flavor. These include the raising of chickens, the price of a hospital cafeteria meal in the early 1960s, an old car, a questionable diagnostic tool offered by a prophetic theologian from the mountains, shag dancing, and apple heads. I intend these mundane references and a scattering of remembered conversations to be helpful as I add commonplace hues and cultural color to my personalized CPE review. As well, I introduce occasional snippets of material from letters, names of songs, or dreams in hopes that these items further enlarge the quilted composition of the interests found so far in my life's story.

The photographs exhibited in *Hunkering Down* also purpose to offer an ambient mixture of some highly valued persons. They have impacted significantly the complexion of my personal and professional journey. These include not only CPE persons whom I have known or heard about but also influential individuals from the background of my personal history. One such beloved person was an African-American mothering figure. Therefore, the CPE inheritance from Anton Boisen has been no more powerful for me vocationally than the riches placed into my heart from this particular woman or, for that matter, from a mentoring farmer or athletic godfather once known. The chronological position of these pictures indicates this ongoing atmospheric blend of my personal story with that of CPE's historical flow. Also, the book's alphabetized back index portrays this varied tapestry of influences in my life. For instance, one such block of items contains John Billinsky (a powerful CPE figure several decades ago), Rhoadus Blakely (a rural parishioner), Doc Blanchard (an All-American football player from the 1940s), blessing (a key theological and supervisory theme), body image (a significant issue in psychology), and Anton Boisen (the founder of CPE).

An additional area of broad concern is reflected in the taking of note about critical eras that have transpired in the bridging of the years. Much of my own CPE voyage has been touched by the sweep of particular movements and time periods. Examples of these various epochs include the long season of enormous state mental hospitals, the so-called human potential movement, and the challenges of today's postmodern needs in pastoral care.

Certain historical periods, such as the above, have influenced greatly the stage on which the drama of CPE has been performed. It remains yet to be seen, for instance, how the tides of managed care, privatization, and large mergers in health care systems will affect the next decades of CPE's enriching person-centered approach to theological education.

Furthermore, another feature in the book is that of its pervasive inclusion of memories about various persons met in my travels along the CPE highway. Luckily, life can bring to us friends and colleagues. They enrich us as persons and help shape the vocational sides of our beings. Hence, events peopled by such folks as Obert Kempson, Armen Jorjorian, and Jap Keith are recounted. My CPE life would be deprived if had not met the likes of a delightful Joe Woodson, a caring Wayne Oates, a vivacious Urias Beverly, and many other unforgettable persons.

An added theme is that the project places periodically into its material references and interpretations about Anton Boisen. This is due to the lasting appreciation that I have had for this founder's thoroughgoing influence on the history of the overall clinical pastoral movement.* In one way or another, any participant in CPE has been touched by the bequeathed contributions from this complex progenitor. Beyond my use of Boisen's conceptual perspectives, I also draw occasionally from the resources of other valued theorists. Some of these include Karen Horney, Harry Stack Sullivan, Thomas Malone, William Kilpatrick, Gordon Allport, and Daniel Levinson.

A further emphasis found in *Hunkering Down* is its including now and then some developed assumptions and methods derived from my own practice of pastoral supervision. Illustrations of these appear particularly in chapters 8 and 9. Considered there are such topics as a playground assessment, story, the competency drive, severe mental illness, and ministry in social care.

---

*The term *clinical pastoral movement* is occasionally used in the book to denote the more comprehensive historical thrust that grew from Boisen's aiding the interface of theology and pastoral care with the clinical dimension. The CPE movement is one aspect of this larger clinical pastoral enterprise as is also pastoral counseling and clinical chaplaincy.

As I locate this personal story at a union with the broader historical CPE context, I have gratitude for information from various literary resources. Invaluable perspectives from a historical standpoint have been gained from Edward Thornton's *Professional Education for Ministry*, Allison Stokes's *Ministry After Freud*, and Charles Hall's *Head and Heart*. Also helpful have been the insights from *A History of Pastoral Care in America* by Brooks Holifield and Boisen's own *Out of the Depths*. I have rummaged also through my own files and memory in order to capture further bits of embedded history.

However, my project endeavors not to duplicate another comprehensive work about CPE history such as that found in books already excellently crafted and extensively researched by the above authors and others. Rather, my main effort is in the sharing of just one individual's personally oriented sojourn through this fascinating CPE initiative. The Seventy-fifth Anniversary of the CPE undertaking is an important aspect of the millennial year 2000. It is my hope that, in being aware of that particular milestone, this book might possess potential value in adding some historical reflections.

Thus, I now invite the reader to hunker down with me (no crouching required) as I attempt to tell my tale about CPE.

Chapter 1

---ᖡᖡᖡ---

Embraced by a Family
and a River, 1934-1952

My overall story in clinical pastoral education starts naturally with my early personal beginnings. As Thomas Moore's *Care of the Soul* suggests: "The family is to the individual what the origins of human life are to the race. Its history provides a matrix of images by which a person is saturated all through adult life."[1]

I can vouch for Moore's contention, because the legacy of my family history and its cultural and geographical placement have remained within me as almost daily influences. The lore about ancestors even provides a rich fiber to my own identity both as a person and a minister.

This chapter intends to explore such personal origins. Also the historical birth of clinical pastoral education is described. A third focus offers an analysis of the influence that my primary personal roots have had on my participation in the CPE movement.

NEAR THE EDISTO

In being stitched firmly to the fabric of the Deep South, the quaint town had inherited the stark social evils of racial segregation. In the scorching heat of the summer months, shoes were strangers to most of its young townspeople. Heat would ripple into a wavy blur above oven-hot county asphalt roads. Much family life in the late afternoons of those sultry days was spent in rocking chairs on front or side porches of homes.

The flowing, dark currents of the Edisto River cut a sensuous swath through the western side of the community. The fertile soil of the geography was known for its abundancy of pecans, cotton, soybeans, and corn. As background music to such vegetative fullness, the melodies of crickets were chirped throughout expansive fields.

It was in this setting that I was born and raised in the county seat town of Orangeburg. The slow-paced municipality—a habitat where expected politeness reigned as a social lubricant—was located in the lower part of South Carolina. The town contained more than twelve thousand citizens—most of whom delivered their colorful words in a slow-motioned southern drawl. Kudzu was sculpted curvaceously across ditches, telephone poles, and old billboards like a sea of smooth greenness.

The year of my arrival into the small, white, wooden-framed home of Anabel and Carroll Summers was 1934. The house nestled in a medium-sized neighborhood less than a mile from the flow of the Edisto. Only two years before my birth, Franklin D. Roosevelt had entered into what was to become a twelve-year presidency of the United States.

A Father under the Bed

Family legend indicates that my father was missing from my nativity scene in the home's back bedroom. A tale has it that an elderly family doctor requested adamantly that, while I was being born, my father stay situated in another part of the house. The reason for this decision was that, when my brother had made his appearance in the world three years earlier, the physician apparently had called out for assistance from the anxiously waiting father.

This unusually calm man dashed from the living room into the bedroom, saw what was going on, and fell to the floor in a faint. The frantic doctor quickly decided to shove him under the bed so that my mother, already laboring enough, would not become too distressed by the sight of her unconscious mate. This was reason enough to keep him later from my birth arena.

No Night Baseball Yet

When I came to life, the nation barely was beginning to creep out of the Great Depression. My father had made a trip two years earlier to Washington for the witnessing of President Roosevelt's inauguration. However, he was forced to come home quickly, because he received a troublesome cable informing him that the Orangeburg banks were shutting down.

In terms of the social climate in that era, I was born into privilege—an entry made as a Caucasian, a male, and one later able to acquire an education. A time for more equitable social power and justice had not yet arrived for African Americans nor females.

Night baseball had not yet made its way into the major leagues. An invincible Joe DiMaggio, the graceful "Yankee Clipper," had not yet gotten there either. He was still toiling in the minors. In Germany, democracy was plummeting as Adolf Hitler's depraved assault on human dignity was rising.

Fifty miles north of Orangeburg was the site of a large state mental hospital in the capital city of Columbia. A hospital chaplaincy career had begun there a year before my birth by a young, blonde-haired Lutheran pastor by the name of Obert Kempson. Our paths would cross fortunately some twenty-five years in the future. This place and person would play a vital role in my later ministerial development.

Ancestral Clay and Moss

My father, who was born and raised in Orangeburg, had started a law practice during 1926 in his hometown. He had graduated earlier from Trinity College (now Duke University) and studied law at the University of South Carolina. This steady man, known for his impartation of wisdom and guidance to relatives and others, met Anabel Hill soon after starting his legal career. She was a dark-haired, attractive woman; and she had arrived in Orangeburg immediately after her Coker College graduation in order to begin work as a secretary with the county highway department.

Her boarding was in a house that was next to my father's original home. She sparkled with energy and beauty; he exuded patience and a pervasive cheerfulness. It did not take long for them to meet and fall in love. A marriage in the Upper State was held at her family's old, two-storied home in Laurens County.

Her origins were from the environment of rolling hills, pasturelands, and red clay; his were those of the picturesque flatlands. The latter featured hushed swamps, gray moss, croaking frogs, and the occasional sight of quail fluttering through fields.

My father's ancestral background included characteristics of classical education, the legal profession, and appreciation for the recounting of family stories. My mother's was influenced by farming, mercantile store ownership, and a similar fondness for genealogical tales.

The antecedents of my father came to America from Chester, England, in 1760. Their migration may have been due partly to religious divisiveness at that time in some parts of England, because they were listed in records as being "protestant immigrants." The small clan arrived in the new country probably near Charleston, South Carolina.

The group went deeper into the territory and made its trek, it is assumed, near or up the Edisto River. This particular river, which the reader will see as an important constant in my life's ongoing story, was named after a Native American tribe. Its refreshing waters empty into the Atlantic Ocean approximately forty miles below Charleston. Going upstream for almost sixty miles, the little Summers band settled in nearby lands—less than fifteen miles from the area that is now known as Orangeburg.

This town had begun being settled thirty years earlier. It was named for the Prince of Orange, a son-in-law of King George II of England. The community was laid out at the intersection of two major Native American paths. Some of my ancestors moved eventually into the little town.

My direct paternal South Carolina lineage goes back to an early patriarchal figure killed in the Revolutionary War by Tory snipers. He had joined the military forces of General Francis Marion, the "Swamp Fox." The enemy soldiers discovered my ancestor on the porch of his home in the lowlands while he was visiting his family. The young father had come back home on a brief furlough to visit the family before the impending birth of a new son. Supplies also were to be replenished before planning a return to the battlefront. One piece of family lore is that the family buried him where he had fallen. A tree was cut down and hollowed out for the preparation of his coffin.

The maternal Hill forebears traveled down from either Maryland or Virginia into upper South Carolina. They were Irish in origin. My mother's father grew up on what was once a prosperous farm in Newberry County. The family's fortunes, however, were decimated by the time that he was a child due to the ravaging of the countryside by the Civil War. Nevertheless, my grandfather retained a love for horses, industrious work, and fox hunting. As a young man, he moved to a small railroad town in Laurens County named Cross Hill. There he began clerking at a general store. In due time he possessed his own in addition to acquiring a sizeable amount of land for farming.

Cross Hill, which is one hundred miles north of Orangeburg, offered me the gift of many enjoyable boyhood days. These experiences included rambling through fields and deep woods, the nurture of family gatherings at Christmas and other times of the year, and riding with my prized grandfather in his Model-A Ford. My grandfather, Archie Mason Hill, affectionately was called Papa. He was short and had a gray mustache.

In contrast, not many pleasant memories remain about a persistently angry hog that roamed in Papa's thistle-covered backyard. The burly and squealing sow, even in old age, would continue chasing me in an attempt to knock me down as I made hasty dashes to an outhouse—a locale for which I at times had much strained yearning.

Papa could not hear well, so I had to holler loudly close to his ears. When he took me fishing with him on steamy summer days, we often concluded our outings by stripping off clothes and delightfully jumping into the partially cool water of a lake. Cold baths on Saturdays were taken with the pouring of well-drawn water over me in an outdoor tin tub. In his middle eighties, he died when I was fourteen. A funeral service was held in his home. A three-person choir from the small town's little Baptist church sang on a stairwell the familiar hymn, "The Old Rugged Cross." My heart would intensely miss him.

THE DAWNING OF CPE

Probably few, if anyone, in the tranquil sites of Orangeburg and Cross Hill knew about the birthing of clinical pastoral education. Its genesis in the 1920s took place in the northeastern section of the United States—a far different setting from that of southern clay and moss.

Anton Boisen and Richard Cabot

The initiation of CPE took place around the formative labors of a highly sensitive, complex, and introspective Congregational minister—Anton Boisen (1876-1965). His family was centered educationally and professionally within academic life at the University of Indiana. During his years of growing up there, he was familiar with extreme shyness and moments of some emotional distress.

Boisen's later clinical pastoral strivings emanated remarkably from the courageous opportunities that he had made from a profound 1920 mental breakdown. Recovering from the horrors of this psychosis and hospitalization in Massachusetts, he became quite focused with a passion for removing barriers that may have separated medicine, psychology, and religion. One writer describes Boisen's theology as an interesting amalgam of moralism, liberalism, mysticism, and empiricism.[2] He brought to his devoted project a strong element of research.

His efforts were assisted greatly by a well-known physician— the Harvard professor Richard Cabot. Even though Cabot's formidable organic views were in disagreement with Boisen's strong psychological and theological perspectives related to mental illness, Cabot facilitated Boisen's receiving employment as the hospital chaplain at Worcester State Hospital near Boston. In those days there were hardly any clergy functioning in such a capacity. This eminent physician-humanitarian had already created for his own medical education approach a case study method for examining an individual's illness. Boisen adapted this model to his own subsequent teaching with theological students.

Cabot spearheaded an interest for clinical pastoral training; he sometimes used the term a *clinical theology*. Cabot himself already had begun teaching courses in social ethics at Harvard. The versatile professor desired to throw open windows and allow a narrow medical atmosphere to be influenced by the educational breezes of healthful contributions from the outside world. Boisen once wrote that, without Cabot's fervid support, the CPE movement "could hardly have gotten underway."[3]

The Launching Pad for CPE

Not only were the pathways of Anabel Hill and Carroll Summers beginning to draw closer in South Carolina but also a momentous happening in theological education had already occurred about that same time in the summer of 1925. It was then that Boisen placed four theological students in clinical training at the Worcester hospital. A published indication about CPE's advent was seen that year in Cabot's famous article, "A Plea for a Clinical Year in the Course of Theological Study."

William Keller, an Episcopal physician in Cincinnati, several years earlier already had introduced a training format to seminarians. This activity was slanted in the direction of involvement with social agencies. Keller's work, however, has been generally remembered as a first step *toward* CPE; Boisen's 1925 program has gained the historical prominence as CPE's genesis. Chapter 9 includes further amplification about Keller's significant legacy to CPE's history.

The students in Boisen's early programs functioned during the day as recreational personnel and ward attendants with the mentally ill patients. At night they held their case study and research seminars with Boisen. Sometimes medical staff representatives were present. In these conferences Boisen examined the critical causations of patients' illnesses through the case materials. After the first five years, the number of enrolled students in Boisen's program had risen cumulatively to more than forty. Some of the former students by then had established their own clinical training programs in hospitals and clinics. In a rather short period of time, a new and vivacious movement in theological education had sprung to life.

Throughout his career Boisen's continuing research approach was central in his clinical training efforts—those particularly related to the religious and psychological study of schizophrenia. Further, he did not neglect a sociological interest. However, the new movement would not ultimately be restricted to merely Boisen's preferences and methods.

Cultural Influences

The success of Boisen's clinical training in the 1920s was assisted by some of the prevailing cultural influences in that particular era. For instance, a preparative Emmanuel movement in the northeast represented one such beneficial resource. The developed Emmanuel clinics in some mainline Christian congregations were emphasizing at that time a collaboration between medicine and religion. This was prominently so in reference to a psychotherapeutic healing ministry. Boisen himself had received pastoral psychotherapy from Reverend Elwood Worcester—rector of the Emmanuel Episcopal Church in Boston and the recognized founder of the Emmanuel movement. Incidentally, Richard Cabot was a strong supporter of Reverend Worcester and the Emmanuel outreach.

Furthermore, Boisen's pioneering work was fortified partly by an excitement over the newly found area of psychodynamics. Sigmund Freud's groundbreaking concepts about the unconscious became instrumental in fueling the nation's growing fascination with psychology.

Other surrounding factors that enabled Boisen's efforts in initiating CPE included the following dimensions: William James's enunciation of the religious significance in psychology; John Dewey's progressive views on education with their process-orientation to learning; and a Protestant liberalism that inclined toward both the features of induction and a more immanental—rather than mainly a transcendental—view of God.[4]

The vigorous mixture of these above elements had a major impact in readying the soil into which CPE was planted.

The Study of Living Human Documents

Many CPE historians accent the high priority that Boisen placed on the authority of personal experience. His devotion to this experientialism (see chapter 6's section on "CPE and Experiential Psychotherapy") was wrought not only from the significance that he saw in his own personal breakdowns but also from the many reviews of patients' mental illnesses. He called the examination of these highly personal experiences in persons as the "study of living human documents." This classic phrase has threaded its way throughout the annals of the CPE tradition. For instance, John— the supervised student described in the book's preface—had begun entering more profoundly the authority of his own life's journey. He had started reading, as it were, the pages of his own unique human document with greater acuity.

Boisen was not actually that enraptured with wanting to ignite a movement. He had little desire of replacing anything substantially in theological education. Rather, his main motive was that of forming a method. He hungered to make a systematic search through persons' mental travails from a theological view. Such ripened themes as sin and salvation attracted him in this particular inquiry. No abstract theological study captured this creative man's interest. Instead, he wished to read actual chapters from human life documents through the intersecting lens of theology and psychology.

(Taking rise from the background of these aforementioned CPE historical origins of the 1920s, today's CPE endeavors have evolved into a variety of structural forms. For instance, a completed CPE unit for a student currently amounts to at least four hundred hours of pastoral care visits, peer group seminars, individual pastoral supervision, lectures, staff meetings with other professionals, conducting worship services, developing written materials, readings, and other educational activities. The students are assigned to a designated pastoral role. The predominant context currently for much of this clinical training happens to be in general hospitals. Today at least six thousand CPE units in the United States are produced annually by the Association for Clinical Pastoral Education in its more than 360 accredited centers.)

Organizational Birth Pains

By the early 1930s, the organizational thrusts in the fresh CPE movement had begun to experience a difficult rupture. Several years prior to my birth, the clashing of leadership roles within a fledgling Council for Clinical Training of Theological Students (CCTTS) had split the young movement. This separation took place only two years after some of the early leaders had incorporated the movement into the CCTTS. There consequently emerged two rival groups, namely, a New England group (later to be designated the Institute of Pastoral Care) and the Council for Clinical Training. Obvious in these struggles were Helen Flanders Dunbar, Philip Guiles, and Richard Cabot. Dunbar and Guiles had been two of Boisen's earliest students.

The Council's focused leader became Dunbar, and her favored environs were New York City. On the other hand, Guiles found relatedness with a New England contingent and the Boston area. Dunbar was said to be very precocious, while Guiles put much energy into developing strategies. There previously had simmered much competition—and eventually bitterness—between these two strong personalities.

The prodigious intellectual prowess and creativity of Dunbar allowed her to acquire three academic degrees (a theological degree, a Ph.D. in comparative literature, and a medical degree). In order to maintain her schedules and busy pursuits, she had two personal secretaries. She was a noted scholar in medieval symbolism, and her wide range of scholarly interests covered Dante and psychosomatic medicine. Dunbar played a major professional and personal role in Boisen's life.[5]

Guiles possessed an outgoing style. In the late 1920s, it was his genius that had brought financial resourcing and plans together for the forming of the CCTTS. He was instrumental also in ushering CPE into seminary life. This was due to his gaining the first seminary appointment as a director of clinical training at the Andover Newton Seminary in Boston.[6]

Regarding Cabot's preference with these organizational dilemmas, he moved toward support of Guiles and the New England group. Those colleagues began to be identified with the matters of training for the general pastoral ministry and also the general hospital setting. The Council for Clinical Training was stereotyped with a psychoanalytic label and had a leaning toward training in mental hospitals. As the two associations became more differentiated and Boisen's role later began to wane, he more or less showed no partiality to either.

Leaving Worcester

By the time that I entered Orangeburg life, Boisen had already moved two years earlier in 1932 from the Worcester hospital. He transitioned his chaplaincy and CPE model to the Elgin State Hospital near Chicago. He remained there until his death in 1965. A factor that prompted Boisen's move to Elgin was that of Cabot's growing disenchantment with Boisen over another breakdown episode in 1930. Also, the biological and psychological differences in their views regarding mental illness remained.

Boisen was attracted principally to the Chicago area because of an enduring relatedness that he had had with the Chicago Theological Seminary. Furthermore, he had possessed for a consider-

able time an idealized love relationship in that city. This particular
person—so prominent in a large portion of Boisen's life—is introduced in chapter 4.

Boisen suffered another acute mental episode in 1935. After this
brief upheaval, he never had further psychosis. The remaining years
of his life saw a vast amount of productivity come out in his writing
and teaching.[7] Due to the exceeding contributions that he offered to
the whole clinical pastoral movement and CPE in particular, Boisen
reappears in some of the oncoming chapters of my account.

EARLY INFLUENCES ON MY
CPE PILGRIMAGE

After taking a look at CPE's beginnings, *Hunkering Down* returns to
a review of my personal origins. There were many roots from
those early years that had a hand in the later shaping of my life in
the remarkable movement of CPE. Hence, the appraisal about
these connections is placed in this opening chapter. I do this now,
rather than locating it later, so that the reader might be prepared to
sense more fully the relationship that these presaging personal
themes have had with my vocational narrative as it becomes gradually disclosed in subsequent chapters.

The features of interrelationship between my young life and
my later CPE interests have included these following matters:
wounded healing, human growth and development, the partici-
pant/observer polarity, racial oppression, a dearly loved river, the
nature of story, and my family context.

Wounded Healing

The blended history of my parents' two family backgrounds provided me with an implicit sensing of the values that were to be
later discovered more explicitly in the pastoral care concept of *the
wounded healer*. This specific term offers a perspective on the role
that one's own suffering has with the deeper reaches of providing
care to others. The concept was espoused by Henri Nouwen, and
it is utilized as the title of his popular 1972 book on pastoral care.

My parents' lives were impressively devoted to the showing of care for others. Furthermore, both of them encountered some critical losses early in their own lives. Because of their personal knowledge of early grief, loyal outreach thereby was subsequently engendered from them for others in suffering. They knew instinctively how to be with people walking through some dark valley of pain. I have come to feel that a substantial aspect of my parents' healing support was well-grounded in the base of their firsthand knowledge of similar valleys.

For instance, my mother's own mother was swept into death at age forty by breast cancer. My mother was only seven years old. Naturally, medical treatment for cancer was limited in those days. Therefore, my grandmother was sent from a little county hospital in South Carolina to a larger one in Richmond, Virginia. Nothing remedied her illness.

Thus, Papa traveled by train to bring his very ill wife back to the family in Cross Hill. She died there within two weeks, and my bereft grandfather was left with the rearing of his four young daughters. Much assistance was provided by his deceased wife's mother. She moved into the home; her own husband and all four of her children had already met death. This grandmother saw to it that her four granddaughters received training opportunities in addition to their schooling. My mother specialized in elocution lessons; she learned how to make speeches and offer poetic odes.

My maternal Papa apparently was a reliable conveyer of care to others. The tale was told by my kinfolks about his receiving the news, on once returning to Cross Hill on a train from a fox hunt in the Lowcountry, that his wife's brother had died suddenly out in Arkansas. He had been jolted from a wagon that was pulled by a lurching mule. Papa had no sooner jumped off one train when he immediately climbed aboard another that was headed westward. He recovered the deceased relative and brought him back to South Carolina for a proper burial.

My own father also knew about sudden tragedy—especially in his teen-age years. As World War I was winding down in Europe, his brother Tom entered the army while in college. He was sent to Belgium, and there he was killed just a couple of months prior to the declaring of Armistice. Garbled news concerning his death was received by the stunned family. A couple of anguished weeks passed before the loved ones knew with finality that this promising young man indeed had lost his life.

Several years ago I discovered a faded letter written by a comrade of my uncle. The injured soldier had described to the Orangeburg family how he had heard my uncle, in the waning moments of his life, request the medical personnel to leave him and give care to the less wounded. This heroic information about his courage deeply touched me. Also the classical mythology term known as the *hero's journey* has long fascinated me.

Within three months of this horrible battlefield death, my father's father—Abram West Summers—died by contracting influenza as a result of the 1918 epidemic that swept through the nation. However, many in the family and the little southern town felt that this esteemed lawyer also had been crushed by a broken heart. Grief was heavy over the dying of a dear son in a distant land. He had earlier attempted so diligently to dissuade his second-born from entering military service, in the first place, at such a late stage in the war.

My bereaved father entered college the next fall at seventeen years of age. A lifetime of loss had been compacted in one sorrow-torn year. He had immensely loved both his father and brother. They had engaged together in many activities; the group gardened and often took Sunday rides in a horse-drawn carriage. The purpose for many of their buggy trips was that of spending the day with nearby relatives. My name—Thomas Abram Summers—was fashioned from these two significant people in my father's life.

In growing up around my parents, I never heard them dwell much on their former losses. However, I was with them on numerous occasions to observe their compassion shown to friends and relatives in times of distress. Intuited in those moments was a sense that their special touch of gentle care came somewhere from their own inner depths.

This precursive glimpse of support from my parents for other persons going through troubled times no doubt prepared me for a later sensitivity to the pastoral care dimension of ministry. I have fathomed that theirs was a healing care very much informed by their own personal knowledge about life's distressing vicissitudes.

The Phenomenon of Growth

Although Anton Boisen's training concerns rested mainly on his research and case study methodology, the CPE initiative after a time went beyond his singular direction. It began to incorporate an emphasis on both the pastoral and personal growth process of the student.

Richard Cabot, who has been seen as a powerful force in forming the nascent stages of the CPE movement, possessed a growth perspective related to education. For instance, he utilized his medical knowledge about the reality of jagged human tissue growth to coin the popular educational metaphor a *student's growing edge* in the learning process.[8] This phrase has been adopted for much usage in CPE conversation related to experience-based knowing.

As a child much of my cognizance concerning the matter of growth was derived from the plentifulness of natural growth that I saw around me in my home environment. For example, a large vegetable garden and chicken yard on my family's property were the earthy entry-points into an enduring love for observing the powerful mysteries of growth and development in plants, animals, and persons.

Far and wide was my father known for his diversified crop of luscious vegetables and fruit. They were brought forth from the earth in the spring, summer, and fall seasons. At an early age, I became attuned to watching him plant small seeds in fertile soil—inflicted with no chemical fertilizer—that would result in the natural sequence of green plants and a bountiful harvest. More was grown than our family of four possibly could devour. On many childhood Saturdays, my brother Carroll and I would sell vegetables to grocery stores or throughout the neighborhood from our wheelbarrows. Many of those evenings, *sans* television, were spent by the radio listening to such hillbilly favorites as "The Wabash Cannonball" and Eddy Arnold's yodeled cattle-calls.

The chicken yard contained approximately twenty-five laying hens that offered a copious supply of fresh eggs. On occasion we hatched fertilized eggs in homemade incubators. We would watch the new chicks eventually grow into hens. When I was nine years old, my father invited me into a business relationship with him concerning the large number of eggs that were being supplied by our productive flock. We agreed that, if he put forth the money for the chicken feed, I would develop customers for the purchase of eggs that remained after our family's needs. The bargain was that I could keep most of the money from these sales. For five years my weekly egg route with eight customers garnered enough money to be spent conservatively on savings bonds and frivolously at the annual county fair—replete with its midway barkers, greased pigs, and Ferris wheels.

As for other chickens that were fryers rather than layers, they would serve the family as a ready supply of fried chicken for Sunday dinners. When we had an opportunity to vacation at the beach, we would put into our car trunk a coop containing a dozen live fryers. Having the chickens to accompany us to the beach would provide us—in those days before frozen food—with the ongoing delicacy of fried chicken for the entire week at a rustic beach cottage. It might be added that any such automobile trip during the World War II years often was beset by a flat tire due to weakened rubber tires. While fixing the disabled hoop of rubber, we would put our coop of chickens under a shade tree. The next chapter reveals, by the way, how I utilized this experience with changing tires in the first sermon that I ever preached.

Just as in an earlier watch over the unfolding of a life cycle in a garden and a chicken yard, I have remained interested in CPE with watching students flourish and develop their own progressive wings of personal and pastoral growth.

Participant/Observer

My interest in CPE's values regarding the *participant/observer* concept more than likely has some of its roots in those years of growing up in Orangeburg. The actual production of this specific term was aided by the theoretical work of Harry Stack Sullivan in his focus on an interpersonal view. It was developed by him from the 1920s through the late 1940s. An extensive bibliography of this well-known psychiatrist's literature can be found in Patrick Mullahy's 1967 book *The Contributions of Harry Stack Sullivan.* From the Sullivanian perspective, the therapist (or supervisor) uses a third eye, as it were, to observe and monitor one's own participation amidst the interaction with a client (or supervisee).

In my childhood and high school years, I started off early with this duality of both observing and participating in activities at the same time. This was done mainly through the avenue of sports. As a youngster I was enthralled with the opportunity of participating in athletics. A calendar year for me was perceived very seasonally. The fall existed for football; winter was ordained for basketball; and, certainly, the warm months were created by God for us baseball pitchers and second basemen. I must have held a gene that was in constant harmony with any activity resembling sports! In its gender values, the culture had a strong affirmation of these heroic battles for males. It would take at least thirty more years before Title IX ushered in the same for females.

I relished being around the sports atmosphere. For instance, many boyhood hours were spent in the delightful environs of the neighboring Mirmow family. In this Jewish home, I was happily captivated by the countless stories about sports that were spun by Eddie Mirmow. He would also show me major league baseball scorecards from New York games seen at Yankee Stadium or Ebbets Field in Brooklyn. He and my father made it possible once for me to shake hands with Jack Dempsey when the famous heavyweight boxer visited Orangeburg during the war years.

My sports mentor, Eddie Mirmow, established me as the batboy for his managed American Legion Junior baseball squad. Before each home game, I would ride with him and his wife Beck throughout the county in his car in order to transport some players to Orangeburg. In a spiritual sense, he has remained in my heart as my athletic godfather. Proudly, my middle name—Abram—maintains a strong tie to the Mirmows' Jewishness. In the late 1940s, Orangeburg leaders built an acclaimed baseball stadium and appropriately named it Mirmow Field. This field of dreams would be the exciting battleground not only for the Legion team but also for Orangeburg's semipro legends—the Braves of the old Palmetto League. It would be the hallowed place, where on a steamy August evening in 1948, I heard the stadium's public address announcer hesitantly offer the trembling news about Babe Ruth's death.

Spring days would see not only lush azalea and dogwood blooms throw a blanket of splendor over the town but also the thrilling presence of a New York Yankees' farm team—the Binghamton (NY) Triplets. The squad would grace the townspeople with much anticipated days of spring training at this sports arena. Many an hour would see me there watching how far some of these diamond heroes could spit their tobacco juice or with what speed some noted rookie could sprint in the outfield pastures. Paradise actually touched earth on one hot Saturday afternoon—a bevy of future major leaguers came to town with the touring AAA Kansas City farm club to show off their talents to the Orangeburg crowd. On almost all of these occasions, Eddie Mirmow would be nestled somewhere in the stands looking out at the fruits of his devoted labors.

During this same period, I had the enjoyable task of distributing soft drinks and sandwiches to the out-of-town sportswriters covering the annual Orangeburg County Fair football game between the University of South Carolina's Gamecocks and The Citadel's Bulldogs. My educated guess now is that Eddie Mirmow and my father probably arranged this opportunity for me. They were the best of friends and were fishing companions on many Saturday afternoons.

The fairgrounds stadium held ten thousand screaming fans for this state rivalry. As I carried out my duties with the food and drinks, I was enamored with witnessing these writers as they talked with one another behind their rickety typewriters in the small tin-roofed press box. I became acquainted one year with the sports editor of the Columbia newspaper. For several years thereafter, he would publish my submitted football All-American selections in his regular sports column.

Concurrent to my fondness for conversing about or playing in sports, I had a passion for writing about this exciting area of life and its rich history. In my late grammar school days, I began writing—after the games—some accounts of various sandlot or league events in which I had a chance to play. This unusual interest required me carefully to observe the game while being right in the middle of it. It is no small wonder that, when I much later came across Harry Stack Sullivan's theories about the participant/observer, it rang a bell with my own history.

Little did I know in those 1940s that, while pursuing baseballs in my barefeet on a southern sandlot and also hungering to write about the observed action, there also were some other folks across the country doing similar things. Except they were engaged in something called "clinical pastoral training." They were not talking about laying down a bunt, but these ministers were teaching pastoral care. While in the middle of their interactions, they were

observing their own work. The playing field for such CPE supervisors as Fred Keuther, Seward Hiltner, and Wayne Oates was in
the clinical setting of conference rooms with pastoral students; but,
from all reports, they wore shoes.

Racial Oppression

An additional sway that my anteceding environment had on my
future clinical pastoral directions was that of the devastating racial
oppression of the Deep South. My beloved hometown had been
bequeathed the searing effects of slavery. African Americans and
Caucasians were not to mingle together in the lingering volatility
of such a social atmosphere. Throughout the South choked-back
resentments on the part of countless Black persons were seen.
However, across the dangerous chasm of the region's ingrained
and legally sanctioned system of injustice, I witnessed immense
moments of kindness and care shown between the races. But
everyone knew that if Black persons tried to move upward from
the rear of so many designated lines, their lives literally would be
in danger. My young heart could make no sense out of this death-
ly battle between fear and kindness.

This was especially so since I grew up fortunately in the presence of a special mothering figure—Louise Montgomery Spann.
She was present when I was born in my home's back bedroom.
Hers were among the first arms ever to embrace me. This cheerful
African American woman—possessing no more than a third grade
education—was a domestic worker and cook with my original
family. She worked in this capacity for nearly forty years prior to
her retirement. As a child I heard her daily songs of religious joy
and struggle. We spent much time laughing and joking with one
another. Acquaintances of the family often would remark about
the strong and special bond between the two of us.

In the summer months of my boyhood days, she would go to
Brooklyn in order to stay with a sister. She could work for some
families in the New York area and make almost more money in sev-
eral months than she could during a whole year in the South.
Occasionally she would mail me picture postcards that depicted a
Coney Island scene or some other visited site around New York
City. I was fearful that she might not want to return to Orange-

burg; however, she always came back on the train in the early fall. My soul* would leap with thanks.   In excitement she would describe to me the wondrous marvels of New York—a roller coaster at the beach, the Statue of Liberty, Ebbets Field, and other favorite places.

A mixture of joy and heartbreak sometimes would visit us on Saturdays. One of the greatest loves in our common life was that of the movies. Never to be forgotten, however, was the specific pain that was a part of our many trips to the theater. I would wave goodbye to her before she ascended to the dusty confines of a racially segregated balcony; my seat was to be found in a more comfortable section below. My throat still carries a lump in it to this day when I think of that demeaning scene.

I never heard Louise say anything about the ruthless racial system in our surroundings nor did I see her take any specific action against it. But it was our devoted relationship with each other that persuasively mentored me toward a plunge into social justice later in my ministry.

The River

A theme hovering over my ongoing vocational process can be seen in my abiding love affair with the Edisto River. As mentioned previously, it was this river that the first Summers family came to know upon descending on American shores. In the long ago, a Native American tribe—the Edisto—patiently fished from its riverbanks and energetically swam its waters. Back then, it was called the Pon Pon, or "black" river.

Its lustrous darkness streams through Orangeburg on a rippling journey southward to the waiting arms of an expansive ocean. The home of my birth and rearing rested less than a mile near the allurement of these enticing currents.

I learned to swim them at the age of three by first holding fast around my father's neck. He then would propel us back-and-forth across the flowing river. This action allowed me in time to experience trust and support in her nurturing buoyancy.

---

*In the use of the word *soul* throughout the book, I am not referring to the split so often seen in a body/*soul* dualism. Rather soul is seen as the unifying and cohesive inner life principle that expresses itself in the depths of one's being.

Most of my boyhood and early adolescent days in the sum-
mertime, when not playing baseball or tending to chickens, were
spent in or near this venerated place. This aquatic mother was in
my soul like a temple of worship. I often would plunge into its
depths and explore the sandy bottoms; and, on bright sunlit days,
I could look up through the waters and witness the shafts of cathe-
dral rays glimmering above me. On many occasions, peer friends
and I would dash through a nearby swamp for engagement in mud
fights with each other and "enemies."

It is no surprise that my heart clutched an enchantment with
Tarzan movies. What a constant treat it was to see on the silver
screen Johnny Weissmuller race through a jungle, swing swiftly
from a sturdy vine, bellow that famed melodious yell, have the
constant companionship of a playful chimp, and—above all else—
dive into clear waters whenever he wanted to do so.

In my twelfth year, six friends and I carried out a vow to jump
into the Edisto each month of the year—regardless of any wintry
freezes. In the cold season, these leaps of faith were always accompanied by a quick retreat to a riverbank's log fire and the smoking
of rabbit tobacco. To this day, some of us reminiscing compatriots
still speak fondly about the sustaining power of our hardy pact.

Since the river nurturingly spawned many of my friends and
myself, my narrative pauses to explore more broadly this peership.
(This description helps to form the foundation for the reappearance
of the preadolescent theme seen in chapter 8. I discuss there a particular CPE assessment model that has a rootage in this particular
age range.) This same coterie of young peers—including Jack Mob-
ley, Watt McCain, Jim LaCoste, Will Kelly, West Summers, Dick
Harvin, and myself—had had a background of prior years before
this twelve-month loyalty to jumping bravely into the Edisto.

For instance, many weekend nights had been spent roaming
into our neighborhood's darkness in the making of adventurous
plans for youthful daring. Trenches and underground passageways sometimes were dug in vacant lots—perhaps catering to
some burrowing or tunneling instinct. The World War II years
would see us don makeshift military uniforms and march forth as
a serious platoon of young infantrymen into the Carolina woods
looking for any lurking foes. Harvin's bird dog, Major, was a constant companion in all of our exploits. There also was a summer
ritual of boarding a train for a fourteen-mile trip to a smaller town

that proudly owned a swimming pool. Even though the pool's bottom had rock pebbles on it, our daylong frolicking in unfamiliar contained waters—in contrast to the flowing Edisto—offered an annual novelty.

Our tender sides would shine occasionally in the neighborhood streets as we pulled, by strings, small shoe boxes. With the radiance of light glittering through the varied color tones of the paper-covered windows in the boxes, it appeared to the neighbors as if a multi-colored processional of glowing trolley cars were passing by into the darkness of the night.

Since money was limited, these early days saw us youngsters making many of our own toys and games. For instance, a long-range missile could be constructed from the placing of several turkey feathers on one end of a corn cob and the insertion of a nail into the other. One could rear back and heave such a flighted wonder in a twirling trajectory for more than forty yards. Also, a thick rope often was thrown over the sturdy limb of a tall, hillside pine tree. A running dash with the rope in hand could result joyfully in a wide pendulum swing through the rushing air. A hollow bamboo segment every now and then would be employed for a weapon in its expelling of a forcefully breath-propelled pea or chinaberry toward someone's unwarned arm or neck. Many of the shadows from our enterprising toils rested not far from the watchful and graceful care of our constant home—the Edisto.

Located not far from one of its riverbanks was a rustic bathhouse. A juke box there constantly emitted lusty jitterbugging and soulful tunes in the summer. My peers and I would watch the older dancers sway and smoothly create their own titillating steps to such melodies as "The House of Blue Lights," "Sixty-Minute Man," and "I Don't See You in My Eyes Anymore." I dreamed of the day that I might be so lucky to do the same.

In the early 1980s, the river's potential contamination by seepage waste from a nuclear weapons plant (located sixty miles westward) prompted my strong interest for tying together a clinical pastoral relationship to the environment and other critical social issues. This matter receives further description in chapter 9. As can be seen there in that particular reference, it was the combination of my love for the Edisto and Louise Spann that would serve as my central inspiration in this later searching out a greater integration of pastoral care with social justice.

I felt honored when Howard Clinebell in 1996 included material about my bond to the Edisto River in his book *Ecotherapy*. That focus implies that the warm memory events of our deep, natural ties to the earth and water "live" in us. These nourishing energies thereby strengthen us in our attempts to be both interpersonally present with others and to deal with today's alarming environmental crises.

This river, undoubtedly like an archetype to me, has remained over the years as a resourceful treasure in my inner life. From its memory and sustenance, I continue to receive significant support in attempting to swim into the challenges found in my personal life and clinical pastoral vocation.

Story

A further contribution from my initital culture and atmosphere was that of storytelling. Innumerable moments during these years were spent sitting around with relatives, elderly friends, and peers in the swapping of stories and tales. I was wrapped up in a southern cloth that included vibrant threads of foot-stomping yarns of humor and irony, endless narratives of personal victory or *near* defeat, and family histories.

One of my most tender remembrances about Cross Hill is that of sitting with relatives on Papa's front porch in late summer afternoons. We would watch the one daily bus come slowly down the road to pick up its usual number of one or two passengers. Then amidst the telling of family stories and the anticipation of fireflies at dusk, we would rock the time away in our chairs. Eudora Welty accurately describes this regional inclination: "I think it is the southern nature to tell stories. We all love to talk."[9]

My affection for storytelling also was yielded from an early experience with the church. My first occasion of speaking in a church was when I was twelve years of age. I had been asked to describe to my Methodist home congregation the schedule of activities that our youth group had maintained for a week's stay at a camp in the mountains. I discovered that the boring routines of what time that we campers arose in the morning and the hours set apart for crafts were not so appealing to the listeners. In midstream I discarded the original outline for my presentation. Instead, I moved into the story about how some of us took some new campers on a deceptive snipe hunt late one night. Actually, a snipe is a fictitious bird. Therefore, the congregation immediately perked up. I began to see the power of a natural story within the religious context, and that perception has yet to fade in my life of ministry. This cultural allurement of story also would prepare me later in my vocation to regard a narrative emphasis as being indispensable in dealing with theology. I gained an affinity with Robert McAfee Brown's following perspective on the relationship that story has with theology and, consequently, with the ministry of pastoral care:

> Our faith, after all, did not initially come to us as "theology." It came as story. Tell me about God: "Well, once upon a time there was a garden." Tell me about Jesus: "Once upon a time there was a boy in a little town in Palestine called Nazareth..."
>
> Out of such stories the systems begin to grow, with results we know only too well: stories about a garden become cosmological arguments; stories about Jesus become treatises on the two natures.
>
> In losing the story we have lost both the power and the glory. We have committed the unpardonable sin of transforming exciting stories into dull systems...
>
> We must recover the story if we are to recover a faith for our day... Our theological task is to find ways to "tell the old, old story" so the listener says, "Aha! That's *my* story too."[10]

The many layers of activity in clinical pastoral education have allowed me to remain attracted to the human richness of stories. For instance, in my nearly four decades of pastoral supervision with students, I have had the rare privilege of listening to or reading about their awesome personal and pastoral life stories. An inestimable number of such intermingled narratives have pervaded my collective CPE hours in seminars, reading autobiographies in application materials, individual supervision conferences, interviewing applicants, evaluation retreats, reading verbatim accounts of pastoral care visits, and generally hunkering down in hallways or around coffeepots. These shared accounts of students have been laden with powerfully hewn meanings. They consistently have sewn the life-giving elements of struggle, hope, and humor into the cloth of the students' pastoral care development.

A major gift provided from these years of listening and responding to these rich human stories has been that of their advancing, at the same time, my internal life's story—with its own unique soul journey, questions, and search for meanings. Time and again, I have experienced this phenomenon proven true: Another's story has the potential to move and energize your own. Above all else, we humans seem to be "story creatures" at the very core of our beings. Indeed, our dreams come to us as nightly tales.

Temperament and the Family System

A concluding feature concerning the interaction of my personal origins with my life in CPE is related to the combination of my personality style and my early family unit. As long as I can remember, I have been aware of the trends of both extroversion and introversion as competing forces within me. In the early years and through high school, I relished many adventuresome moments with peers. At the same time, I also was protective of space for times of solitude and introspection.

The inseparability of these outwardly and inwardly directed trends was no more obvious than that which was seen in the high school annual's "senior superlatives." I was selected paradoxically by classmates not only as the best all-around and most popular student but also as the most bashful. Absorbing strongly a surrounding parental nurturance, I knew both the warmth and burden of sensing a specialness about my life.

I tended generally to avoid severe conflicts and showed little of a rebellious streak to my parents. However, it was in sports and adventure where I felt the sheer enjoyment of competition. Entry into my pubescent days was delayed. For a period of time, I feared that an eagerly sought sports career for high school would be lost. But even at one hundred pounds and just a few inches over five feet tall, I still went after an early spot on the school's football team. In once sustaining a knee injury, a doctor told me that I had a "Cadillac motor with a Ford body." However, I began to grow rapidly in my fifteenth year. My dreams for playing high school football, basketball, and baseball then became fulfilled. Nevertheless, I carried for some time the scar of that body image predicament.

My mother's strong optimistic and outgoing style contained much talent for developing social networks in Orangeburg. She also possessed enduring values for maintaining close connections with kin and friends. More than forty-five years ago, the Orangeburg newspaper wrote an article concerning her kindness and community service. Contained were the words: "… the part about her that has endeared her to innumerable friends and acquaintances is her everlasting thoughtfulness—the little things she does for people that mean so much. A little visit, a little gift … or just a kindly word—these are the things for which she will always be remembered."[11]

My mother was executive secretary of the county Red Cross chapter during World War II. She was selected as one of twenty women throughout the nation to serve on a national planning committee for the American Red Cross, and they met in Washington to carry out their work. On some of her automobile trips throughout the county, I often accompanied her on her visits to families of overseas servicemen.

A central demeanor of my father was that of his laid-back style. He and I spent many moments in just sitting down and talking. I have often wondered if the closeness that we felt for each other was not only fostered by our strong relationship but also by the fact that I bore the first name of his much loved brother—one so dreadfully snatched away by the ravages of World War I. In the early 1950s, our family was proudly present in the county courtroom to witness his installation as the new Orangeburg County Judge.

Although my brother Carroll and I had many common interests as youth, his even more daring nature eventually carried him into more forays away from home than I undertook. My educational goals focused more on the classics and the humanities while his studies invested him in the direction of a civil engineering degree at The Citadel.

Both of our parents strongly encouraged Carroll and me to make periodic visits with nearby elderly relatives. In visiting with one, I would find myself often bouncing up-and-down on a swayedback joggling board, while she—seated on a porch close by—recited a plethora of stories that were handed down to her about the Civil War and other genealogical matters. Every now and then, she would break out in a high-pitched song and ask me to sing it along with her in my even more wailing voice.

A paternal first cousin and I were the same age. Too, he and I had a bond as if we were brothers. We both loved swimming in the Edisto River and were known as "river rats." Some folks who were not that familiar with our families actually thought that maybe West Summers and I might have been twins.

Our parents supported Carroll's and my work interests. His high school summers were spent with a construction company, while mine were with the county highway department or in baseball coaching on the city playgrounds.

Early life within the family mileu, in addition to my own emerging personality, facilitated within me an interplay between sociability and a tendency for contemplation or pensiveness. My interest over the years in the clinical pastoral education model of action/reflection more than likely has a connection with these earlier personal tensions. Some of my closest professional colleagues have reminded me that, at times, I seem to offer a combination of being both very active and keeping issues close to my chest. The mixture in my background prompted a style of seeking leadership roles in a quiet manner.

Because of the power that early features can exert on one's future development in life, the reader likely will see some of these seven preceding themes from my origins reappear in other chapters throughout the book. Furthermore, their manifestation more than likely will be sensed in various subtleties of the material.

INNOCENCE AND THE SHADOW

The years of growing up in this geographical, social, and familial context could have provided a backdrop for a regular Norman Rockwell painting. The ingredients for such brush strokes would have been many: World War II patriotism, shooting marbles on grammar school playgrounds, hunting and fishing, a linkage with kin, familiarity with my grandfather's outhouse, searching for frogs in ponds, mud fights in river swamps, barefooted days from May through August during grammar school years, raising chickens, ball games, and more ball games. Throughout the years I have felt fortunate for these gifts that have contributed to my life.

However, lurking below the innocent southern surface of such a charming Rockwell scene would have existed, as already noted, the wrenching reality of racial division in the culture. Hence, in pastoral supervision I have held a keen interest in encouraging CPE students to grasp not only the strengths of their primary contextual heritage but also its latent shadowy side.

(Incidentally, racial unrest in Orangeburg erupted out of the shadows thirty years ago. An attempt by African-American college students to integrate racially a local bowling alley resulted eventually in the tragic shooting deaths of three students. The intervening years have shown intentional and hopeful efforts on the part of leading townspeople for greater racial reconciliation. One such project in 1999 was the "Let Us Heal Ourselves" campaign.)

REFLECTIONS ON EARLY LIFE

I have attempted in the section of "Early Influences on My CPE Pilgrimage" to convey some lasting motifs that emerged from the commencing stages of my life. In order for the book's effort to have an early experiential value for the reader, I now invite you to pause and do some reflecting about your own unique and early life experiences. In other words, in what ways did any wounds known by your forebears assist you in learning how to better care for others? How have you become fascinated with the phenomenal mystery of human growth and development? Has an early awareness of social oppression ever seared into your soul? What special place in the natural environment has remained eternal for you? And I particularly have great regard for such a question as: How would you describe your early culture's shadowy dimension—as well as its innocent and nurturing side?

As mentioned in the preface, you are encouraged to consider throughout the rest of *Hunkering Down* the unique issues in your own developmental life-stages as mine unfold.

LETTING GO OF A FAMILIAR PLACE

One of my joys in high school athletics was that of being able to play basketball under the tutelage of an Indiana-bred coach, Earle Steckel. He came to Orangeburg and rescued the hapless team of my sophomore year (only two games won that season) by taking us eventually into South Carolina's Lower State championship finals in my senior year. I also became a defensive halfback for Bill Clark—known by some as the Silver Fox or the Silver Colonel. His disciplined and loyal football squads won nearly eighty percent of their contests in his first four years in Orangeburg.

In my senior year, I fell head-over-heels in love with a high school girlfriend. I announced to my amazed baseball coach and friends that, for that last spring season, I was hanging up my glove and cleats so that I could spend more time with my sweetheart than with sports. Matters of endearment apparently had gained more prominence in my young soul than those on the base paths.

Many delightful sock-hop dances were held in the high school's gymnasium. The school orchestra cast popular tunes long into the night air, namely, "Again," "Too Young," "Hey, Good Looking," "Blue Moon," "Because of You," "The Tennessee Waltz," and "Cold, Cold Heart." However, the music did run warmly through our hearts as well as our shoeless feet.

College days also were to arrive in that year of 1952 as I made ready to depart from the secure garden of Orangeburg. By the way, it was around this same time that the so-called Committee of Twelve in the CPE movement had begun its tough deliberations in hammering out nationally approved CPE standards for the first time. This committee contained representatives from the following national organizations: the Council for Clinical Training, the Institute of Pastoral Care, the Lutheran Advisory Council, and the Association of Seminary Professors in the Practical Field.

Thus, as I prepared to leave my early securities, such clinical pastoral education luminaries as Ernest "Ernie" Bruder, John Billinsky, Fred Keuther, Tom Klink, Carl Plack, Paul Johnson, and others were also moving into a new and uncertain territory. Their committee work represented a negotiation from the protection of separately organized turfs toward a common set of groundbreaking standards. The rift of the early 1930s between the Council and the Institute—described earlier in this chapter—had moved a long way into some healing. The Committee of Twelve would meet eight times between 1951 and 1957. The standards would become adopted in 1953, but fourteen years would remain before there would be a national unification of the whole CPE movement.[12] Into the present day, CPE has historically found its systemic, funded home in health care and generally not in the seminaries nor the religious faith groups—although at interface with them.

I said goodbye to my familiar surroundings on the eve of a trip upstate to Methodist-supported Wofford College. Packed into a trunk and a little suitcase were my baseball glove, clothes, a fragile radio, and a few other belongings. My heart did some grieving over taking leave of my sweetheart and the Edisto world.

Without knowing it in the early 1950s, my formative years had set a stage for future decades of interaction between my vocational journey—with its clinical pastoral emphasis—and such durable issues as my family origins, a wounded healing, a river, and storytelling.

Chapter 2

———— ✦✦✦ ————

Swimming through College, 1952-1956

The undergraduate days at the small liberal arts school in Spartan-burg, South Carolina, were savored by me. A range of diversified friendships was established—some for a lifetime—during these commonly called Eisenhower years. Studies, athletics, and campus life became the valued paths on which I walked at Wofford College.

The campus at the all-male school contained not only a student body of approximately five hundred students but also a leafy over-flowing of trees. The professors generally fostered in our studies a freedom of thought and inquiry.

This portion of *Hunkering Down* considers some important features in these collegiate years. The main themes include the areas of learning within the classroom, the accompanying campus culture of the 1950s, the continuance of a special fondness for sports—with an emphasis on a courageous swimming team, an emerging interest in ministry, the noting of CPE's uniqueness in this particular time period, and a description of my experience prior to entering seminary years.

KING LEAR AND SCROOGE

The classroom atmosphere at Wofford was very appealing. The persuasive studies generally opened new windows of ideas, and many of the capable professors offered a lifelong model for embracing fresh learning.

For instance, Shakespeare's King Lear, Lady MacBeth, and Othello all danced around in the student's mind as William Hunter—exuding a creative sarcasm—put forward a penetrating analysis of the bard's handiwork. One also could not help but attempt mastering the intricacies of Spanish through the disciplined and patient push of John "Fish" Salmon. C. C. Norton, a scholar in sociology, showed his playfulness and versatility every December by giving the student body a Christmas gift through his animated rendition of Dickens's Scrooge.

With a humorously measured and exploratory style, Dean Philip Covington whet the appetite for English literature through the likes of Coleridge, Tennyson, and Wordsworth. For two semesters Gordon May's clear instruction in mathematics actually allowed me surprisingly to fall in love—momentarily—with algebra and geometry. Lewis Jones's informed passion for history sowed countless seeds in preparing graduates' future sensitivity to the historical human pilgrimage.

Inside these classrooms, a thriving of intellectual processes lived. I have heard it said that, in the teaching relationship, those who have torches pass them on to others. I will always be grateful for that which was handed to me by Wofford's fine professors.

OUTSIDE LEARNING

Outside those buildings, the campus culture of this period spread an active smorgasbord for other kinds of learning. Around this particular table, education—in its different and vivacious forms—socially took place as well. If a time capsule from that era of more than forty-five years ago were opened today, its content themes would reveal a variegated array of such moments.

The Thumb-Thing

As an illustration, a body part that was very instrumental in transportation during my college years was the thumb. Since cars were somewhat scarce on campus, hitchhiking—sadly now almost a lost art due to societal dangers—often became a mode of getting a ride from town to town or even from the campus to various parts of Spartanburg.

If the thumb had a lucky Friday or Saturday in negotiating the 135 miles between Spartanburg and Orangeburg, I could successfully make the occasional trip in almost four hours. The mixture of Good Samaritans rescuing me from many a roadside ditch was housed in a wide assortment of emancipating vehicles: logging trucks, funeral hearses, hog trucks, or an occasional Cadillac. Actually, any chariot with four wheels was quite all right with me.

The thumb became a reliable ticket to many critical places. For instance, hitchhiking dispersements were made with college classmates so that one's family car could be proudly brought back to campus for a week of constant usage. The weary auto sooner or later would be returned to a transportation-starved family. The thumbs then would fetch these college travelers back to Wofford.

This digital form of conveyance also wrought once a moment of blessing in my early college days. After the first several weeks of freshman life, my heart began to pine intensely for the sight of my former high school's football team and its renowned coaching mentor. The pigskin combatants had not been faring well so far in their young season. At the end of classes on a Friday, I could not entertain this agony any longer. I spread down a hitchhiking carpet that whisked me eventually to the faraway field of skirmishing—just in time for the latter part of the first quarter.

The Silver Fox, pacing anxiously up and down the sideline in a fretful coaching state over his team's lack of zip, spied me standing nearby. He ran quickly over and said, "Tom, we're in deep trouble. I need you badly." In obedience to what I thought was his call to action, my first impulse was to consider dashing out on the gridiron with street clothes on and jumping into the fray for my recent and fearless leader.

Instead he continued, "Check with me at halftime." The team happened to perk up as the first half progressed, but he still carried the wrinkles of worry and wanted me to accompany him at halftime. Little did I know that I soon would be transferred from being a former charge of his into the newly recognized status of laboring side-by-side with this esteemed football wizard. It was then that I would find a most important transition moving into my life. In a locker room atmosphere—dripping with September sweat—I became a coworker in the football vineyards with my hero.

"Guys, Tom—who was a part of that bunch last year that spilled their guts out on many a field—is going to give us some words of courage," he passionately preached, "so that we can go out there and take that second half! Take over, Tom."

My Knute Rockne-inspired speech probably did little to assist in the team's ultimate victory that evening. Instead, it was the Silver Fox who, as usual, pulled another win from the jaws of defeat.

It had been the thumb, however, that got me there in time for a momentous baptismal ceremony—one that ushered me into a new adult mutuality at an early season's halftime.

Choppy Waters

My delight in participating with sports continued in college. Later in my freshman year, I attempted to make a place on Wofford's basketball team. Not having a scholarship nor envisioning strong possibilities that I might play much on this highly capable squad, I terminated after a time my courtship with the college roundball activity. Nevertheless, it was exciting to have been on the same floor in scrimmage with one of Wofford's all-time greats and a future pro, Ellerbe "Daddy" Neal, and other such stalwarts as Bill Moody and Dennis Mathis.

Had I not later experienced a focus toward ministry, I may have followed a career of sports writing. As in high school, I both participated in athletics and was the sports editor of the student newspapers. My regular column in high school and college was titled "Summing up Sports with Summers."

The latter part of my second year brought me to an unforgettable opportunity for a unique expression of my athletic interests. Each spring, Professor William Scheerer of the athletics department would sponsor a call for interested Wofford students to compete for entrance into the nation's honorary collegiate athletic fraternity—Sigma Delta Psi.

Many contenders on registered college campuses were given a three-week span in which approximately fifteen strenuous athletic requirements were to be successfully completed. Certain dictated times or distances were directed to such diversified activities as track dashes, swimming events, rope climbs, broad jumping, baseball throwing, shot-putting, and other compulsory tasks. Occasionally a few Wofford students might make it through these rigors; I fortunately succeeded in this venture.

Sometimes now if I am ever asked the question about what might be among the most significant events in my life, my soul quickly drifts back to the particular memories of those dashes, throws, and other athletic strains of yesteryear. Their lingering sustenance has helped to shepherd me through some of life's tough times.

But it was back to the water where I found much of my athletic life in college. The currents of the Edisto were still coursing through my spiritual veins. At the beginning of my sophomore year, the college's athletics department announced that there would be forming, for the first time in the school's history, an intercollegiate swimming team. This bold undertaking attracted me. I would be able to maintain my love for swimming, and there also was a part of me that found it appealing to help create something completely new. I was made captain of the team for the next three years. I swam freestyle in both the fifty and one hundred yard events in addition to a relay race.

In our opening meet at Clemson University, we were forced to place an observer near the entrance to our locker room. His appointed mission was that of peering out at the pool and reporting information back to the rest of us. Particularly were we interested in how the opposing team went about its preliminary exercises in approaching the water. We required such a model since none of us had had any previous involvement in competitive swimming. When our initial tribe of only twelve members dived into the pool to show off our distinguished skills in this inaugural warm-up period, we almost lost our new swimming suits. The athletic office had ordered ones that contained too much cotton, and they soaked up water like sponges. Not a single race did any of us win in that first undertaking.

The only drawback to the college's swimming dreams was that it had no swimming pool! Our swimmers, instead, bravely practiced and held home meets in the Spartanburg YMCA pool. It was only twenty yards in length, whereas the collegiate pools of that day were at least twenty-five yards long. The choppy waves at the Y pool sometimes seemed to swell to English Channel proportions. But the tumultuous seas in this minature natatorium did little neither to dim our team's hopes for an unachievable victory during the three years of Wofford's winless dalliance with intercollegiate swimming nor did they cause any drownings.

However, our scoring improved with each year. We competed throughout the state and the Southeast against the likes of Clemson University, the University of South Carolina, The Citadel, Emory University, Davidson College, and East Carolina University. The challenges were invigorating—even the wrenching 43-41 defeat handed to us by the University of South Carolina. It was caused by our team's losing the last race at a meet in my junior year. I can still see in my mind's eye how we were beat by almost a fingertip.

This aquatic sojourn of long ago has assisted me over the years in holding dearly to a metaphor: *creating something out of nothing.* Form has the possiblity of emerging from chaos. The perspective of building and rebuilding has been present—as will be seen in various parts of the book—during some critical times in my life when faced with personal or systemic confusion.

Incidentally, simultaneous to the time that I was relishing the swimming team adventures up in Spartanburg, there happened to be a future clinical pastoral giant *diving* into the clinical context of ministry down in Columbia at the South Carolina State Hospital's clinical pastoral education program. John Patton, who recently had been involved with Seward Hiltner's graduate program at the University of Chicago, was participating in a CPE unit in the 1955 summer program under Obert Kempson's pastoral supervision. Patton later was to become one of the nation's leading authors and leaders in the pastoral counseling and pastoral theology areas. Being a professional friend of mine for years, he is introduced again in chapters 6 and 8.

The Back-You-Down Trip

Engagement in a favorite escapade sometimes made with college friends was another part of the social banquet outside the academic hallways. We called this occasional activity the "back-you-down trip." An auto jaunt to one of the Atlantic beaches, Atlanta, or some other distant destination would result for a carload of merrymakers in such an undertaking. The trip became fated if no one person backed away from a capricious late-night dare to start off on such a pilgrimage.

One journey, for instance, was arranged very quickly for Myrtle Beach with the expressed purpose of listening for several hours to the popular juke box music of the Platters, Joni James, or supremely Roy Hamilton's version of "Unchained Melody." An added benefit was that of hearing a splashing ocean's soothing accompaniment to the heartfelt music.

Nicknames were used rampantly in my college days. These were just a few among a varied assortment: Gut, Swamp Rat, Tub,

Light Bulb, Colonel, Flip, or Duck. Mine was Tomcat, or Cat for short. The moniker was bestowed on me by Knife. On such back-you-down forays, likely never to be heard were any real first names. However, plausible travelers could have been a Bull, Rock, or a Whip.

For the sake of my studies, thank goodness there were only about six or seven such hasty ramblings that transpired from these uncertain—but delightful—maneuvers.

Springtime Breezes

Although this collegiate environment could not exactly hold a candle to the exaggerated high jinks as depicted in the movie *Animal House,* there was a kinship to this life of pleasurable diversion—above all, in the springtime. Not only did the sap exuberantly rise in the lavishment of campus trees at that season but also there was a comparable elevation in the playful realm of prankishness. The warm breezes invariably brought with them an outbreak of contagious mischief. The art of fashioning innocent antics was profusely practiced.

Not uncommon, for instance, was the sight of a water-filled balloon—descending in almost slow motion from a dormitory window—targeted with uncanny accuracy near an unsuspecting head below. Student cars, which might have been nocturnally parked in front of a dormitory, mysteriously had an itch—unknown to the owners—to find a different habitation during the late hours in another harbored place of refuge.

Further, dormitory rest rooms represented a danger zone in the spring, especially if the anxious seeking of a certain fixture had an immediate priority for the user. Unbeknownst to one in such a seated vulnerability, there could be the sudden flush of a sizzling firecracker from the intricate plumbing on the above floor. This slight pop, however, would be enough to *bowl* one over—at least by surprise.

One particular spring saw a masterminding group of planners—using honed logistical skills from its student military training—stage a most remarkable excursion to the nearby women's college. Marching secretly under the cover of night, the clandestine and stealthy battalion deployed itself quietly, with the aid of walkie-talkies, into its point of destination. Some prior reconnoitered information revealed the exciting news that a door to the student dormitory inexplicably just might likely be ajar.

Through this readied portal streamed the exultant invaders into the confined domain. They dashed quickly through the forbidden halls and snatched victoriously the sensuously coveted trophies from the awaiting fingers of cheering accomplices. Panty raids, such as this ingenuously orchestrated effort, were tantalizingly sweeping the nation on warm springtime evenings in these 1950s.

Also there was peril present when the lingering influence of such spring cavorting cast its spell on some students' summer weddings. Social fraternity colleagues were less than brotherly in pitching some grooms into lakes or pools just a few hours before the wedding music was to crank up. Sardines also would be strategically placed on car motors so that, when a bride and groom made their quick exit, the bonded twosome soon occupied a roadster that resembled an odorous fish market in transit. As a loyal best man, I did my utmost to protect my roommate from some breathtaking wrestling attempted by our eager fraternity brothers and other college tricksters at his wedding reception's receiving line.

Such was the extended period of rambunctious adolescence for many of us in this post-World War II phase. Yet, not all of life outside the classroom contained such innocent playfulness. We took on some serious issues. For instance, as veterans of war-torn Korean hillsides trickled back to campus, some besieged souls periodically would be assaulted unpredictably by long-continued bloody images that were planted in their minds by the catastrophe in Asia. Their silent misery would discover the balm of a supportive ointment of care—applied from the touched hearts of fellow students. Also some campus editorialists crafted strong denouncements of the state's protracted social obedience to racial segregation. In a survey of the student body, more than sixty percent of the respondents indicated that their presidential preference was not for President Eisenhower. There dwelt an underlying desire for a chief executive with more overtness in social consciousness. Campus projects, such as the collecting of used books for overseas missions or the mobilizing of recreational events for economically deprived sections of Spartanburg, were constantly being developed by students.

The mixture of this spirited campus life—so diversely alive near the stimulating halls of intellectual learning—provided an animated microcosm through which a student could test out wings for a future flight into later engagements and responsibilities with the broader world. I might add that, for the sake of society's sanity and security, the breezes of spring helped to cleanse somewhat the propensity for prankish antics from our beings. No unsuspecting world deserved such balloons, firecrackers, or sardines.

MOVEMENT TOWARD MINISTRY

Not only did sports writing hold a career interest for me but also a second-year affection for embryology led me to think about a vocational pursuit for research in that area. However, the lack of a leaning in chemistry soon dampened that agenda. Perhaps, those earlier times of collecting eggs and caring for the chickens in Orangeburg had sustained this curiosity about ova, eggs, yolks, and such. Even ancient civilizations, too, thought of the egg as holding the secrets of new life.

A Turning Point

However, nearing the latter part of my sophomore year, I began considering the study of religious life. I entered college with hardly any thought of ever entertaining this inquiry—much less the ministry. The strongest factor that began moving me in this direction, however, was that of a private and illuminating prayer moment on a spring evening. I sensed, what I interpreted to be, God's reconciling nearness and impacting presence during a phase of some personal turmoil. I had just lost a political race on campus for a student body office in addition to having some disappointment over a dating relationship.

I add this particular focus on the above unsettledness due to my long-time appreciation now held for William James's classic book *Varieties of Religious Experience.* In his material James indicates that deep religious transformations frequently take place within the combustible disharmony of internal conflict.

The inexplicable nature of tasting an inwardly growing spirituality did some cartwheels at the time with my more intellectual bent. As a Methodist, John Wesley's historical discussions of the "warm heart" made some semblance of sense to me for the first time. I discovered much later in my life—as described in chapter 8—that this affective emphasis known emotionally by me in college would prepare me for a similar trust in the uncanny and extraordinary insights later derived from the wondrous dimensions of Jungian dreamwork, gestalt therapy, bioenergetics, sensory awareness training, and such. Further, there likely had been a river's preparation of me for this later fascination with being apprehended by awe. The Edisto's benevolent adornments of shimmering underwater shafts of sunlight were enough to set any young heart toward an ongoing search for mystery and meaning in life.

At the beginning of the next school year, I sought a major in English and a minor in religion. I now wanted to risk the studied pursuit of my religious questions. In terms of the religion courses, I favored the contributions from Old Testament archeology and the Pauline materials as offered by Dr. Charles Nesbitt. This hard-nosed University of Chicago graduate was not one to back away from higher textual criticism in biblical examination with college students. The ardor of his searching mind impressed me as being both courageous and challenging to the intellectual process of religious studies.

Even with the background of these spiritual and academic factors, it would not be until the ending of my junior year that I began to entertain possibilities of seeking entry into the ministry. The models were yet rare for me as to what one might do with this sort of experience other than explore it as a minister. Also there was a desire to speak about that which was beginning to nestle faithfully close to my heart.

A Rotation of Tires

It was during my senior year that I had an opportunity to do such speaking. I was invited by a Methodist church in a small nearby town to preach my first sermon at its regular Sunday morning worship service. For three prior weeks, I toiled slavishly on constructing this sermonic effort. Its basic subject was that of prayer. Every word in the four-page manuscript was honed to what I thought was perfection. In the week before the event, I stood before a mirror and practiced this finished product at least a dozen times.

As I located myself behind the church's pulpit on the much-anticipated day of disclosing this work of art, my recently shined shoes glistened and the one blue suit that I owned was exceedingly pressed. I eagerly anticipated arriving at that concluding place in the sermon where my consummating illustration would render full light on the entire content of this focus on prayer. In reaching that point, I had unfalteringly uttered every memorized word.

With a demeanor of attempted erudition, I said, "We resort to prayer sometimes like we deal with our car tires in an emergency." (Apparently, I was still recalling those World War II days when my family had constant problems with the weak rubber tires on our car.) "When we come down with a *spare* tire," I said, "we open our trunks and pull out the *flat* tire." As soon as this brilliant homiletical statement fell from my lips, I knew that something did not sound right. Indeed, these tires needed rotation. So I started over again to make sure that this momentary glitch would not torpedo my handiwork.

I continued, "I need to back up a minute." Lo and behold, the same set of tires rolled out, "When we come down with a *spare* tire... pull out the *flat* tire." In feeling as if I wanted to hold up a white flag and surrender, I gasped, "I think I need to give up on that one."

A sainted deliverer on the front row—sensing that this young man had been waylaid by these uncooperative tires—came to my rescue in his saying barely above a whisper, "Preacher, go ahead and let the jack down. You've done a great job, and it ain't no use to pull out another flat tire!" In our corporate laughter, I quietly retorted, "Well, you can't win 'em all. But I did want to 'drive' home that point."

I continue to have thanks for that congregation's letting me know, early in my religious life, that preaching can be something more than trying to create an artificial effect or the putting on of airs—or tires, for that matter.

A Seminary Award

In response to a request from Emory University's seminary for recommendations on candidates for a full scholarship award, Dr. Nesbitt and the religion department submitted my name to the

Candler School of Theology at the start of my senior year. That spring I was given the news that the school in Atlanta was desirous of my accepting such a scholarship offer.

I was delighted with these tidings, but I also carried some quiet skepticism about the ministerial role. I wondered whether too much of my life and interests would become constricted by a cultural stereotype. Due to these issues, I felt some ambivalence creeping slightly into my young soul. However, an inner assurance of my own spiritual realizations remained alive for me even amidst moments of wrestling with some doubts. I accepted gladly the seminary's award and concurrently requested from the United States Army a deferment on my second lieutenant's military commission gained from the college's ROTC program.

DOING, KNOWING, SAYING, AND BEING

Since there existed the backdrop of a historical drama in clinical pastoral education at the same time that I was engaged in back-you-down trips or deciding about seminary studies, this section now takes a look at some features of that concurrent CPE story.

In a summary of CPE's history thus far, one view held that each historical phase had contained consistently a distinguishing characteristic of uniqueness. For instance, the 1925-1935 era had shown students and supervisors generally asking, "What must I *do* in providing pastoral care to the patient?" The 1935-1945 theme was, instead, flavored by the issue of "What must I *know*?" The next span of 1945-1955 generally promoted the emphasis of "What must I *say*?" The earlier *doing* represented the historical tone of emphasizing techniques; *knowing*, theories; and *saying*, counseling responses. The suggested 1955-1965 motif, however, contained a completely different thrust in its question of "What must I *be*?"[1]

When I was in college, the CPE enterprise apparently had begun integrating an emerging value about the *relationship* in the caring process between the pastoral representative and the person receiving the pastoral care. The explosion of the relational psychotherapies following World War II had its influence on CPE's development. Hence, the personhood, or the *beingness*, of the pastoral-care provider assumed more prominence in the 1950s. By then, Anton Boisen's original research focus in his wanting to

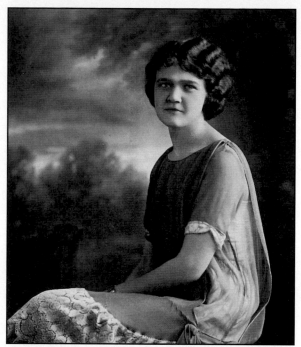

My mother Anabel Hill Summers at twenty-one years of age.

My father Carroll Erwin Summers prior to entering college.

Thomas Raysor Summers, a paternal uncle whose first name was given to me, was killed in World War I.

The Orangeburg home is the 1934 birthplace of my story in clinical pastoral education (CPE). By the time that I was born, the young CPE movement had split into two rival groups; namely, the Council for Clinical Training and the Institute of Pastoral Care.

Anton T. Boisen (1876-1965) is the recognized founder of CPE in 1925. (ACPER)

My maternal grandfather, affectionately known as Papa, sits on the porch of his Cross Hill home in 1936.

Louise Spann holds my son Mason in 1973.

The Edisto River has remained as an inspiring resource throughout my life.

Baseball had captured my heart by the age of four.

Bob Brinkman (left) and Seward Hiltner in New York City during the 1930s. Brinkman was director of the Council for Clinical Training, while Hiltner served as its executive secretary from 1935-1938. (ACPER)

My first cousin West Summers (right) and I sit on the bumper of a family car in 1938.

An adoring—and mischievous—glance is given to my older brother Carroll when I was seven years old.

Fred Keuther (right), who succeeded Bob Brinkman as director of the Council for Clinical Training in 1947, was a formidable leader in the clinical pastoral movement for decades. He is seen in a pastoral supervisory conference with a CPE student in the 1930s. (ACPER)

► *West Summers (right) and I are blessed in 1945 by the All-American football player and Heisman Trophy winner Doc Blanchard of the famed Army teams. My maternal aunt lived next door to the Blanchards in Bishopville, South Carolina.*

The henhouse on my family's property in Orangeburg was the source of my egg-selling business.

Obert Kempson did supervisory training under Ernest Bruder at the St. Elizabeths Hospital in Washington during the summer of 1947. Bruder is seen on the first row, third from the left; while Kempson is fourth from the left. (ACPER)

◀ *Anton Boisen (left) makes a consultation visit—probably in 1947—with Ernest Bruder at St. Elizabeths Hospital. (APC)*

▶ *In 1947 my baseball team won Orangeburg's City Playground Championship. First row (left to right): Bert Gue, Will Kelly, Eddie Rushton, Boby Pearson, and me; second row: Marion Funderburk, West Summers, Al Wilson, Jim Bryant, and Glen Lake. Notice the bare feet.*

CPE groups from Massachusetts General Hospital and the Boston City Hospital—both related to the Institute of Pastoral Care—gather in the summer of 1947. Rollie Fairbanks, the IPC director, is on the front row, fourth from the left. John Billinsky, the CPE supervisor of Boston City Hospital, is fifth from the left. (ACPER)

▲ *Obert Kempson (far left) leads a CPE seminar at the South Carolina State Hospital in 1949. (APC)*

▶ *Eddie Mirmow, my Orangeburg athletic godfather, speaks to a sports club in Charleston, South Carolina, in 1948.*

Louise Long—one of the first women certified as a CPE supervisor—is on the first row, far right. She holds a discussion in the 1940s with a group of her students. (ACPER)

restrict rigidly the study of living human documents to that of patients had been radically transformed by other CPE developers. Added in the 1950s was this corresponding concern for the CPE student's own personal and pastoral growth process. A sense of *being*, thus, had gained more prominence for the religious representative than just that of *doing* ministry. The pastoral supervisor began to give attention not only to the student's acquiring pastoral care skills and techniques but also to the student as a growing, relational person. This emphasis would be similar to what James Ashbrook later would write: "The deep necessity of relationship depends more upon what we *are* to each other than upon what we say to each other."[2]

APPROACHING SEMINARY

Following my college graduation, the summer of 1956 found me returning to Orangeburg. With the complex mix of both eagerness and some reservation, I anticipated nevertheless my beginning in the fall with theological studies. During the first half of the summer, I labored with a construction company in the pouring of concrete for the building of a grain elevator. The latter phase was spent administratively assisting the director of a nearby Methodist nursing home.

An Ashtray

Also during that summer, I completed my Methodist studies for the seeking of a preacher's license. The undertaking was under the auspices of a district examining committee. This activity of pastoral scrutiny would be my first exposure to a committee appearance. It proved to be later in my ministry an exercise often repeated in the clinical pastoral tradition—as seen in my description of a certification committee in chapter 5.

The licensing occasion also saw my first brush with the subtle edges of incongruities in church officialdom. The committee was asking me about some of my doctrinal and policy beliefs. I noticed that, when the question came up about my reaction to the church's ideas on abstaining from the use of tobacco, several of the ministerial examiners sheepishly waved away some remnants of smoke that had hovered over an ashtray. As the years have unfolded, this inconsistency has served to remind me that the church as an institution seeking to offer grace, after all, is far from being perfect!

A Growing Disquietness

As seminary days approached, there were some perturbing pressures that began to mount in my personal transition. For one thing, I was beginning to feel a trace of unclarity about my choice of moving in the direction of ministry. However, my customary style at this time of my life was that of not easily revealing to others that there were such moments behind a calm demeanor. Further, there was a dimension of the commitment yet stirring in me that restrained any turning away from a social and religious covenant made with both my indicated path for ministry and the scholarship award. Secondly, the end of that summer brought a finality to the intermittent relationship with a woman—the cherished person described as a girlfriend from my earlier high school years. The merging of these distresses was kept clutched within as I began my pilgrimage to seminary. In contrast to the fire in the belly with the anticipation of former back-you-down trips or other expeditions, the day that I voyaged toward Atlanta was not an easy one.

At the time of my searching, there coincidentally was another venture being undertaken in the South. During that year, Gus Verdery had become the chaplaincy director of the Georgia Baptist Hospital in Atlanta. He had entered an extended form of clinical pastoral training with Charles "Chuck" Hall at the Georgian Alcoholism Clinic that same year and completed a similar program under the pastoral supervision of Charles "Chuck" Gerkin the next year at Atlanta's Grady Memorial Hospital.[3] Woven later throughout portions of the book is the described impact that Verdery, Hall, and Gerkin would have on my future clinical pastoral life.

In completing the walk across the stage of the four collegiate years, I now was preparing to step into perhaps the most turbulent—but molding—arena of my whole life. The next chapter explores that tumultuous crucible.

Chapter 3

Prepared by a Storm,
1956-1960

Little did I know that a major resource in my ministerial development would not be discovered primarily in books and seminary courses but mainly from an unanticipated whirlwind. This next interval of time would see a ragged personal and pastoral growth process hammered out arduously on this anvil of intense searching and suffering. Chapter 3 describes that precarious passage made in my early twenties.

A WELL-INTENDED PRESCRIPTION

Midway durng my initial 1956-1957 year at Emory University's Candler School of Theology, I confided with a trusted faculty member about the twinned quandary of my personal hurts and faith questions. I had not yet realized fully enough that these two particular issues often go hand-in-hand with life's crises. He heard for a long moment my plight, but his well-intended suggestion of my needing just more time in prayer was not discovered in the long run as being the remedy. However, I had taken a step in reaching out for responsive support. I also had the assurance of knowing that someone else in my setting realized that I was in a struggle.

It would take the following year before I would try again. This strained hesitancy reflected the degree of stunned shame over what I sensed to be the loss of my faith. I was now feeling an isolation from the previously discovered spiritual wellspring in college. In addition, I carried the aforementioned burden of a historical resistance in letting others know much about my personal perplexities.

Interestingly enough, my academic studies were kept at a rather significant level during this distressing time. Also I played as a starter on the Circuit Riders—the seminary's highly regarded basketball team in the graduate league. The squad played against teams that included some formerly outstanding collegiate players from such universities as Vanderbilt, Cincinnati, and Florida. Our team was invited occasionally to compete in some tournaments around Atlanta. During that year I also was one of four seminarians employed by a Methodist district in Atlanta. Our task was that of surveying the northeast area of the city for an eventual organizing of a new congregation. Within a year it would become the Saint James Methodist Church.

ACADEMIC SPARKS FANNED

Beginning in my second year, the untended tumult that was quietly brewing within me became a strong persuasion that sparked my desire for enrollment in pastoral care courses. My faith questions took on more relevance as I entered those studies that involved the providing of care to persons undergoing ragged times. I could deeply identify with this particular human need.

Discovering Anton Boisen and Carl Rogers

Along with my other required and elective courses, I sought those classes that dealt in particular with religion and psychology, pastoral perspectives on personality development, pastoral theology, and pastoral counseling. These offerings in seminaries had begun to grow as a result of the preludial groundbreaking labors seen in such pioneers as Anton Boisen and his proteges. My participation in this curriculum was made with Floyd Feely. He was a professor who had a graduate school exposure at the University of Chicago with both the psychologist Carl Rogers and the pastoral theologian Seward Hiltner.

During this particular era of the 1950s, much of the focus in pastoral care and counseling was placed on a Rogerian, nondirective method in providing pastoral response. This approach implied stereotypically that the pastoral care-provider gives little interference in order that the recipient of care can find, through such a non-threatening atmosphere, an inner release of growthful strivings. Some took this client-centeredness to the extreme by parroting verbally back almost exactly what was said by the parishioner. At least, the practice of this trend allowed some pastors to gain greater listening skills and a competency in developing rapport. However, Howard Clinebell's 1966 *Basic Types of Pastoral Counseling* would greatly assist in later revising and diversifying the models of pastoral care and counseling.

Developing such term papers for Feely as "The Psychological and Religious Aspects of Guilt" and "The Schizophrenic Break" was quite stimulating. It was through the research efforts on the latter project that I first became acquainted with the history and contributions of Boisen. Early materials on schizophrenia from Silvano Arieti (his 1955 *Interpretation of Schizophrenia*) and Freida Fromm-Reichmann's *Principles of Intensive Psychotherapy* proved extremely helpful to me. My first exposure to the writings of Harry Stack Sullivan and Wayne Oates (*Religious Dimensions of Personality*) also took place around the preparation of these papers.

Freud Talks with Shakespeare

Another faculty member who was vital to my learning process was William Mallard. My involvement in his course on "Christianity and Literature" has endured to this day as a key resource for me. Mallard encouraged the weaving of my psychotherapeutic interests in such writers as Karl Menninger, Sigmund Freud, Abraham Maslow, Rogers, Gordon Allport, Boisen, and Erich Fromm with the literary materials of William Shakespeare, John Milton, Henrik Ibsen, and Eugene O'Neill. I have remained indebted to Mallard for the combination that he offered, at this early stage in my pastoral development, for a dual focus on systematized writing and a correlation of meanings between two disciplines of thought.

My academic inquiry was further enhanced by such professors as Fred Prussner and Wyatt Aiken Smart in the Old Testament curriculum. Albert Barnett and Merrill Purvis captured my imagination. Barnett was an authority on the Gospel of John, while Purvis offered analysis on Rudolf Bultmann's textual explorations of *kerygma* in the New Testament.

However, the seminary experience of these 1950s was dominated largely by a lecture methodology. There was little emphasis on the integration of materials by small group work or seminar dialogue. My involvement with intentional group learning would take place later within the resources and methods of clinical pastoral education.

CPE IN HIDING

I heard about CPE only vaguely while in seminary. By then, this kind of pastoral training had been in existence for barely thirty years. I knew about the engagement of two fellow students for a couple of months in a "hospital visitation program" at Grady Hospital in Atlanta. It was mentioned to me that a new chaplain by the name of Charles Gerkin had arrived there from Kansas. By and large, the Emory theological students were engaged in stealth fashion with CPE. Hardly anyone at the seminary seemed to know much about it. There were no noticeable signs of proactive encouragement given to students by the seminary leadership for the pursuing of such experiential involvement in those days.

Nevertheless, due to Emory's growing support of CPE over the past couple of decades, its center for pastoral services currently possesses one of the largest and most recognized CPE programs in the nation.

A WRACKING STORM

Although remaining outwardly quite related to academics and student government, I continued in my second year to be grasped by the greater encroachment of an inner distress. The experience at this time probably represented an increasing depression that had been gradually gathering its storm clouds for more than a year. Before leaving for the summer, I met a couple of times with Professor Feely and shared with him the fear that I was falling apart. I wondered with him if I would be able to survive the oncoming several months. I was poised to become for that period of time a student associate for two churches in South Carolina. He indicated that he knew of some psychotherapy provisions in Atlanta, but I resisted using them at that time.

Touched by Pastoral Care

Feely displayed deep appreciation for my dilemma. His availability in listening represented to me the most significant moments of care than any previously received from a pastoral representative. There were times when my fright could only be expressed in the silence of tears in my eyes. As I now examine this heightened crisis, I view it as a season in my overall life's journey when I first touched the life-enhancing benefits of the clinical pastoral movement. Due to his background, he indicated that he would be starting a therapy group in the upcoming fall quarter. I was assured that I could become a part of this endeavor upon my return to Emory. With a glimmer of hope to grasp, an embattled twenty-three-year-old young man left to face the uncertainties of the summer.

Life Caves In

However, my anxiety heightened as those months in the churches progressed. By the latter phases of that sweltering season, restless and sometimes sleepless nights appeared as unwanted visitors. A family trip with my parents and a cousin had been previously planned so that we could be present for my brother Carroll's wedding in Laredo, Texas. He had been stationed there as a jet pilot instructor with the air force.

Not yet knowing very well how to safeguard my own limits, I undertook this 1958 trip with a queasy trepidation. I had worked feverishly that summer without taking in nurture. By the time that we arrived at our destination, I felt that my whole inner world was collapsing. My structures and securities had imploded from within, and there was little left but an abyss. Gloom set in like heavy clouds, and gastrointestinal upheavals raged exhaustively. My family approached the return trip with much caution.

When we arrived back in Orangeburg, I entered into physical examinations. No medical reasons were discovered for my travail. This lack of finding was basically no surprise to me. I was beginning to feel that, whatever it was, I was in a different and foreign kind of trouble. Antidepressants—such as they were at midcentury—provided only slight comfort. I stayed in bed for more than a week. Worry and prevailing despair were constant companions. I had lost more than fifteen pounds over the summer months as these stormy winds ripped away much fleshly strength from my moderate frame.

I began to wonder if this devastation was akin to what was mentioned in those days, a "nervous breakdown." I have often pondered if what I encountered—undiagnosed years ago—was not only a profound depression but also it felt as if I had approached a state of near madness. Regardless, I came to know at a young age what uncontrollable terror was like. My parents, not knowing what was happening to me, were extremely concerned and offered me quiet support. My father must have undoubtedly known perplexing moments as he saw me struggle. I cannot imagine how his soul might have quivered in seeing his second-born—once years ago warmly holding close to his neck in learning how to swim the Edisto—now almost being swept out to sea. I learned some years later that he had had a couple of close relatives whose own young adulthood years earlier had broken open with much apprehension.

A TIME OF REBUILDING

A drive back to Atlanta that September was made hesitantly. But my starting again at theological school for that final and third year proved to offer me an attempt to pull a shattered life together. At the same time, I felt that I was moving out into unknown territory with no map. Were these storms also portending a need for the ragged redemption of some neglected inner regions of my young adult life? There were long moments when I was aware that I was trying primarily to hold on for survival's sake. I just hoped that I would not get blown away by such fierce forces.

You'll Never Walk Alone

I discovered that I was able to study and concentrate only for a couple of hours each day for the first several months. I learned how to pace myself and measure my energy. Solace was to be found from phonograph records that emphasized courage. For example, Roy Hamilton's "You'll Never Walk Alone" became a nurturing melody. So great yet was my bewilderment over what I was encountering that I mentioned to only a few of my South Carolina seminary friends anything about the surface dimensions surrounding my situation. My young, troubled soul could find no meaningful reconciliation between this particular dark night—where little faith frequented—and the daybreaking of an illuminating faith discovered unexpectedly four years earlier in college years. However, I learned much about life's vulnerable and fragile qualities.

A great sense of loss further was realized in the late fall when it became apparent to me that I would not be able to play my last year on the Circuit Riders basketball team. Not only had my legs relinquished their spring but also much coordination had failed me in both dribbling and shooting. My athletic life, so long an external bedrock around which I had built much of my interests, had been crippled. This detour from sports, however, promoted at the time more sensitivity to searching patiently for the life of inner resources.

A Safe Harbor

Thankfully, a principal place where I was to find movement toward gradual hope and health was that of the regular therapy group formerly mentioned. I discovered therein an anchor to which I could bring my brokenness. Five other participants and myself wrestled with the depths of strenuous moments through Floyd Feely's facilitation. In a ragged course of time, I began to grasp new understandings related to some unattended dimensions. For instance, I grappled with my dependency, ambivalence, and intimacy needs. These insights were pulled from pain's grip. I felt a resurrection of hope when I learned how to cry openly. This lamenting had been entombed in a long hibernation.

Slowly in the spring of that final seminary year, I began to sense some portion of the dreadful fog lifting from my crushing burden. I attributed much of this to the group engagement with my fellow strugglers. Energies of directness, compassion, anger, and nurture were among the living waters found in this clustered harbor. I had come some distance during that year, but I also realized that there may yet be a long way to travel.

Sermons Born from Fire

That senior year also was accompanied by my being an associate
pastor on Sunday mornings with four churches of the North Georgia Methodist Annual Conference.   This Bethlehem Circuit was
essentially in a rural setting; I was able to establish my own stride
and not find great weariness. I preached at one of these churches
each Sunday, and I often remained for a hospitable dinner with one
of the church families. In now reviewing my sermons for that year,
I notice where I spoke invariably on such themes as hope arising
out of suffering, the relationship of faith and doubt, the unpredictable vicissitudes of life, and God's loving acceptance of us.
These sermonic efforts truly were born from the fires in my own
ragged experience.

In once sharing a meal around a family's table in this parish,
the father offered me a moment of graceful care and encouragement. He had no education beyond the eighth grade and had
known some rocky roads in his own life. However, he was an avid
reader and held a special infatuation for his own self-educated
craftsmanship with words. He said softly, "Preacher, when I hear
your sermons, I always feel that you know *whereof* you speak. For
the sake of us who know what hurting's about, please never *desist*
from doing that." I have known no greater perspective about the
powerful opportunity of preaching than that which his utterance
indicated.

Literature That Touched the Soul

It is no small wonder that my academic focus continued for some
further elective courses in pastoral psychology and pastoral care.
My own personal raggedness was instrumental in a search for literature that had primary meaning for the questions that were resident in my struggles. Speaking volumes to me in those days were
such books as Boisen's *Exploration of the Inner World*, Carl Michalson's *Faith for Personal Crises*, Carl Rogers's *Client-Centered Therapy*,
David Roberts's *Psychotherapy and a Christian View of Man*, Karen
Horney and her *Neuroses and Human Growth*, Henry Guntrip's *Psychotherapy and Religion*, and *God's Grace and Man's Hope* by Daniel
Day Williams.

Central to me mainly were those literary accentuations that

emphasized a potential present for reconstruction in the midst of severe upheaval. Enduring for me has been this early exposure, for instance, to Boisen's psychogenic perspective. This thrust indicates that psychic disturbance can result in positive implications. Like fever in a physical organism, Boisen suggests that the unsettledness can be a regressive organismic attempt to move the individual into the lower levels of mental and spiritual life. This backward movement, as it were, is an undertaking to assimilate certain hitherto unincorporated masses of life experience. The disassociated meanings clamor for attention and give the sufferer no peace until in some way they receive response.[1] At least, this is what some of my turbulence was like for me.

HARRY EMERSON FOSDICK

As the completion of my seminary days neared, I was blessed by the reading of Harry Emerson Fosdick's autobiography *The Living of These Days*. Recounted was his own breakdown experience in 1901 as a young seminary student. I received his life-giving story as a precious gift, because it gave me a mooring with which I could strongly identify.

Written Care

I began to have a brief correspondence with this retired and once noted minister of New York's Riverside Church. I shared with him an account of my recent years of breaking apart. He offered through the written word his inimitable balm of supportive guidance and care.

Fosdick once included in a five-page letter these following words of encouragement:

> You can come out of this wretched experience a better man and a better minister than you ever could have been without it. This is not an easy achievement. Don't expect an overnight miracle. Work out your problems with patience, and try to keep your chin up and never give in.[2]

Fosdick and Boisen

My later studies in the history of the clinical pastoral movement, by
the way, would reveal Fosdick's vital role during the 1920s and
1930s in that effort. He had helped to shape some of the era's significant issues. In addition to knowing much about the tradition of
the Emmanuel movement, his familiarity with the contributions of
Boisen and Richard Cabot had put him squarely in the middle of
the religion and mental health dialogue.

While teaching at Union Seminary in New York City in those
days, Fosdick once provided critical financial assistance to a young
student named Russell Dicks. As a later important clinical pastoral
pioneer, Dicks would introduce in the early 1930s the written verbatim method to the CPE world.

Fosdick and Boisen personally knew one another. Robert
Moats Miller notes that Boisen took some courses that were taught
by Fosdick at Union in the early 1920s. In feeling gratified that
Fosdick once mentioned his own earlier breakdown, Boisen
recalled to him that "... you graciously told me of your personal
acquaintance with the little-known country between mental disorder and religious experience which I have been trying to explore."[3]

A further indication of Fosdick's appreciation for the emerging
contributions of pastoral psychology was seen in how he viewed
his preaching role. He perceived it as being heavily directed
toward personal counseling on a large group scale.

I have remained grateful for what Fosdick's caring correspondence meant to me in my special time of need in seminary. A
request from Riverside Church has been made for one of the letters
that he wrote me to be placed in its archives.

In preparing to graduate from Emory's Candler School of Theology, I gave some consideration to entering doctoral studies in
Boston University's theological program of personality and religion. Had I moved into that geography, the likelihood is that my
early identification with the clinical pastoral movement would
have been with the northeastern tradition in the Institute of Pastoral Care. However, a stronger pull within me pushed my attention to a direct pastoral care form of ministry rather than academic
pursuits.

Toward the latter part of this third year, I was humbled to be
selected as one of twenty Outstanding Seniors at Emory Universi-

ty by a campus publication. Another surprise was that of an induction into Theta Phi—the international academic and honorary theological society. How these events were able to take place during the strenuous storm through which I had been traveling remains for me a mystery to this day. I had seen my ordeal mainly via the lens of a religious quest with such themes as exile, hope, and sin.

PAUSING WITH THE ARMY

Regardless of the subsequent pastoral pathway that I would walk, a time of hiatus occurred upon my completing the seminary years. As already stated, I had received a military commission at my college graduation. These six months of active duty were postponed until the completion of my theological degree. At that point, I had the choice of converting the original commission into three years of military chaplaincy with the United States Army or retaining the obligation of six months as a second lieutenant in the Infantry. I chose the latter, because the three intervening years at seminary had produced a decision in me not to engage in a prolonged military tour.

I entered the army at Fort Benning with a hope that I had recovered fully enough to withstand the upcoming rigors of basic officers' military training. This return to Fort Benning represented a much different tour from that made four years before. Following my junior year in college, I had spent that summer in encampment there as an ROTC training cadet. The requirement of jumping off towers with the paratroopers, dashing through woods with rangers, or bivouacking in fields was encountered with a certain sense of accomplishment. Further, I had enjoyed being one of several competitive swimmers from our training battalion to enter into a base-wide swimming meet. We went up against some noted University of Florida swimmers from another battalion.

To say the least, the summer of 1959 instead was radically different. There initially were some vulnerable moments. In one instance I passed out due to fatigue. I came very close to seeking a medical discharge in those early phases. Consultation was sought with a clinic's social worker, and his understanding spirit contained much supportive interest. By phone I conferred with my father; and his caring, pragmatic suggestions were found to be helpful. Perseverance was made with the training. I soon learned that I could hang in there—if only sometimes by a slender thread. The years of preceding capabilities and physical confidences had evaporated somewhat like fog at noon. But I decided that I would attempt to complete this unclear situation. I learned much about patience. Fosdick's earlier written encouragement of "not expecting an overnight miracle" became like a spiritual mantra with its upholding buoyancy—much like the Edisto River had been.

Those 1959 summer months of July and August infantry training saw much trudging through the swampy woods of southern Georgia and the steamy fields of the fort. During this same time period, South Vietnam officers occasionally could be seen at the military base. We were told that these visitors were meeting with United States advisors so that assistance could be received in response to "some problems" arising within their slightly known region in the Far East.

My remaining four military months were situated at Fort Jackson in Columbia, South Carolina. By then, the Army was trying to decide what to do with the now almost obsolete infantry lieutenants serving six-months tours. A first sergeant's question greeted me amidst his laughter, "What in the crap are we supposed to do with these young six-monthers—plus one who's a preacher!"

On occasional weekends I went to Orangeburg to be of assistance to Carlisle Smiley—the Methodist minister now at my home church. He had known of my going forth—with apparent strength—three years earlier to seminary. I shared closely with him some of the rugged details of my recent years, and this generous clergyman listened with a warm interest to my pilgrimage. I will always hold a special place in my heart for this kind man whose pastoral blessing helped to embolden my own faith journey—at a time when broken places in it were strewn within my soul.

At Fort Jackson I began to embrace the emergence of more inner security. The schedule of a military regularity in my external structures and the realization of the successful completion of the Benning months were helpful contributions in my gaining more balance. Some of this increasing strength also grew out of my entrance into psychotherapy with Dr. Frank O'Sheal of Columbia. The therapy undertaking opened up much further my search for direction and health. Later I would learn that the CPE tradition strongly valued that its participants utilize the resources of psychotherapy for continued personal and pastoral growth. Further, my seminary studies and group involvement had given me appreciation for the therapy field. My self-initiated entry into the therapy experience contained some mixed features of both trust and desperation.

As the decade of the 1950s came to an end, I started grasping a greater sense of hope for my journey. This awareness rested within the realization that a frightening nightmare—swirling with its potentializing energies—had crashed in and through my young life. Only the years ahead could reveal whether Fosdick's following affirmation would bear fruit: "You can come out of this wretched experience a better man and a better minister than you ever could have been without it."

In many ways my future ministry and CPE supervision were prepared by this stormy span of time.

Chapter 4

———◦◦◦———

A Model from Rhoadus, 1960-1961

The closure of my military sojourn ushered in the opportunity of my receiving a parish appointment to three country churches. They were situated in South Carolina's Williamsburg County. The Trio (pronounced "Try-O") Methodist Charge was located in one of the most poverty-ridden sections of the nation.

Entertained in this segment of my account is a look at how I became more interested in a sustaining form of ministry. Although my stay was not a prolonged one, I was influenced very positively by the Trio parish and a most unlikely teacher.

A SUSTAINING SEASON

My 1960 wintry arrival date at this village of the lower state was accompanied by a freezing rain. The parsonage was placed several hundred yards away from the only paved road in the community. The three folks sitting around a stove at the little post office mentioned to me that it would be impossible to drive my car to the house. The vehicle, they confidently said, surely would bog down to its axle on the muddy dirt roads. They further indicated that even tractors were known to be submerged in such mud for a whole week. In silently thinking of my seminary courses, I was tempted to feel that the bearers of such sadistic tidings to a newcomer were in need of Seward Hiltner's "precounseling" approach as described in the seminary-assigned book *Pastoral Counseling!*

I rolled up my pants legs and walked barefooted through a frozen cornfield toward the parsonage. In reflecting again on my seminary learnings and attempting to see further humor on this dismal day, I began to sense strong reservations about what the seminary curriculum earlier had transmitted regarding Paul Tillich's notion *the ground of all being*. I saw the ground slipping away from within me—not to mention literally from under me.

However, the less than two years as pastor in this rural setting offered me a growing measure of personal and pastoral centering. A new appreciation for the sustaining function of pastoral care emerged to more than balance my strong devotion to its healing and reconciling natures. The churches contained many elderly and some unemployed persons. Many members were stuck away in rather isolated places. Much of my pastoral time was spent visiting people in their homes. We sat around dinner tables, in rocking chairs on front porches, or around stoves in cold weather.

The congregational members were desirous for their minister to be with them for the hearing of boundless stories and reminiscences. The leaders of the churches were not focused heavily on expansion nor seeking marked budget increases. There was just not that much money available. I was paid annually $3,300; the Methodist Conference contributed an additional $200. My pastoral stay with these delightful people was featured by a *being* form of ministry rather than getting stirred up over great expectations for a *doing* style. Hence, my sustaining of others became the most paramount mode of my pastoral care attempts.

DODGING WASPS

This parish presented me with natural memories and images that have endured to this day. One such image would show up more than thirty years later in a published short story of mine, "Riding to New Salem." The main figure in the story is Lukie, an eleven-year-old son of a rural preacher. Sitting in church one day, this free-wheeling observer comments to himself:

> Pap will probably preach about the same thing he did awhile ago down at Oak Hill. Now that's preaching for you: how those dry bones laying around in this valley, where these *profits* lived, all of a sudden could rise up and be put together! Pap likes to preach on quick things like that, things that happen all of a sudden. Like the *profit* Paul getting hit by a bright light on a road or a wall in *Jerry Go* falling down suddenly when you blow a trumpet at it.
>
> By the way, maybe some *profit* somewhere could make a sermon about the blamed wasps hanging around this New Salem church, waiting to zap you all of a sudden. It was some bad stuff last summer when one of those stinging babies fell out the hanging light and dive-bombed Pap on the nose when he had just got started preaching on how *Jay Cup*

pulled a fast one over on his daddy and his brother, the *profit E Saw*. Pap hollered just a little bit, and he could hardly make it in time for the piano *inner lube* before his nose swelled up.

Course, that was nothing like what happened at the end of the summer when one of 'em bounced off the ceiling and headed right down the front of Cornelia White's blue dress. She squawked a loud one and everybody just looked at her and done nothing. It sure weren't going to be me to reach down there and get that sorry dive bomber and get stung all of a sudden. Course, there's also manners to think about.[1]

Like Lukie's father, I tried to dodge many a summer wasp in the middle of a sermon at one of the churches of the Trio Charge.

A CHERISHED MENTOR

The Trio mileu also possessed a charming character who led me into cultivating a greater sense of presence with other persons. His name was Rhoadus Blakely. This gangly, southern-drawled farmer was a bus driver for the county schools. He constantly reminded me that what folks basically want is to have somebody listen to them talk about what interests them. In this respect, I have known no better teacher in pastoral care than Rhoadus.

He also gave me a lively metaphor about pastoral care that stuck with me throughout the majority of my later clinical pastoral education days. His particular symbol is the main title of this book. The natural instructor saw a teachable moment with his protege on a hot Sunday morning. It occurred when I hurriedly was dashing out of one of the churches so I could quickly jump into my unpredictable car and speed away to a second church for its morning worship service. Before I could open the car's door, I heard a familiar voice ring out from under one of the nearby shade trees. It included a term that was new to me at the time. The words were transmitted in his usual slow speech: "Preacher, come on over here and *hunker down* with us. You look like you're too much in a hurry."

Out of the corner of my eye, I could see that, sure enough, it was Rhoadus. He was crouching down with several of his cronies. In this squatting position, they were engaged in the spontaneous exchanging of stories before going back into the church building for Sunday School. Much useless information was being thrown around. Their discourse ranged in speculation about the weather

to that of baseball scores, national politics, or the reference that I
made about some fellow named Tillich in my just-completed sermon. Nobody was doing anything; they were just being. When I
joined the small group of squatters on that day, I encountered my
own innate ties with the early memories of sitting around with kin
or passing time away on my grandfather's front porch.

During my later CPE and chaplaincy years, an interest in a hunkering down ministry would not be, of course, from a literal posture of crouching. Rather, it has been rooted in the sustenance
exchanged between persons via a natural mode of relating and
conversing. Hunkering down—or the art of doing absolutely nothing—may appear on the surface to be irrelevant. But authentic
hunkering requires a great deal of awareness by the pastor about
the nature of facilitating supportive and trustful moments. Hunkering offers a mode of beingness amongst persons. In providing
consultation to various staffs and groups, I have often asked the
question: "In your busy work, how well do you hunker down
together?" Naturally, this gives me an opportunity to introduce
them to the memory of my dear friend and one of my best pastoral
care teachers—Rhoadus Blakely.

Although now deceased, the recollection of him remains in my
soul as a reminder of the importance of persons naturally and
spontaneously talking with each other. What he taught me
metaphorically about the unsophisticated art of hunkering down—
or doing nothing—would show up in my CPE teaching a dozen
years later.

BROKENNESS AND OPENNESS

In a continuing effort to consider the theological questions arising
from my recent years of deep struggle and entrance into psychotherapy, I maintained at this time some correspondence with
Floyd Feely back at the seminary. He wrote some very pastoral letters in which meaningful theological perspectives were made in
response to my questioning. Some of his themes spoke deeply to
my spiritual search. For instance, on one occasion, he wrote:

> In an effort to be genuinely supportive, let me share the thought
> with you that perhaps the very traumatic experience of brokenness with
> which you are now grappling is *in itself* an entree to the deep kind of reli-

gious certainty for which you have longed. In other words, the brokenness can be an openness to a new range of experience.[2]

Over the years I have given thanks for the substantial pastoral
and theological support that I experienced in such written words of
guidance and reflection from Feely. They met me profoundly at the
intersection where I was attempting to bring some theological integration into my splintered personal experience.

OUT OF THE DEPTHS

It was during this period that I also read Anton Boisen's newly
published autobiography *Out of the Depths* (1960). Contained were
the flavors of torment that he knew as an adolescent with his social
awkwardness and an almost fatiguing internal monitoring that he
made of his feelings.

The book revealed further that his vocational life remained
unsettled up to his middle forties. Included in this prolonged disjointedness were excursions as a forester, a social surveyer, an overseas worker for the Interchurch World Movement, and an unsuccessful parish minister. However, monumental learnings from his
psychotic episode in 1920 ultimately brought to him for the
remainder of his life a concerted focus in the theologically
researched study of mental illness. Boisen sometimes referred to
his experience with his psychosis as being plunged into a "little-
known country."

Much of Boisen's creative momentum was wrapped around a
persistent and, some would say, unrequited love that he had for a
woman named Alice Batchelder. They had met in 1902 at the University of Indiana when she was there as a YWCA worker. From
the time of their first meeting until her death in 1935, Boisen held
fast to this idealized relationship.

When he moved in 1932 from his chaplaincy at Worcester State
Hospital to the Elgin hospital near Chicago, she had been working
in that city for a long period of time. In the epilogue of *Out of the
Depths*, he refers to her as the "guiding hand" behind much of his
life and his creative labors. A year after her death, Boisen crypti-
cally dedicates his momentous book *The Exploration of the Inner
World* to her with the use of her initials—A.L.B. It is my opinion

that, if any student of Boisen's work neglects the import of Alice Batchelder's influence on him, then much of the gist pertaining to his strong motivation and energies will be missed.

From the seed of Boisen's passionate theological and psychological inquiry about the scantily known territory of mental illness, there blossomed a clinical pastoral movement of enormous proportions. It was Boisen's bright intellect and bravery that allowed a light to start flickering brightly. Those students early around him—such as Carroll Wise, Philip Guiles, and Helen Flanders Dunbar—gathered it into a larger torch. Due to their insights and organizing labors, a powerful enterprise was born. In the course of time, mighty streams of not only clinical pastoral education but also clinical chaplaincy and pastoral counseling would flow from this main and nascent clinical pastoral tributary. Hence, my overall clinical pastoral life has remained indebted to that original spark which became truly ignited from Boisen's depths.

Further gained from my time in Trio was the meeting of someone destined to become the most significant person in my life. The next chapter contains an introduction to this treasured one. Also, my direct entry into the overall CPE movement is depicted.

Chapter 5

—◦◦◦—

My CPE Beginnings, 1960-1962

As described in chapter 1, my personal commencement began within the supportive bosom of the Summers and Hill clans and on the prized banks of the Edisto River. On the other hand, my origins in clinical pastoral education and mental health ministry had their start within the murky shadows of a huge state mental hospital. It is to this time of vocational preparation for such ministry and education that I now turn.

A KNOCK ON CPE'S DOOR

While serving my Methodist parish in 1960, I began conversation with Obert Kempson about my interest in clinical ministry. I received his name from Floyd Feely; he indicated that Kempson was the only CPE supervisor in South Carolina. As a matter of fact, he was one of just a few in the whole Southeast. Kempson, who had begun his chaplaincy at the South Carolina State Hospital in Columbia during the early 1930s, had developed in 1946 the first approved CPE program in the Southeast by the Council for Clinical Training.

The hospital teemed with more than thirty-five hundred patients. Its chaplaincy effort was a part of an almost unbroken chain that stretched back to Elias Hort—the institution's first chaplain of the 1840s. The South Carolina culture had held a long interest in making available the presence of a pastor for these distressed persons.

As I met with Kempson and shared with him my interest and my story, this white-haired interviewer remarked that he felt like I was not yet ready for clinical training. The dapper Lutheran, who was then in his early fifties, wondered whether I had yet integrated fully enough my recent years. It was through persistence and further contact that I was accepted by him several months later for the hospital's training program. Over the span of our subsequently long relationship, Kempson and I would laughingly acknowledge on occasion that he "knew a very young guy that he once turned down for CPE."

As I entered clinical training, I became more aware of how my own tribulations had become a compelling force to seek a ministry related to human suffering. I felt that I knew, on a firsthand basis, some of that particular terrain. The term *wounded healer,* which was mentioned in chapter 1, aptly reappears as I now review my clinical pastoral beginnings. Henri Nouwen's symbol represents an enormous truism for a countless number of pastoral representatives entering CPE through the portals of their own brokenness. This search has led many into a ministry of devotion to pastoral care.

I undertook that year two consecutive quarters of CPE in the fall and winter seasons at the hospital in Columbia. At the same time, I commuted to my parish in the Lower State on the weekends and some other weekdays.

MINISTRY BEHIND A HIGH WALL

For the time spent in Columbia, I resided in a student dormitory that was high atop the hospital's ancient administrative building. Adjoining this edifice on both sides were wards that housed hordes of long-term, chronically disturbed patients. In the same building were not only the hospital's staff offices but also the office of the hospital superintendent—Dr. William S. Hall. This tall, courtly, and nationally recognized mental health leader had been on the hospital staff for more than twenty-five years. Before sallying forth to the wards for pastoral care moments with the patients, I sometimes would have a casual hallway dialogue with Dr. Hall—always showing interest in students—or some other mental health official in the same building. The hospital's monthly stipend of one hundred dollars barely saved me from poverty, but the staff cafeteria meals (seventeen cents each) greatly assisted my pocketbook.

A Dark Corner of Society

The large hospital had been developed for nearly a century and a half in the form of an intact community. The sprawling campus contained its own laundry, library, morgue, medical-surgical hospital, auditorium for dances and worship services, canteen, horticultural nursery, and a nearby farm. The sidewalks constantly incorporated the busy traffic of patients being escorted to various activities. Some psychiatrists and their families lived in cottages that were located on the grounds.

There was a high wall that encircled much of the campus. It tended to isolate the hospital from the encompassing city. In those days society placed these aged institutions upon its marginalized borders. Even though financial support from the State Legislature had its limitations, the hospital staff generally exhibited a motivated and humane spirit. Available for educational discussions were such persons as psychologist Elmore Martin.

My training in clinical ministry occurred in a place that was packed with human misery. However, it was not unusual for the darkness to see some rays of light breaking through in moments of a patient's recovery, release, or a staff member's constant and courageous skills. But the nation's state mental hospitals in this era were very similar to the ancient Babylon rivers where the exiled could not find in their hearts songs to sing "while in a foreign land" (Ps. 137: 4 New International Version).

In that time of lingering racial segregation, this hospital housed only Caucasian patients. Another setting, which was five miles away, admitted African Americans. The latter facility—the Palmetto State Hospital—was in much worse physical shape than even that of the South Carolina State Hospital.

Since community mental health outreach was minimal, state mental health treatment was confined largely to these two major hospitals. This centrality meant that huge numbers of mentally ill citizens streamed through the gates of these antiquated treatment settings. Many of my clinical training days were spent in making initial pastoral care visits on the wards where newly admitted patients entered. It was there that I attempted to offer a supportive presence to multitudes of persons whose tormented souls had been pushed into such a dark corner of society.

Flying by the Seat of My Pants

But nowhere were the excruciating ravages of severe mental illness so apparent than in the areas known as the "back wards." During this part of the century, almost every public mental hospital in the nation contained similar tombs of hell. These back wards were a ghastly systemic reminder of society's strong neglect of the severely mentally ill. They represented the bottom rung on a tall ladder of public disregard.

Even though some of the hospital's admission and exit services attempted a comprehensive interprofessional treatment and training approach, the contrasting and overcrowded back wards writhed in isolated agony. Psychiatric diagnoses and adequate medications were limited in those days. Therefore, many of these warehoused and regressed patients aimlessly wandered around. Some looked dazed and were incessantly babbling. The dismal diagnostic labels of catatonia and hebephrenia were applied rampantly by courageous, but spent, personnel. I had many moments in these dark recesses of the hospital trying to learn more about establishing contact with such unanchored lives that were confined there.

These crushed persons taught me invaluable lessons in the area of expecting unpredictability in pastoral care. In short, I was forced to "fly by the seat of my pants" in my ministry with them. No reasoned comment on my part could adequately penetrate their stony stares or jumbled words; there was no compass in this flying.

In one of my first visits to such a back ward, a woman with anger almost smoking out of her nostrils, walked up immediately and exclaimed, "You're the sorriest thing on the face of this earth! You ain't worth spitting on." She then proceeded to implement her latter statement. She turned around and walked away. Leaning up against a far wall, she never took a fixed stare off me as I made my way around the noisy ward awkwardly trying to strike up a conversation with others. I never had felt so naked and stripped bare of reasoned thought in all of my life. She also had gone straight to the heart of a foremost issue in my overall personal and pastoral learning quest—that of dealing with someone's anger. These exiled folks eventually became my guides in how to risk being available to others' unconscious and primitive thought processes.

Peer Learning

As mentioned in chapter 3, my seminary curriculum had been dominated generally by a lecture methodology. However, the clinical pastoral training emphasis of daily seminar discussions and interactions with a peer community of four or five other students became very appealing. The reception of feedback by peers and supervisors about my actual pastoral care with patients helped to propel me simultaneously into some needed personal growth areas. One of the major hallmarks in the evolving CPE tradition has been the focus on such peership. It is in such an environment where the student tastes, in a lively and experiential way, the theology of community-building.

The Reign of Freud

The most prominent psychological theories presented in the inter-professional training mileu were those of Sigmund Freud's intrapsychic thrust and the interpersonalism of Harry Stack Sullivan. My theoretical readings in those days were in harmony with a writer's following assessment: "I came of professional age when Freud was God, Jung was his sometime prophet and the diverse archangels, Fromm, Sullivan, Horney, Reich, and Perls, hovered high in the firmament. It was a golden age. Or so it seemed."[1]

Within a couple of decades, some of the Freudian conceptual structures would begin coming under critical review. One author even would go so far as to surmise that "... Freud's ideas, which dominated the history of psychiatry for the past half century, are now vanishing like the last snows of winter."[2] Other critics have not been as harsh. However, *Hunkering Down's* chapter 9 reveals how the emergence of brain research in the early 1980s began to show the lack of relevance that Freudian psychoanalysis would have on treatment of the severe mental illnesses.

Growing Edges

By the next fall season of 1961, I had departed from my parish appointment in order to begin six consecutive, full-time quarters of clinical training at the hospital. Kempson was primary supervisor for five of my total periods, while Jarvis McMillan supervised three. I received from Kempson supervisory assistance in attempting to develop further listening skills and also pastoral care approaches with persons in particular crises. With McMillan, attention was placed on my growth areas of self-assertion and authority development.

A pastoral supervisory evaluative report once noted perceptively two of my most important growing edges, namely, a "proneness to delay making decisions until he is over his head" and a need "to develop a way to take hostility directly without being immobilized." The observations were right on target with some of my personal/pastoral learning struggles at the time.

BETWEEN KANSAS AND CAPE COD

During this particular two-year span of CPE, other varied events transpired that embraced special significance for me in my evolving clinical pastoral venture. These occurrences included a memorable trip to Kansas, supervisory education, my first regional CPE conference, marriage, an interesting event on Cape Cod, and the search for chaplaincy employment.

Memories of Hall, Klink, and Caldwell

Midway through my training in South Carolina, I became acquainted with information about the extraordinary mental health treatment and clinical education taking place in Topeka, Kansas. That locale was developing notoriety as a national mecca in mental health circles. Receiving much attention were the Menninger Foundation and the Topeka State Hospital.

With a desire to explore training possibilities there, I arranged an airline trip in the summer of 1961 to be interviewed by Charles Hall—the CPE supervisor at the state hospital. In order to travel by a propeller flight to Topeka from Columbia in the early '60s, it was necessary to make stops in Augusta, Atlanta, Louisville, Cincinnati, Saint Louis, and then finally Kansas City. I caught a Greyhound bus for the last leg of the trip to Topeka. Upon arriving in this land of promise, I felt as if had made a pilgrimage that was halfway around the world.

During my stay in Topeka, Hall developed an array of interviews for me with his CPE supervisory colleagues in the area. For instance, I spent some time with Tom Klink at the Menninger Clinic. His resonant voice and a fixed attention—while listening intently—was a noted trait of his. It allowed others to feel quite comfortable in his presence. Ten or so years later, it was quite startling to learn of Klink's untimely death. At that point he had become regarded nationally as perhaps the leading theoretician on pastoral supervision.

Klink's insights about such supervisory issues as "cross-grained experience" endure even today. This notion implies that anxious learnings of a student move against the earlier foundational understandings in the person's experience. It probably is no coincidence that, in the same years when his perspectives on supervision were being crafted, the Menninger setting also was the 1958 birthplace for Rudolf Ekstein's and Robert Wallerstein's monumental collaborative book *The Teaching and Learning of Psychotherapy*—a basic supervisory bible. Many a fledgling pastoral supervisor has cut her/his teeth on such themes from this book as "parallel process" and "learning problems."

Another resource person for Hall was Joe Caldwell of the Boys Industrial School. Charles Gerkin of Atlanta had been an earlier CPE supervisor at this particular institution. Caldwell's method of getting acquainted was that of touring me around his facility. He used effectively an approach to hospitality while walking. In addition to focusing on my clinical pastoral interests, some of our conversation revolved around his prior North Carolina heritage and my own South Carolina history near the Lowcountry. It appeared that Caldwell knew instinctively how to hunker down.

(About five or six years later, Caldwell left Topeka and moved to Atlanta with the opportunity of building a pastoral counseling training program. The undertaking was a part of Gerkin's innovative development of the Georgia Association for Pastoral Care. Caldwell's giftedness was cut short in the early 1970s by a tragic bout with cancer. Obert Kempson and I attended his funeral that was conducted back in Caldwell's North Carolina roots at a small cemetery cuddled on a little hillside.)

Charles Hall's interviewing time with me was confronting in a clarifying sense. It aided me in grappling with some ambiguous issues in my current CPE. He left few stones unturned. As I met in a closing conference together with the three colleagues, some unresolved themes related to my considering leaving South Carolina had begun to coalesce in my and their thinking. This Kansas exploration led me toward a decision in due time to remain in South Carolina.

I have intentionally extended the description of this Kansas trip that was made years ago. This has been done, because those brief days in Topeka offered me—young in my career development—a glimpse into the strong connections that so strongly thread themselves throughout CPE's overall history. The historical phenomenon of how persons are so firmly interrelated in the clinical pastoral movement remains yet a fascination with me. For instance, the ties between Anton Boisen, Carroll Wise, Philip Guiles, Helen Flanders Dunbar, and Seward Hiltner are vivid aspects from the early days of the CPE legacy. The Kansas colleagues represented a second and third generation with a common grounding.

The sojourn in Topeka brought me directly and impressionably into such an arena of connections. There were these aforementioned Kansas bonds existent between Hall, Klink, Caldwell, and Gerkin. (By the way, chapter 2 mentioned Hall's brief move to Atlanta in the late 1950s with the prospect of starting a CPE program at the Georgian Alcoholism Clinic. This was done about the same time that Gerkin had initiated in Atlanta a program at Grady Hospital.) Not only did the Topeka base offer historical links between these particular CPE supervisors, but one could just as well consider the ties that have emanated intergenerationally from so many other places around the nation. To name but a few, Houston, Philadelphia, Louisville, Boston, Minneapolis, and Birmingham, have been such locales. As a further example, the renowned programming of Armen Jorjorian in Houston years ago produced later from his proteges the rippled-out waves of intergenerational contributions from an Al Anderson in Omaha or a Pat Prest in Richmond. Prest was Jorjorian's first supervisory student in 1956; and following a brief stint in New York City, he started a productive career at the Medical College of Virginia.

An Itch for Becoming a Supervisor

The fall of 1961 brought an emerging desire in me to seek training with the goal of also becoming a certified CPE supervisor. I began to explore with my own supervisors the possibilities of my eventually entering what the Council for Clinical Training then called an "assistantship." This supervisory training implied that one began pastorally supervising CPE students while having his/her supervision of those students brought under supervision. Conceivably, this certification process could be completed within a year and a half. In the spring of the next year, I was recommended to be reviewed regionally for entrance into an assistantship at the South Carolina State Hospital.

My First Regional Conference

In that season I rose up again from Carolina roots in order to travel. Not toward Kansas this time was I headed, but to Virginia. Avoiding another complicated airplane route, I chose to drive my unpredictable Chevrolet to meet a reviewing committee in Richmond. I had not met a committee for vocational purposes since my 1956 encounter with the Methodist district group that had an accompanying ashtray on its table.

I made it barely on time for my Virginia committee appearance, because my untrustworthy vehicle became disabled on a lonely North Carolina road. Even though the car's resistance was frustrating, I might add that it was difficult to be totally disappointed in it. It had served me well for a long time. For those of us growing up immediately after the Great Depression, belongings such as a baseball bat were held in special devotion. Many persons had great fondness for their cars. Some were given names—like "Old Betsy" or "The Blue Flame." (Incidentally, from 1973 to 1996 I drove a total of only two automobiles, as some of my amused friends could verify.)

I met an evaluation committee that was composed of sponsor Ed Dobihal of St. Elizabeths Hospital, Knox Kreutzer of Washington's Pastoral Institute, Pat Prest of the Medical College of Virginia, and Ralph Carpenter of Richmond Memorial Hospital. Rather than known as a "certification" unit back then, this group was called an "accreditation" committee. Even though this twenty-seven-year-old candidate was granted the assistant's status, I left the session scratching my head. I was partly puzzled by Kreutzer's gruff comment that I "seemed wet behind my ears." For a young man in a hurry to impart the stirring wisdom of Anton Boisen and Seward Hiltner, I felt that any observed need for additional years of seasoning should not be a distraction from enthusiasm.

Not only awaiting me in Richmond was this particular committee appearance for an assistantship review but also an opportunity to experience afterwards my first southeastern CPE regional conference of the Council for Clinical Training.

For instance, I learned that the Council's borders reached extensively from Delaware down through Georgia. Florida soon would be brought into this regional nexus when Frank Cook would become the CPE supervisor at Avon Park's alcohol treatment center. Roy Raymond was in the Region's most northern outpost at the Delaware State Hospital. Kempson of South Carolina and Gerkin of Georgia were the main representatives from the far southern tentacles of the Region.

I have long cherished the hospitality shown to me by the experienced supervisors at this particular conference in their reaching out to us younger ones attempting to come through the ranks. The reciting of CPE "war stories," hearty laughter, firm handshakes, and the taking of interest in the novice's background were some of the gifts offered by the elders. Some of these supportive persons included the Washington area's Herb Hillebrand, Dobihal, Dave Gregory, and Bob Robey. Richmond was well represented by Prest and Carpenter.

Parenthetically, in considering the intergenerational life that I have been privileged to witness in the professional pastoral associations through the years, I have developed the metaphorical term *holding on with both hands*. From this frame of reference, organizational life is imaged as a drama stage upon which the activitites of that association are played out. The currently active members have the role of reaching out with one hand, so to speak, to hold in care and memory those members whose entrance onto the stage preceded theirs. The other figurative hand is extended—at the same time—to cultivate relational ties with younger ones newly approaching organizational life. I felt that Prest, Robey, Gerkin, and the others offered encouragingly their hands to help shepherd us newcomers onto this CPE stage.

I also was particularly impressed at the conference with the strong influence and panel leadership shown by the seminary personnel—John Soleu of Virginia Episcopal Seminary and John Gessell of the Sewanee Seminary. Much of the whole conference focused on the seminary students' learning process in the single summer quarter of pastoral care formation in CPE.

The existence of a broader CPE world outside of the Council for Clinical Training became a reality for me at this conference. For example, I heard references being made about a rival clinical training organization—the Institute of Pastoral Care. An aggressive Institute leadership, which rested in the person of John Billinsky, was mentioned. Billinsky, incidentally, had followed Philip Guiles at Andover Newton Seminary after the latter's death in 1953.[3]

Comments also were heard in hallways about a Southern Baptist CPE emphasis in the form of Richard Young's program in Winston-Salem, North Carolina. Naturally, I was quite alert to any information about job openings. I could not believe my ears when I heard about the one at Mendota State Hospital in Wisconsin with its exorbitant salary range of up to $8,900.

Following the time in Virginia, my appetite became whetted for delving into materials that reflected both the history and current issues as related to CPE. My reading of the 1956 proceedings that were generated from the Fifth National Conference in Clinical Pastoral Education greatly assisted me in gaining some basic perspectives. I discovered therein the wealth of papers and discussions by such persons as Paul Tillich, Wayne Oates, Tom McDill, Rollie Fairbanks, Tom Klink, Earl Loomis, Fred Keuther, and Charles Gerkin. Creative writing had been so powerfully produced by a former generation in the likes of such frontline pioneers as Boisen, Cabot, Dunbar, Guiles, Dicks, and Don Beatty. But as I read the works of the ensuing leaders from these 1956 presentations, I perceived a similar enthusiasm from these emerging and passionate architects. They were adding the benefits of their additional philosophies, methods, and amplifications into an earlier clinical pastoral heritage.

Wedding Bells

It was also in these early 1960s that I began to entertain the most important relational experience of my life—that of marriage with Marilyn Boyd. Our now long-time companionship has its origins when I became pastor of the three churches in lower South Carolina. Marilyn was mentioned at the end of chapter 4 as being the "treasured one." Her family had its membership in one of the churches, and she was making preparation to begin collegiate life at the University of Georgia. We fell in love eventually and married following her sophomore year in 1962. Ray Charles's then popular song of "I Can't Stop Loving You" served as a constant background muse to our courtship. Marilyn's playful and vivacious spirit, warmth, and direct honesty about feelings were among her many qualities that captured my heart. Jack Meadors, later to become a United Methodist bishop, officiated at our wedding. He was a pass-slinging quarterback in Wofford intramurals, and I teamed with my friend as an end.

Beginning Pastoral Supervision

Following the Richmond conference, I began the spring quarter of 1962 as Kempson's first supervised assistant CPE supervisor. Much of my time was spent in making preparations for the oncoming summer quarter. I read Ekstein's and Wallerstein's excellent book on supervision and also a paper by Hiltner concerning the functions of anxiety. Another book in which I found great insights was Karen Horney's *Our Inner Conflicts.* Her remarkable concept *the idealized self-image* has been one that I often have utilized in pastoral supervision. Horney posits that many persons carry with them an elevated and unrealistic sense of self that serves as an internalized buffer against the enormity of such unconscious dimensions as loss, rage, low esteem, and anxiety.

In the summer quarter, I supervised my first CPE students. They were four seminarians, and Kempson supervised two additional students. As a conglomerate, we all met together daily as a total group for regular seminar meetings. I struggled during the first half of the summer with the residuals of not making a fuller claim on my own authority in supervision. At times I felt some intimidation by Kempson's long history of supervising students. The latter part of the quarter brought forth an increased display of my supervisory presence and role security. Both Kempson and myself felt like an additional quarter for the supervised assistantship would be helpful in order to build on the evolving growth during the summer.

Marilyn and I married between the summer and fall quarters

that year in the Methodist church at Kingstree, South Carolina. After some engine trouble on our honeymoon trip, my courageous Chevy car eventually whisked us away into the cool North Carolina mountains. My stipended monthly riches now had risen from $100 to $150 due to my elevation into the assistantship. Although causing my new nine sisters-in-law and brothers-in-law to wonder about our poverty status, the sparse financial resources did allow for a $60 monthly rental of an apartment in Columbia and weekend celebrations with hamburgers and the movies.

I discovered that some hospitals were willing to interview persons still at the assistantship level for the purpose of an eventual CPE development at those centers. While in my summer and fall quarters at the South Carolina State Hospital, I began to enter into such a job search. I traveled to Nashville on one occasion to talk with the staff of the Central State Hospital about a position that also carried an adjunct appointment to the Vanderbilt Divinity School. The chaplain coordinating my visit happened to be the now-deceased Ken Mitchell. He later joined the Menninger Clinic staff with Tom Klink in Kansas. Mitchell would become after a while a noted author in the pastoral care and counseling areas.

However, I became more interested in exploring a chaplaincy and CPE supervision position at the Milledgeville State Hospital in middle Georgia. Doug Turley, who had been certified by the Southern Baptist Association for Clinical Pastoral Educators, had been recently hired there to plan an extensive chaplaincy and CPE program in the nation's second largest mental hospital.

The Council and the Institute on the Cape

A memorable aspect of that fall season in 1962 was that of the trip that Marilyn and I made to the annual meeting of the Council for Clinical Training. The conference was conducted near Hyannis Port, Massachusetts, on Cape Cod. The site was not very far away from President John Kennedy's home. Travel was ably facilitated by the fatigued car. This particular meeting has held a certain enchantment for me due to various reasons.

For one thing, the meeting represented my first involvement with a national CPE conference. Over the next thirty-five years, I would miss only five such conferences. At the 1962 meeting, I felt a measure of professional identity. This was due to having access not only to Council supervisors previously met in my own region but also becoming familiar at Cape Cod with prominent leaders from other parts of the nation. Some of these supervisors included Armen Jorjorian of Texas and Herman Eichorn of California.

Another interesting feature about this gathering was that the locale was one wherein both the Council and the Institute of Pastoral Care had decided for the first time to hold their individual annual meetings in the same location. As described in chapter 1, these two groups had had a long history of rupture between them. There had existed competitive stereotyping of each other: the Council (too psychoanalytical) and the Institute (too pietistic). The miracle in all of this prejudice was that the two fussing camps were considering moving toward a merger.

They had conducted previously joint executive committee sessions for several years. The preceding labors of the Committtee of Twelve, as sketched in chapter 1, were finally paying off. However, both groups contained members harboring some resistance over these interorganizational pursuits. For instance, as the combative John Billinsky of the Institute walked by the common cafeteria tables, I could see some of the Council supervisors bristle. When the comparably energetic Jorjorian of the Council appeared, the Institute folks had grimacing looks of stony silence. These two separate families—finally now in the same proximity—did not know exactly what to do with each other. It were as if those divisive energies from the enormous organizational split thirty years earlier between Philip Guiles and Helen Flanders Dunbar were still hovering in the interactive atmosphere between the Council and the Institute. However, the two national associations were able to move along with enough trustful healing so that, by the next year, they shared a *joint* annual conference program together.

The meeting on Cape Cod also allowed me to become acquainted with one of CPE's legendary figures. I was sitting at a cafeteria table and became introduced to Joe Woodson—an Institute supervisor. He had been trained in Boston; and, from my earlier seminary readings about the eminent writings of Paul Johnson from that area, I looked forward to Woodson's northeastern knowledge. As soon as he opened his mouth, the acclaimed Mississippian spewed forth that slow and hoarse southern twang of his. What Institute prejudice that I had inherited from the Council quickly melted. He talked continuously about grits, coon dogs, and other important matters. He carried on almost without pausing to catch a breath.

For many years afterwards, I would see Woodson at various meetings. We would pick right up immediately with the sharing of our southern stories. In 1984 he was presented the distinguished Boisen Award by the Association of Mental Health Clergy in Los Angeles. Making the trip to the West Coast from Boston was no small thing for this humorously intuitive genius in his latter years. But he was just as funny as ever. On several occasions some of us conferees—including Woodson—piled into a car and did some sightseeing of the city in miniscaled back-you-down trips. He spun his yarns exuberantly as he offered a running commentary on everything that he saw in addition to almost everything that any-body else would see or say. He is now deceased. I will always regard him as being a delightful and fascinating part of CPE lore.

A further uniqueness about the Cape Cod conference was that many of the attendees stayed in the homes of local townspeople. The conference center did not have a wealth of lodging rooms. Marilyn and I stayed with a very hospitable family; and, thereafter, correspondence was maintained with the members for many years. Al Shevre—a Council supervisor from Minnesota—and his wife also stayed in the same home.

In so many ways, the quaintness of that overall time on the Cape remains to this day as a favorite memory of mine.

As the curtain descended on my total of eight CPE quarters in the two years spent in training at the South Carolina State Hospi-tal, I looked southward to Georgia for my initial full-time employ-ment in clinical pastoral ministry and teaching. The intervening six years since I had departed from the small swimming pool in Wofford College days indeed had led me into some powerful waters of vocational preparation.

Chapter 6

Milledgeville Days, 1962-1965

In the fall of 1962, I was invited by Doug Turley to join his chaplaincy staff at the mammoth Milledgeville State Hospital in Georgia. The hospital housed more than twelve thousand mental patients, and it was located on the outskirts of Milledgeville. There were only several mental hospitals throughout the world that were larger.

This chapter purposely takes a prolonged look at the Milledgeville phase of my CPE story. For one thing, these several years represent to me never-to-be-forgotten times, because my full-time professional foundations were being early laid. Vocational friendships were established that would endure for years. Secondly, exciting CPE developments were abounding in Georgia. In addition, this early part of the 1960s offers a further historical snapshot of the era's gigantic state mental hospital apparatus containing some of its chaplaincy and clinical pastoral education flavors. The glimpse of the huge system represents a vista prior to the rapid dismantling influences seen in the deinstitutionalizing of the public mental hospitals.

BREAKING NEW GROUND
FOR RELIGIOUS CARE

Immediately before finishing my training period at the South Carolina State Hospital, Marilyn and I drove down to Milledgeville so that we could attend the groundbreaking ceremony for a main chapel. A golden shovel used by the governor's wife hardly pierced the frozen turf on that cold day.

Turley, who was in his early thirties and previously the head of a mental hospital chaplaincy program in Ohio, had been at the Milledgeville facility for six months prior to my December arrival. Henry Close, who had achieved his acting CPE supervisor's status with the Council for Clinical Training, joined Turley earlier that fall. Close had completed his CPE training program at Grady Hospital in Atlanta and was supervised by Charles Gerkin. Chappell Wilson and Jim Travis—both having received their supervisory training through the Southern Baptist Association for Clinical Pastoral Educators—came to the staff in the following summer.

I was appointed by Turley to head up chaplaincy and CPE assignments in one of the hospital's overcrowded major units. It contained more than two thousand patients. There were daily interprofessional treatment team meetings on new admission wards. Many of these conferences were led by very personable Cuban physicians; they recently had fled from the Castro Revolution in their homeland. Some psychiatric residents from Emory University were assigned to clinical rotations through these heavily populated admission wards. Also, students from other training programs, for example, music therapy internships and social work field placements, functioned actively in the clinical areas. The hospital had already begun encountering some revolutionary change. A newspaper reporter from Atlanta had published in the late 1950s a series of scathing articles related to some of the highly negative conditions found at this immense institution. The commentaries originated from the guise of the reporter's having been admitted as a patient into the treatment program. The expose resulted in a public outcry for a transformation of this ancient habitation that was holding countless tormented minds.

One of the actions taken was that of improving radically the religious care of patients. A statewide financial campaign with Georgia congregations was planned. Funding resulted in the eventual construction of the major hospital chapel and four other chapels that were scattered across the sprawling campus. State monies also became committed for an extensive cadre of staff chaplains, CPE supervisors, and internships.

MEMORABLE VIGNETTES

As I consider my time span of ministry and CPE at this hospital, numerous moments—so drenched with poignancy—remain etched in my memory. The few that follow serve as illustrations in an attempt to convey the ambience of hospital life in this unusual setting.

Fishing on a Back Ward

Part of my attention was captured by an ongoing interest in my unit's back wards. These desolate areas were pregnant with masses of persons hospitalized for years. Many empty faces looked similar to those that I had known at the hospital in South Carolina. They were like castaways—much forgotten by their families and communities.

Through consultation with the unit's chief psychiatrist and nurse, I began conducting regular group meetings with a dozen female patients on one of these tightly secluded wards. The majority of the patients were not very emotive and tended to be quiet. In utilizing the then emerging therapeutic approach of "remotivation" (a focus on sensory stimulation for the regressed patient), I attempted to use the concrete elements of touch, hearing, smell, and sight. The effort was that of attempting to build on the positive memories and resources within those persons whose energies had become eroded due to their long-term illnesses.

An example of one such session featured the subject of fishing. I brought to the group a bowl of goldfish, and they could be seen swirling with their rich colors in the water. The group members then were led corporately to construct a fishing pole from a cane, lead sinkers, and a cork. I then showed them various pictures of some fish. We looked at a whale, a trout, a dolphin, and others. Some of the patients' eyes showed an increased sparkle as they observed these marvelous and long-forgotten creatures from the watery depths.

Even today I can still picture a sullen woman—heretofore depressively mute—offering a whisper. She uttered, "Yesterday me and my uncle went down to a pond in the pasture and caught us some catfish. We fried 'em and ain't no fish never tasted better what me and my uncle caught." Moments such as these in that group led the hearer to stand on sacred ground. It mattered not whether what was faintly said rested in a memory trace, a hope, or a fantasy. The mystery of life was at work in the human drive for a familial grounding and a remembrance of kin. How well I knew that from those rocking-chair hours spent with my loved ones on my grandfather's front porch in Cross Hill.

Shocking Moments

An excruciating time, however, was experienced several times weekly on the new admissions ward. An elongated procession of patients would be readied there for a regular ritual—the use of electroshock treatment. The persistent use of this therapy was a common national feature in overcrowded public mental hospitals. A man whom I had gotten to know rather well would provide consistently his gallows humor as I stood with him in his wait. Often he would say, "Preacher, I'm going to 'live better electrically' today!" He was emphasizing the slogan used on billboards throughout Georgia by a major power company. However, for most patients the prospect of that shock button being pushed sent chills into their souls.

A Proverbial Accent

I had many opportunities fortunately to work with Dr. James Craig—the hospital's assistant superintendent and an ardent Catholic supporter for the chaplaincy program. I spent considerable time with him in the forensic section where hundreds of persons with penal and criminal concerns were sent for evaluation and treatment. He was an intuitively caring person and demonstrated a constancy of support and humaneness to patients. Occasionally I would travel with him down to Reidsville State Prison in order to ascertain whether some disturbed inmates there were in need of transfer to the state hospital in Milledgeville.

Throughout the hospital Dr. Craig exhibited an applauded talent for his skilled use of proverbs in helping to form an opinion about a patient's clarity of thought and cognitive functioning. One of his favorites was seen in his asking for the meaning of the saying, "a rolling stone gathers no moss."

A mental health worker—wanting to emulate this master of proverbs—once asked that he might try his hand with the technique. In a lengthened Georgia accent, the question rolled out slowly, "What is the difference between a lie and a *meeestake?*"

The questioned one looked puzzled for a moment. The forthcoming reply indicated that the first thing mentioned was the telling of an untruth. The latter item, it was suggested, was something from the killing of a cow, then cooking it, and finally eating it. The wrinkled brow of the interrogator signaled that such a macabre response contained dire diagnostic proportions. However, the observing group quickly surmised that a language blunder had been made. The novice was reminded about the difference between a *mistake* and a *beefsteak*. Also, Dr. Craig kindly told the questioner that he should shorten his southern accent when using proverbs.

The diagnostic perils in the huge hospitals of those days were many. However, there were numerous staff persons, such as Dr. Craig, who brought care and dignity to many persons around them in such overwhelming conditions.

A Matter of Time

Another penetrating moment—similar as seen in a catfish or beefsteak image—broke momentarily into the large hospital's highly charged atmosphere in one of the chapel's worship services. A new CPE seminary student had prepared diligently a sermon that was characterized by strong features of existentialism as influenced by Paul Tillich's systematic theology. The background of the message was built upon Tillich's perspective of time as found in the Greek words *chronos* and *kairos*. The student's seminary curriculum had included the study of Tillich's popular series of *Systematic Theology*.

Poised to demonstrate his high level of theological interest for the patients, the young preacher delivered this opening question in a very serious demeanor: "What *time* is it?" Immediately a paranoid-inclined patient, waiting to attack any sign of smugness or condescension shown by anyone around him, jumped out of his seat. He hollered loudly, "You fool, don't you have a wrist watch? If you can't tell time by now, get the hell out of this church!"

Shaken for days, the CPE student eventually began to remove—stone by stone—his high wall of intellectual defense. His pastoral care growth subsequently got underway. I had empathy for the preacher as I thought back to the college experience of my trying desperately to convert a spare tire into a flat tire during my initial crack at a sermon.

Chaplains also learned that, if a rhetorical question were asked during worship on the back wards, one invariably could expect a direct, honest answer to emerge.

I once queried a small group of Holy Week worshipers on a secluded ward about the seasonal meaning of Lent. A woman, who had worked in a textile mill, possessed a quick answer. She innocently responded, "Preacher, that Lent stuff is what you get in your bellybutton if you work around cotton too long. I betcha' got some in yours right now."

As often was the case in the labyrinth of the state mental hospital, the patients ultimately became the teachers about natural, concrete learning for the chaplains and their CPE students.

Sporting Moments

The town of Milledgeville possessed approximately the same number of persons as that residing in the large hospital. Although there were social and cultural events transpiring in the town, the chaplains sometimes would devise their own recreational activities.

For example, we formed a softball team and challenged other departments in the hospital. One favorite group that was anticipated for competition was that of the Cuban psychiatrists. For days leading up to the game, there would be much affable bantering between the two groups. We would talk about the oncoming contest before treatment team meetings, in the hallways, at lunch, or greeting each other while walking on campus. Sometimes the games would be followed by picnics and much joking. A leader for the Cuban team was Dr. Julian Gomez—later a prominent Atlanta psychoanalyst.

Another athletic memory is that derived from Jap Keith's church basketball team. Keith, who had entered a yearlong CPE internship in 1963, was pastoring simultaneously a Southern Baptist church nearby in a little town. He invited the tall Chappell Wilson and myself to bolster his team's hopes against a formidable foe. These opponents were workers during the day in a kaolin clay mine. The burly basketeers elbowed, pushed, and flung Wilson and me all over the court for most of the game. A fight almost broke out between the two teams and the church folks. From then on, Wilson and I decided to keep our energies focused on pastoral care. We no longer wanted to risk our necks with further involvement in Keith's roundball exploits.

STRONG VISIONS

Some of the religious programming in the hospital mileu contained courageous and visionary dimensions. This was an era flavored by uncharted horizons; two mentioned here include racial and accreditation concerns.

Racial Integration

When the Deep South's religious institutions had not budged toward much racial integration in the early 1960s, Doug Turley's leadership brought forth an inclusive chaplaincy staff at this hospital in middle Georgia. Two African-American clergy, Payton Cook and Charlie Alston, were added following Chappell Wilson's and Jim Travis's arrival in the summer of 1963. Rumblings of consternation rippled through some parts of the state. It was not uncommon to hear such an echoing question as: "What are those left-wing preachers up to at that hospital?" The situation was weathered, and an integrity was garnered. My early ties to Louise Spann aided me inspiringly in this strong momentum for racial justice.

Broad Accreditation

Another far-reaching dream became actualized. It rested in the hope of having the CPE program characterized by a multi-accredited nature. The striving was that of breaking down professional rigidities and healing the gulf that had too long existed between such CPE associations like the Council for Clinical Training and the Institute of Pastoral Care. The dual accreditations of the Council and the Southern Baptist Association for Clinical Pastoral Educators already had made our Milledgeville center one of the first in the nation with this type of CPE organizational consolidation.

A strong attempt was made by Turley to recruit a CPE supervisor from the Institute, but the search was not successful. Many CPE persons were interested in our successful local program model of two accreditations being synthesized at one center. Some speculated that this became a sign of encouragement for planners in their eventual proposals for a later nationally merged Association for Clinical Pastoral Education in 1967.

EARLY DAYS IN THE GEORGIA
ASSOCIATION FOR PASTORAL CARE

In addition to the Milledgeville hospital's attempts for including a wider diversity of CPE training organizations, there were efforts being made by others toward a much higher level of merged or federated matters. One of these was seen in the formation of the Georgia Association for Pastoral Care (GAPC) in 1962. This organization brought together seminary structures, CPE accreditation, health care systems, and religious judicatories in Georgia. When I came to the Milledgeville hospital, Charles Gerkin's leadership in Atlanta already had begun to shape a CPE associational rhombus composed of the Milledgeville State Hospital, Grady Memorial Hospital, Georgia Baptist Hospital, and Emory University's hospital.

Part of Gerkin's early interest in the clinical pastoral movement had gotten stimulated as a seminary student when he heard Anton Boisen lecture at Garrett Theological Seminary in the middle 1940s. Gerkin participated later in his first CPE at Elgin State Hospital where Boisen, although retired, was still a presence.

The GAPC monthly meetings of CPE supervisors contained much professional fascination for me. These sessions would include Gerkin and Bob Myers of Grady Hospital; Gus Verdery and Zeke Delozier of Georgia Baptist Hospital; John Patton of the Emory Hospital; and Turley, Close, and myself of the Milledgeville setting. Patton was in supervisory training as an assistant with Gerkin. I still retained my assistant's status while awaiting an acting review at the national level by the Council for Clinical Training. Wilson and Travis of Milledgeville joined the GAPC involvements after their arrival in the summer of 1963. Joe Caldwell later would come aboard after having left Kansas. Bill Touchberry was eventually added to the membership due to his CPE activity with the Youth Development Center in Atlanta. George Dominick soon joined the GAPC grouping by his initiation of a training program at the Georgian Clinic. Tom McDill, the renowned professor of pastoral care and counseling at Columbia Theological Seminary in Decatur, would be present for many of the meetings.

As one yet young in the field of pastoral supervision, it was a robust time to be a part of the strenuous supervisory and organizational discussions related to GAPC's developing its collaborative arrangements. Pioneering work seemed to be at hand. Similarities were felt in this enterprise as that experienced by me in Wofford's stretching toward some swimming horizons.

The varying styles of some GAPC group members were animated and left indelible impressions. For instance, Verdery offered a calm wisdom that consistently was conveyed after clearing his throat. McDill, whose round-faced smile evoked a warmth about himself, was known for a long regional fidelity to shepherding the clinical pastoral movement in the South. Close had an artistic knack for introducing paradoxical humor and metaphors into the discussions. Touchberry's laughter and aggression punctuated conversations as his face quickly reddened. Delozier could be depended on for his producing folksy images about supervision. On one occasion Delozier described unforgettably the parallel meeting of two issues in pastoral supervision as having kinship with the crossing of two quail in flight. I recall becoming impressed with how Verdery smoothly smoked a pipe. There was a period when I also attempted to bring into my young supervisory work a replicated coolness and an abbreviated activity of smoking a pipe.

GAPC would continue its pilgrimage into the next decades; however, it would undergo various revisions. By the end of the 1960s, Gerkin had departed from his role to begin a long and distinguised career at Emory University's Candler School of Theology.

CPE AND EXPERIENTIAL PSYCHOTHERAPY

In addition to my continuing interest in psychotherapy, it was common in those days for CPE supervisors to maintain therapeutic activity for expanding self-awareness—a key foundation in pastoral supervision. Hence, I began psychotherapy in 1963 with Dr. Rives Chalmers of Atlanta. I had first learned about Chalmers after discussing my interest with Gerkin.

The Atlanta Psychiatric Clinic

Chalmers had first been exposed to CPE when, as a young psychiatric resident at St. Elizabeths Hospital in 1945, he was invited by Ernest Bruder to meet on various occasions with Bruder's CPE students at the Washington-based mental hospital. Chalmers later

would become a part of the psychiatric staff that pulled out of
Emory University's medical school in the middle of the 1950s. This
nucleus group soon formed the noted Atlanta Psychiatric Clinic,
and it became housed in a two-story brick house on Peachtree
Road. One of the reasons that these psychotherapists had departed from the medical school context was that their intent on having
medical students engaged as participants in group therapy was not
fully congenial with the medical setting.

Among the other therapists at the newly formed clinic were
Carl Whitaker, John Warkentin, Tom Malone, and Dick Felder.
Their approach had much to do with contributing to the development of an *experiential* form of psychotherapy. In this thrust, the
therapist's own personhood and use of self are crucial in the therapy process. The emphasis, although not disregarding diagnosis,
contains strong phenomenological and existential elements.

Theory Developed from One's History

Still contained in some CPE discussions today are references to
CPE as being an experiential form of pastoral education. When I
hear those comments about experientialism, I often ponder over
the strong influences offered to the clinical pastoral movement by
the early leaders in experiential psychotherapy. They would
include those already mentioned above and also persons like Carl
Rogers, Arthur Burton, Sidney Jourard, Spurgeon English, Sheldon
Kopp, and others from the formative days of the American Academy of Psychotherapists. The early editions of this academy's quar-
terly publication *Voices* contain rich articles from the wealth of
these early pioneers.

Such persons were the heirs of a much earlier philosophy (such
as John Dewey's) that prized both personal growth and the development of theory as being derived from a reorganization of experience within the person. I have much gratitude for Arthur Burton's
edited book *Twelve Therapists* and have special interest in the experiential accounts developed therein by Warkentin, Rogers, English,
and Burton. These writers demonstrate how their theories about
psychotherapy are influenced heavily by their own explored histories as persons. The metaphor of "hunkering down" is derived from
the value that I place on my explored history and a resultant theory.

As rugged discussions over standards were held in early 1952 by the Committee of Twelve in the CPE field, a simultaneous battle that year was experienced by my high school basketball team in its close defeat in the Lower State Championship finals in South Carolina. First row (left to right): Jim Mitchell, me, I. J. Mallory, Jim Bryant, and Terry Dukes; second row: Jim LaCoste, Gene Suttlemyer, Glen Lake, and West Summers; and third row: coach Earle Steckel, Aubrey Reed, John Mallory, and Bill Garrett.

Bill Clark, the acclaimed "Silver Fox," was my high school football coach.

In 1995 I visit the Wofford College campus—my cherished collegiate home forty years earlier.

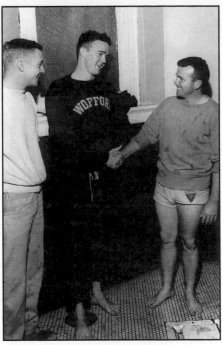

A successful one-hundred-yard freestyle dash is celebrated in Wofford College's swimming meet with East Carolina University in 1955. I am between assistant coach Bill Penny (left) and coach Chet Stephens. (WC)

At age twenty-five John Patton—later to become one of the nation's outstanding authors on pastoral care and counseling—completes in 1955 a unit of CPE with Obert Kempson at the South Carolina State Hospital.

Paul Tillich, one of the theological giants of the twentieth century, preaches at the celebration opening of a new chapel at a CPE center in 1956. (ACPER)

A New York meeting of the Board of Governors for the Council for Clinical Training in 1956. Pictured at far end of the table is Carroll Wise (far left), and Ernest Bruder and Reuel Howe are at far right of the same table with Wise. Obert Kempson is seated in middle of the table at right. (ACPER)

The seminary's Circuit Riders basketball team captured in 1958 Emory University's Graduate League championship in addition to competing in some tournaments around Atlanta. Here an opposing player (left) blocks one of my field goal attempts.

Correspondence with Harry Emerson Fosdick, the noted minister of New York's Riverside Church, aided me during some troubled seminary times in the late 1950s. (RCA)

Rhoadus Blakely, a farmer and parishioner in one of my rural churches, is shown in 1960. He taught me how to hunker down.

As a CPE student in the early 1960s, I resided in the student dormitory of the historical Babcock Building—once the thriving administrative hub of the South Carolina State Hospital. (SCDMH)

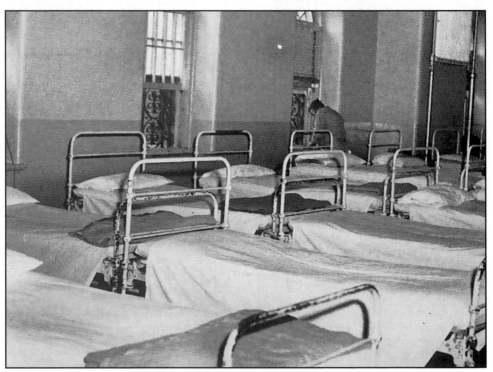

Crowded ward conditions in the nation's large public mental hospitals were common when I was in clinical training at the South Carolina State Hospital. (SCDMH)

Tom Klink, CPE supervisor at the Menninger Foundation from the 1950s into the 1970s, was considered one of the nation's leading theoreticians on pastoral supervision. (ACPER)

A very prominent CPE figure for many years in the northeast was the forceful John Billinsky of Boston. (ACPER)

Marilyn Boyd and I married in August 1962 at the Methodist Church in Kingstree, South Carolina.

One of the first gatherings of the CPE supervisors related to the newly developed Georgia Association for Pastoral Care in 1962 (left to right): Doug Turley, Henry Close, executive director Charles Gerkin, Bob Myers, Gus Verdery, and John Patton. (CSHM)

◄ *Rives Chalmers, an Atlanta psychotherapist whom I have known since the 1960s, and his wife Buba are pictured in 1997.*

The chaplaincy staff at Georgia's Milledgeville State Hospital in 1963 (front row, left to right): Henry Close, Doug Turley, and me; second row: Jim Travis, Payton Cook, Chappell Wilson, and Charlie Alston. (CSHM)

I am conducting a worship service at the Milledgeville State Hospital in 1964. (CSHM)

► *James Craig, a psychiatrist with whom I worked in the forensic section of the Milledgeville State Hospital, is pictured with Jim Travis (right) in the early 1970s. By then, Craig had become the hospital's superintendent and Travis, the chief chaplain. (CSHM)*

A group of CPE students that I supervised in 1966 at the South Carolina State Hospital (right to left): me, Lin Barnett, Finley Brown, and Lavaughn Keisler. Brown became my first student in supervisory training. Barnett would later become a CPE supervisor. (SCDMH)

A meeting with the accreditation team of the Southeast Region of the Council for Clinical Training during its site review of the Hall Institute in August 1967 (left to right): William Hall, George Dominick (team member), me, Burt Newman, Alexander Donald, Henry Close (team member), and John Hughes. Hall was the state's mental health commissioner, while Donald would become the longstanding director of the Hall Institute. (SCDMH)

The initial executive committee in the Southeast Region of the newly formed Association for Clinical Pastoral Education (ACPE) in 1968 (left to right): Charles Gerkin, Henry Close, Frank Cook, Jap Keith, me, Zeke Delozier, Doug Turley, and Obert Kempson. (ACPE-SRR)

▶ *A discussion by leaders in the Southwest Region of ACPE in 1968 (left to right): Ken Pepper, Armen Jorjorian, and Tom Cole. (ACPER)*

Process Theology

Many CPE supervisors resonate theologically with an experiential-ism in their teaching. The trend can be congenially correlated with the perspective of process theology. This theology, which values the tenets of flux and a coming into being, stretches back through George Albert Coe, Dewey, Alfred North Whitehead, Henry Nelson Wieman, and John Cobb. Incidentally, one author asserts that Anton Boisen's academic studies included some courses under Coe.[1] All of this simply is to suggest that the blending of the experiential elements found in psychotherapy, process theology, and CPE supervision has provided a strong interest for many in the CPE enterprise. Indeed, it has for me.

Boisen and Experiential Features

In some ways Boisen could be perceived as having been an experientialist. He so painstakingly examined the experience of his own inner world in almost everything he did and wrote. For him, there was an ultimate authority in one's own experience.

However, those who knew him well could not have viewed him as having had a congruence with a relational form of experiential teaching. A student of his once wrote:

> In a sense Anton set himself up as a case to be studied, not as a relational person... Cascading human emotions were to be controlled, not embraced as great gifts... While he was grateful to a few devoted friends who protected him in time of crisis, he nevertheless excluded those friends from his inner world. Their only entrance to his world was by a study of his case.[2]

Hence, Boisen was—and at the same time—was *not* an experientialist in his pastoral teaching. It was an ambiguous position for him to occupy. Although he profoundly regarded the realm of personal experience, it was no easy matter for him to entertain bringing his own inner experience into the interpersonal teaching role.

Recovery of Soul in Supervision

Partly due to a perceived dimming of the experiential dimension in CPE supervision, some supervisors and others formed in 1990 the College of Pastoral Supervision and Psychotherapy (CPSP) in order to highlight more strongly the supervisor's use of self.

Some critics of the organized CPSP movement contend that an undue emphasis on the self—both the supervisor's and the student's—overburdens the task of educational supervision. However, the CPSP presence offers a vital reminder about CPE's evolved heritage in including the strong use of one's own personhood in the supervisory task of pastoral learning. I include some further comments in the latter part of the book concerning a hope for more dialogue between the Association for Clinical Pastoral Education and the CPSP. I feel that a special theme in such explorations could be that of a subjective "recovery of soul" for pastoral supervision amidst today's more objectified educational climate in our culture.

Concerning my earlier mentioning of the 1963 entry into psychotherapy with Rives Chalmers, I have remained deeply aware of how that relationship has been a key resource in my life. We have known each other now for more than thirty-six years. He has been intermittently with me during some stirring times in my life's journey.

Many persons who have been related to the CPE process in Georgia and some other parts of the Southeast Region of ACPE have appreciated him for his availability and the continuity of his interest in the clinical pastoral field.

CERTIFICATION AND FIRE TRUCKS

The spring of 1963 not only included my entrance into therapeutic work with Rives Chalmers but also it contained an appearance before the Council's certifying committee—yet called the "accreditation" committee. I was seeking in this review the next professional level as an acting CPE supervisor. Since this was an off-season business and review session for the committee, most of its members were all present in one room rather than being in a subcommittee format. I had submitted materials prepared from the previous supervision of students during the 1962 summer and fall quarters at the South Carolina State Hospital.

When I walked into the dimly lighted New York hotel room, I was amazed to discover that seated before me were most of the certification power figures. They often had been mentioned to me in the war stories told by other candidates. Especially had I heard many tales about a dark-eyed Armen Jorjorian and a cigar-smoking Mack Powell. Among those others awaiting my arrival were Charles Hall, Tom McDill, Henry Cassler, and George Dominick. Cassler's gravelly voice reverberated throughout the room. I recall that also present were Mark Shedron and Maurice Clark. I felt that there were enough committee members to meet two or three candidates all at once.

Part of my inward struggle of feeling occasionally compliant in the presence of an authority figure began to seep into my reactions with the committee. However, the event took a definite tumble when—suddenly in the middle of the interview—noise from sirens and clanging bells in fire trucks began to create an uproar in the New York streets below.

Most of the committee members dashed to the windows to see what was happening. This existential moment threw me into a dilemma. Do I rush along collegially with them to a window or do I stand apart more autonomously? I chose to remain seated. The street commotion soon subsided, but the ambivalence over my own authority had not. Eventually a committee's decision of not granting me the acting supervisory level was rendered.

My encounter with this 1963 queasiness over inner authority would become seventeen years later the inspiration for my published writing about the "grasshopper syndrome" in the certification process.[3] This perspective infers that a time of flinching can occur for some candidates as they brush against the authority representatives in the pastoral review process. This very unsophisticated diagnostic label is derived from an Old Testament story concerning spies being sent out to scout the land of Canaan. The quivering report brought back by them expresses a danger: "We can't attack those people; they are stronger than we are... The land we explored devours those living in it. All the people we saw there are of great size. We seemed like *grasshoppers* in our own eyes..."(Num. 13:31-33 NIV).

I returned back to Georgia in a dispirited mood. On the one hand, I was tempted to give up my pursuits for a pastoral supervisory direction in ministry. On the other, I knew that I had a deep hunger to teach in this kind of educational ministry. Almost five years had passed since the time that I had traveled through those stormy seas during my seminary years. I felt that I had come a long, long way down a winding road in searching for further health and faith. A passion had been grasped for this vocational arena where such dimensions as suffering, healing, and care rested educationally at its very foundations. Doug Turley assured me that he was aware of my strengths; he indicated that he would be supportive of my developing any further assistantship directions. But for several or more months, I toyed around with the notion of relinquishing altogether the CPE thrust as a career. I considered concentrating instead either on the parish ministry or a primary clinical chaplaincy.

A PIVOTAL TIME WITH McDILL

There was a very fortuitous conversation with Tom McDill that resulted in a moment of ministry during this time of my severe disappointment. Following a Georgia Assocation for Pastoral Care supervisors' meeting in Milledgeville, I asked this quietly perceptive seminary professor of pastoral care to give me his impressions of the New York committee meeting. I mentioned to him that I was considering the abandonment of pursuing any further involvement in clinical pastoral education.

As we met in his automobile and talked at length, McDill encouraged me to look more broadly at this era of my life. He reviewed the committee's efforts with me. He speculated that I probably needed more time. His words offered meanings of hopeful perseverance. Harry Emerson Fosdick's earlier guidance of "keep your chin up" had been a similar refrain.

In now looking back over the four decades of my CPE work, that young heart-to-heart time with McDill represents one of the most pivotal moments that I have experienced. I hazard a guess that, had not such a gift of support and understanding been offered from a representative in the certification field at this early juncture of my professional preparation, I more than likely would have sought another avenue of pastoral focus. McDill was serving as, what Erik Erikson once described, a "guarantor" for me. An elder in the field was encouraging a younger to keep on keeping on. This time of crisis reminds me of an emphasis that has been passed down through the tradition of pastoral care: "Be kind; for every person you meet is fighting a hard battle somewhere."

For the next months, I remained in an unusual assistantship role with the Council for Clinical Training. I basically had no designated pastoral supervisor, although I retained my assistant's title. The situation characterized some of the flexibility existing in the Council's certification work at that time. In retrospect and in reviewing the committee's later correspondence, I feel that the committee was providing me with additional space to work out future directions and gain growth in more independency.

I began to do some occasional supervision with Turley and Close in their work with a summer group of seminary students. One of those students happened to be Boyd McLocklin. He would ably serve the ACPE's Southeast Region as its chairperson twenty years later. I also developed and coordinated a twice-a-year clinical pastoral orientation course in a week's residency for Georgia parish clergy. A pastor in one of those programs was Jack Gleason. He later became a CPE supervisor and eventually a very creative director of the American Baptist chaplaincy division.

GATHERING TROOPS

A remarkable visitor came to Georgia in the noteworthy fall of 1963. Bill Oglesby, who taught pastoral care and counseling at Union Presbyterian Seminary in Richmond, was invited to lead a weekend retreat for the GAPC supervisors at a rural state park. This joking pastoral care leader, who would become an Association for Clinical Pastoral Education president more than a dozen years later, owned an arsenal of homespun phrases. I will always remember him as one of the most humorous persons in the entire clinical pastoral movement. His stories and terms served the purpose of keeping folks laughing and loosened up. In a jocular manner, he would refer to some persons as "cockroaches" or "troops." When he wanted to invite someone to join a group, he might have hollered, "Come on over here and join these other troops."

However, there were times during that weekend when Oglesby had difficulty in gathering his troops. Many resistant supervisors were glued to a television set—a commodity not yet so plentiful in those days—watching Navy's fabled Roger Staubach quarterback his way skillfully through a highly ranked Duke University football team. Oglesby later wrote a book *Biblical Themes in Pastoral Care*. It undoubtedly will remain as a classic in the pastoral care field—as well as the memory of its popular author with the bubbly personality.

Within a month following that delightful time with the Virginian, sadness gripped the nation. President John Kennedy was assassinated in Dallas, Texas. As I entered an admission ward's dayroom at the hospital on that fateful day, a female patient ran up to me. In distress she put her head on my shoulder and cried out that she had just heard the news on television that our young president had been shot. Our national innocence has never been the same since this horrible tragedy burst out from lurid shadows.

REVIVING PASTORAL SUPERVISORY INTEREST

Beginning in early 1964, I started discussing my interest with Charles Gerkin concerning his possible supervision of my assistantship at the Milledgeville State Hospital. Since I was not located in Atlanta at Grady Hospital, he indicated that he could not be my supervisor per se. However, he did invite me to be a part of an Atlanta weekly group wherein two other persons at the assistantship level were sharing audio tapes of their supervision of students for the gaining of peer feedback and interaction.

I made such a Milledgeville-to-Atlanta round trip of two hundred miles from early spring through the summer to be in these sessions with John Patton, John Crow, and Gerkin. Incidentally, Gerkin and Patton would start emerging by the 1980s as two of the nation's most noted authors in the fields of pastoral care and counseling. Their early respective books—*The Living Human Document* and *Pastoral Counseling: A Ministry of the Church*—show up consistently in bibliographical materials. Further, Gerkin's *An Introduction to Pastoral Care* in 1997 is viewed as a groundbreaking exploration of postmodern pastoral care.

I began to develop plans for supervising a 1964 summer group of four seminarians. Chappell Wilson and Jim Travis also were shaping two similar groups at the hospital. Since we young supervisors now were becoming well acquainted with the CPE rubric of committee evaluation, we required the twelve students to meet individually our supervisory troika for the rigors of a midsummer evaluation appearance.

THE WASHINGTON CONFERENCE

At the Council's annual meeting of its Southeast Region in Washington that year, several key themes were noticed. One was that of the Region's expansion over the past couple of years. By now, Frank Cook had started his CPE program in Avon Park, Florida. It was the Region's southernmost outpost. The influence of the Georgia Association for Pastoral Care had influenced further CPE development around Atlanta. Also a familiarity between the various clinical pastoral training organizations increased. For instance, the Southern Baptist certified supervisors from Milledgeville participated in the Council's regional conference in Washington.

Another significant matter was found in a dramatic report that was made at the business meeting. It was announced that a group of persons in the clinical pastoral field was moving steadfastly toward the forming of an additional organization with a sole focus on pastoral counseling. Some of these national planners mentioned were Howard Clinebell, Fred Keuther, and Knox Kreutzer. A few regional members scoffed at the notion that such a new and controversial undertaking could ever get "off the ground." The issue brought forth the age-old discussion about education versus therapy for some regional members. Also there was some bemoaning of the fact that the Council could have incorporated the dimension of pastoral counseling into its structures had there been an earlier acceptance of it into the Council's standards.

Nevertheless, the bearers of the tidings said that an organizing meeting would be taking place soon in Saint Louis. The group was going to call itself, someone seemed to recall, The American Association of Pastoral Counselors. It seems that, after more than thirty-five years of outstanding history, AAPC did more than just rise above the ground.

A further issue that emerged was represented in the lingering concern about the breaking away of the CPE program at St. Elizabeths mental hospital from the Council's accredited membership category. Ernest Bruder, who long had been a leader in the entire CPE field, resisted the requirement of the students' tuition fees going directly to the Council's central office in New York. The specter of a fracture seemed to linger over much of the business and hallway conversation.

An additional recollection from that meeting is that of my having met Harold Yoder for the first time. He was engaged that year in supervisory training with Bruder. In the early 1970s, Yoder would move to Columbia in order to establish the first chaplaincy and CPE program at Richland Memorial Hospital. For a long period of time, this slow-talking Lutheran minister has been a devoted colleague and a persistent encourager in my writing efforts.

ON A LIMB WITH JORJORIAN

Nearly eighteen months after my first encounter with the Council's accreditation committee in the dim New York room, I appeared again before the committee seeking acting CPE supervisory status. This Chicago meeting represented the first time that the Council and the Institute of Pastoral Care functioned together in interviewing certification candidates. A segment of the committee review provided me with an indelible memory that is described below.

I appeared before a four-person group: John I. Smith and William Rogers of the Institute, and Armen Jorjorian and Tom McDill of the Council. I also recall a couple of Institute observers sitting in on the interview: Henry Brooks and Jud Howard. I felt fortunately a refreshing sense of inner openness and creative anxiety in meeting with these folks.

The unforgettable 1964 moment for me was when Jorjorian, in the closing phases of the conference, indicated to me that he wanted to take a risk. He said that, although I was asking to become an acting supervisor, he was willing to go out on a limb and consider any interest that I might immediately have in requesting instead the full certification. Although his colleagues did not show visibly any outward signs of gasping for breath, their eyes leaped in surprise. They probably could not believe that they were being put in a position of allowing a candidate to hurdle over one certification level and into the next.

The delightfully assertive Jorjorian and I wrestled around with such an offer. His dark eyes seemed to relish such an unusual moment. I ultimately reckoned with the group that what I wanted was that for which I had come asking. I told the group that naturally I was interested in the full status, but that I would come back next year to talk about that.

Jorjorian and I laughed in a soul-stirring manner amidst the committee's affirmation of my receiving that which "I had come to Chicago to claim." I always have held a warm spot in my heart subsequently for this stocky man—known widely for his energetic and caring encounters in the CPE process. Jorjorian once described a supervisory encounter as an act equally founded "in love and in guts and in health."[4] I found this description to be one that he lived out in his own life. It was quite a loss to the CPE world when he died nine years later. This occurred a year after his prominent program at St. Luke's Hospital in Houston was rattled with an attack on its budget.

Perhaps Jorjorian's approach to such spontaneous moments in the certification process cannot be replicated so readily anymore in today's more cautious and litigious climate. No doubt, newer certification processes have brought more accountability to the enterprise of professional review. Yet, there was something about the energy and risk-taking in that certification moment of thirty-five years ago that has touched my heart and memory for all these years. It all might have had something to do with *blessing* (a theme that is more fully explored in chapters 7 and 8). Should pastoral certification ever lose such soulfulness in the review process, I fear that a precious part of the clinical pastoral heritage will have faded.

A CALL FROM CAROLINA

In the winter following my Chicago certification experience, I was contacted by Obert Kempson. He was still heading up the chaplaincy program at the South Carolina State Hospital in Columbia. He invited me to consider the position as director of the CPE program at the hospital. This offer was exciting; but, at the same time, I felt unsettled about it due to my deep satisfaction with the Milledgeville situation.

But after touring the South Carolina hospital's recently constructed Chapel of Hope and the new William S. Hall Psychiatric

Institute on the campus, my decision-making labors began to move me increasingly in the direction of returning north from Georgia to Carolina. I found appealing also the state's envisioning of a more solid linkage between mental hospital treatment and community mental health.

Additionally, the move would provide Marilyn and me with greater access to both of our families. For the most part, they were residing still in lower South Carolina. We retained our longings for such enjoyments as Lowcountry barbeque in Carolina and that section's culture of beach music—so delightfully and rhythmically found in shag dancing and blues. As an aside, my love for this kind of music stays rooted in the work of such artists as Percy Sledge ("When a Man Loves a Woman"), Gladys Knight ("Midnight Train to Georgia"), the Drifters ("Under the Boardwalk"), Otis Redding, Jackie Wilson, Al Green ("Take Me to the River"), Smokey Robinson ("The Tracks of My Tears"), the Platters ("Red Sails in the Sunset"), Ben E. King ("Stand by Me"), and South Carolina's own Drink Small and Brook Benton ("Endlessly"). Juke box echoes of Edisto still remain.

A mixture of trends and happenings also were present as I departed from Georgia in March of 1965. For one thing, Marilyn had just completed her graduation requirements in business education from Georgia College in Milledgeville. Furthermore, the word *training* was diminishing quickly and *education* was on the national ascendancy in the term *clinical pastoral training*. It was at this time that the whole movement was becoming known more clearly and definitively as *CPE*.

Another phenomenon recognized for my five total years in CPE was that of the continued paucity of women and African-American students in the movement. CPE had been peopled primarily by White males. Thus far, I had known only two African-American CPE students and no women in the programs of my involvements. The only CPE-related women whom I had met were Helen Terkelsen (an Institute supervisor from the Northeast) and Emily Spickler and Win Holmes—both of whom managed the Council's central office in New York. Spickler also had spent one summer at the state hospital in Columbia doing some research for Obert Kempson while I was still there in clinical training. The only African-American CPE supervisor known by me up to the middle sixties was Henry Brooks of the Institute.

A further theme to note from the middle 1960s was that of the continuing idolatry of a strong psychological causation for the mental illnesses as generally held by the mental health field. The oncoming biochemical and organic brain importances, as seen in the book's chapter 9, yet were to make their dramatic impact. Some inferred that influences from psychoanalytic theory and the early beginnings of family therapy coalesced, without the benefit of today's brain research, to heap much causative blame for severe mental illness in those days upon faulty parenting. This was especially so in the extreme focus put on the mother. I still shudder in recalling the hideous label of the "schizophrenogenic mother" being brandished by various theoretical and treatment groups.

GRATITUDE FOR
MILLEDGEVILLE CHAPLAINCY

Leaving Milledgeville was not without its grief for me, because the chaplaincy staff was like a familial grouping. In departing I profoundly would miss the daily brotherly contacts with Turley, Close, Wilson, Travis, Keith, Cook, and Alston. From his second year's supervisory training role, Keith would fill the job position that I left in March.

The initial Milledgeville group, however, would not stay intact too long. Turley, Close, and Keith moved to Atlanta in the following fall to develop chaplaincy and CPE at the newly opened Georgia Mental Health Institute. Travis would become the chaplaincy director at the Milledgeville hospital, and he held that position very prominently for nearly eight years. He then would lead the pastoral department efforts at a medical center in Jackson, Mississippi. Wilson moved from Milledgeville in the early 1970s to Augusta for the purpose of initiating chaplaincy and CPE at a state regional mental health center.

Milton Snyder came to Milledgeville from North Carolina in 1966 to join the chaplaincy staff. He was elevated subsequently to the chief chaplain's role when Travis left for Mississippi. Snyder held his post until 1991, as did Wilson his position in Augusta. Alston would eventually leave the Milledgeville Hospital, and Cook remained for years until his retirement.

The days spent in Milledgeville represented very fondly the

early formative years of my full-time vocation in mental health chaplaincy and CPE pastoral supervision. My focus of educational supervision back then primarily was on the intrapersonal and the interpersonal dimensions of pastoral care. The social justice aspects of this caring process would more strongly touch my interest almost fifteen years later.

It has been said that the definition of the word *home* is a place where cherishing is found. As was Orangeburg, Milledgeville was another such location for me. The next chapter indicates my return back to another significant home in my life: South Carolina's public mental health system. It would be there where the majority of my clinical pastoral years would be lived.

Chapter 7

Daybreak at a New Institute, 1965-1970

In his research on adult male development, Daniel Levinson shows that, from the age of the late twenties through the early thirties, many men enter into a particular life-cycle phase. It is a time when energies are heavily directed toward revisions in their lives. Even though the potential of renewal is present throughout one's life, Levinson's designated age range focuses on reconstruction.[1]

This phase has the distinct purpose of building *for the future*. The transition, says the researcher, provides an opportunity for reconsideration of choices and the making of changes, large or small, in earlier-made young adult structures. At this *modifying* stage of personal growth in this specific age span, there is the seeking of a more updated and integrated niche in the adult world.

I prefer characterizing any such pivotal change, like the one I made, as having rootage in one's ongoing "soul journey." Some further chapters in the book depict other soul rhythms, so to speak, that have pulsated later in my continuing adult quest. For example, a later midlife point of soul passage represents another such stirring movement.

I had taken a risk, barely in my thirties, in departing from the appealing Milledgeville setting to seek future potentials elsewhere. I was taking a big leap, but it would be there where I would carve out the deepened revision and amplification of professional dreams.

This segment of *Hunkering Down*, therefore, discusses some of those important features related to the first years of my coming back to South Carolina. Special attention is directed to my involvement in the early beginnings of an exciting mental health training facility—the William S. Hall Psychiatric Institute.

CHANGES ABOUND

In returning to Columbia, I discovered at the South Carolina State Hospital that change was in the air. I felt a sense of excitement about a plunge into the new situation of my clinical pastoral life and the matters that surrounded this part of the 1960s. Transition was apparent not only in public policy directed toward the nation's mentally ill but also in the life of Anton Boisen.

Deinstitutionalization

A major shift in public mental health had begun taking place in the United States at this time. It was due partly to a clarion call made several years earlier by President Kennedy. He had urged Congress to shape a bold new approach in response to the distresses of the mentally ill. Therefore, special federal emphasis was put on the states' need for the development of community mental health centers so that large numbers of hospitalized patients could return to the support of the community. This downsizing of the mental hospitals was made possible due to an interactive combination of newer forms of psychotropic medications, the interest of civil liberties against lengthy hospital stays, and the fiscal hopes of state legislatures. These governmental bodies were particularly trying to save money by the diminishing of huge hospitals.

There were in the 1950s more than 550,000 mentally ill persons in public mental hospitals throughout the country. Between 1963 and 1973, over fifty percent of the people, however, were emptied from those locations. In the 1990s the states closed 37 of the mental hospitals. Fewer than 70,000 patients remain today in designated public institutions for mentally ill persons.

One of the dismal results of this speedy process was that some states were not prepared adequately with enough community infrastructure to handle properly the burdensome influx of so many discharged patients. A positive dimension in deinstitutionalization was the intent by many planners to develop treatment and care systems within the context of mainstreamed community living.

Although South Carolina joined this momentum in the exodus of patients later than some states, its 1965 population of almost

6,000 adults in the two historically major state hospitals in Columbia dropped radically over the next thirty years. The numbers eventually reached its current level of approximately 350 patients in a long-term setting. The census of 12,000 patients at the Milledgeville State Hospital fell gradually to today's population of approximately 1,000 persons.

A New Chapel

Another new earmark in the middle sixties was the presence of an aforementioned worship facility on the campus of the South Carolina State Hospital. This Chapel of Hope possessed a sanctuary that held nearly 450 worshipers. The religious center was constructed from the bricks of the high wall that once had separated the hospital from the surrounding city of Columbia. The Kempson Center, an educational wing adjoining the chapel, became the focus of administering the CPE program as well as providing hospital chaplaincy offices. The Hort Room, a Colonial-style parlor in the center, was named after the hospital's first chaplain of the 1840s.

The dedication of the chapel and this entire facility took place a month prior to my March arrival. Marilyn and I traveled—finally in a new car—from Milledgeville for the celebration event in Columbia.

A Wise Role in the CPE Story

Carroll Wise, who was one of Anton Boisen's early students in the founding days of CPE, was the main speaker at this occasion. The important pastoral care professor was a rather short person, and I remember hardly being able to see him behind the chapel's large pulpit. This section's material describing his prominence is indebted to Edward Thornton's research in *Professional Education for Ministry*. In the early 1930s, Wise was appointed to head up Boisen's developed training program at Worcester State Hospital. This action resulted from Boisen's previously mentioned move to Elgin State Hospital in Illinois. The gaining of this leadership role by Wise disappointed Philip Guiles, because it represented a position that he coveted. Guiles's loss, along with the fierce competitiveness between him and Helen Flanders Dunbar, rested as an additional factor behind the major disruption that split early leaders into the two camps—the Council and the Institute.

As another causation in this early organizational chasm, Wise—remaining as Worcester's chaplaincy director for twelve years—would not agree with Richard Cabot's persistent biological views on mental illness. Therefore, the headstrong Cabot became more disenchanted with the Worcester program. Subsequently, Cabot developed a congeniality with the training activities of Russell Dicks at the Massachusetts General Hospital and with Guiles at Andover Newton Theological School.

Thus, as previously intimated, the initial nucleus of the New England group—later to evolve into the Institute—was that of Cabot, Guiles, and Dicks. A contingent, which was more identified with New York and as the Council, united the efforts of Wise, Dunbar, Seward Hiltner, and others compatible with their views.[2]

Shaking Hands with Boisen

In the middle phase of the 1960s, changes continued in the CPE world. They were contained pointedly both in the relationship between the two major training organizations and in the death of Boisen. These two issues seemed to merge in forming the surrounding CPE atmosphere at this time.

The Council, for instance, held its annual meeting in the fall of 1965 in Miami Beach. The Council and the Institute were beginning to add further healing to their separation by participating jointly now in the certification process. Rather than just observation being offered by one organization with the other, they began making mutual decisions together about certification for candidates.

I sought my full CPE supervisor's status and met a committee consisting of George Dominick, Henry Brooks, William Rogers, Henry Taxis, and John Billinsky. Some other certification members functioning with various subcommittees that year happened to include Joe Woodson, Armen Jorjorian, Emil Hartl, Jack Humphreys, Joe Caldwell, Paul Kapp, John I. Smith, Ed Springer, and Herman Eichorn. I achieved successfully a recommendation of full certification status from the committee. Admittedly, the interaction included little of the energized fireworks known the year before with Jorjorian in Chicago.

I recall particularly two priceless papers being presented by Hiltner and Wise at the Council's annual meeting. They described the debt that the CPE movement had for the life and work of Boisen. He had died at age eighty-nine shortly before this conference.

Hiltner, who had worked for several years in the middle 1930s as executive secretary for the Council under Dunbar's leadership, affirmed the powerful mixture of Boisen's heavy personal loneliness and his brilliant creativity. Wise's paper dramatized some of the towering organizational encounters between such powerful clinical pastoral giants as Cabot, Dunbar, Guiles, and himself. From Wise's remarks I perceived that those early days in the movement were rampant with extraordinary vigors of intellect, jealousy, courage, competitiveness, territoriality, and energies.

I shall never forget Hiltner's parting words to the effect: "It will be a few years hence when a meeting like this will find no one who ever shook hands with Anton Boisen." Although I never had a chance actually to meet Boisen, I felt as if I had on that day when I heard these two legends speak.

Additional Handshakes

Further opportunities to hear persons talk about Boisen's history have held my interest. For example, I heard Wise again make a presentation about him in the late seventies at the annual meeting of the Association of Mental Health Clergy in Chicago. Wise, who had a lengthy and noteworthy tenure at Garrett Theological Seminary, had just recuperated from encountering a severe burn. He described how the element of personal upheaval has the potential of moving the individual toward greater growth within one's personality. This renowned pastoral care teacher reflected that, in recovery from his third-degree burn, he learned once again the truths much mentioned by Boisen—those related to our inner worlds. Wise stated: "...Anton Boisen often emphasized that, in life crises or periods of stress the key to the solution is in the person and the experience, and not outside; in inner forces which are either at peace or war within the person."[3]

Wise had seen firsthand at the Worcester hospital the agony of Boisen's brief psychotic episode of 1930. This breakdown, a clinical pastoral historian suggests, probably was triggered by not only the death of Boisen's mother but also by the convergence of his ambiguous attachments to Helen Flanders Dunbar and Alice Batchelder.[4]

At another AMHC address nearly ten years later, Len Cedarleaf referred to a positive side of Boisen's demeanor: his gracious, gentle manner. Cedarleaf saw this trait in him as he met for a 1943 interview. He was seeking entrance into Boisen's training program at Elgin State Hospital that summer. Always present throughout that summer's session, Cedarleaf said, was Boisen's walking cane. Sometimes the cane would be thumped to emphasize a teaching point. (The subject of this cane again will appear in the book's ninth chapter. The historical significance of this wooden object has been woven into a specific ritual related to CPE's organizational life.) Incidentally, Cedarleaf's roommate for that particular summer program was a young Tom Klink—the same outstanding supervisory theoretician described in chapter 5.

I sometimes have heard persons from an earlier CPE generation refer to Boisen by his nickname of Pappy. Even in that affectionate term, some had known his moments when he could be very cantankerous and aloof

Behind Boisen's death, there had been stored a magnificent and complex legacy in his nearly ninety years. Future generations would have the benefit of mining the plenteous historical riches from such a wealthy stockpile.

THE EMERGENCE OF A
NEW TEACHING HOSPITAL

In terms of chaplaincy and CPE, there was present much transition in 1966 at the South Carolina State Hospital. Obert Kempson, who had been at the institution with his pastoral effort since the early 1930s, moved into a newly created position. He became a pastoral consultant with the South Carolina Department of Mental Health's division of community mental health.

In the meantime, I had begun to have increasing interest in pursuing the starting of chaplaincy and CPE with the recently founded William S. Hall Psychiatric Institute. This facility, which was constructed on the grounds of the State Hospital with an original purpose of being an ultramodern admission and exit service for the hospital, was being legislatively transformed into a separate teaching and research hospital within the framework of the overall state Department of Mental Health.

In August of that year, I was named as its first chaplaincy and CPE director. It would be a position that I would occupy for the next seventeen years. Hence, I packed up my files and moved the length of four football fields from the State Hospital to my new professional home—the Hall Institute.

At the same time, Burt Newman was appointed as chaplaincy head for the State Hospital. Glenwood Morgan, who received his supervisory training with Pat Prest in Richmond, had joined the hospital's chaplaincy by that time. Morgan would become the first African-American CPE supervisor in the Southeast Region.

Since the Hall Institute's CPE program would be a year away from commencing, I continued educational supervision for some of the State Hospital's pastoral students. Before my move to the Hall Institute, my first student in supervisory training was Finley Brown. He received subsequently his acting certification status from the Council in 1966. Since I had received my full certification just a year before, I apparently was either very audacious or not too interested in letting further ripening keep me away from supervising supervision!

The hopes for a CPE program at the Hall Institute came to fruition in the summer of 1967. An accreditation team of George Dominick and Henry Close, representing the Southeast Region of the Council for Clinical Training, spent a day visiting in the setting. Such a survey in those days involved not so much in reviewing a plethora of written documents as it was in gaining a perception of the training center's climate, uniqueness, and the supervisor. Dominick's nature of quietness and sensitive wisdom, coupled with Close's intuitive skills, aided in making this a refreshing accreditation day.

The first yearlong CPE residency at the Hall Institute began with three students in the fall of that year. By the next summer, there was established a summer quarter program for seminary students. One of the participants in the year's residency was Jerry Alexander—a Presbyterian minister from Texas. Alexander received supervisory certification a couple of years later after completing his supervisory training at the Hall Institute. He and I would work as CPE colleagues in the Department of Mental Health for nearly thirty years prior to his retirement. Alexander, a strong regional leader since the early 1980s, was awarded the Southeast Region's distinguished service award in 1999.

From its early beginnings and onward, the Hall Institute would emerge as a premier mental health teaching hospital—gaining both southern and national attention. As my years at the Hall Institute unfolded, I would hold gratitude for the relationship with and general support of the facility's administration. Its long-time director, Dr. Alexander Donald, offered abiding skills and a strong commitment in developing the facility. Dr. Joe Freed, who served as the Institute's director of training and professional services, and myself started off many mornings by hunkering down over a cup of coffee in the hospital's canteen. As the administrator, Forrest "Pete" Newman gave a steady hand to the setting.

I found substantial freedom and nurture at the center in developing the pastoral care and CPE programming. It was invigorating to supervise students in their rich pastoral learning moments on various inpatient and outpatient clinical areas. In addition to the psychiatric residency program, the profuse presence of numerous interprofessional training programs, such as psychology internships and social work placements, allowed the CPE students to interact closely with the variety of students from many mental health disciplines. Noted lecturers, for example, Bert Pepper and Maxwell Jones, frequented the setting. At times the smorgasbord of learning was so bountiful that one of my administering perplexities was that of attempting to shape some manageable narrowing to the CPE curriculum. The abundancy reminded me of my father's lavish garden.

Many of the graduates from these training programs—including various pastoral students—entered full-time service with the state's public mental health system in its centers and hospitals. Due to both a national trend for the reduction of support for training institutes in state public mental health systems and some structural transitions in South Carolina's mental health department, the prominence of the Hall Institute in the mental health educational arena began to be altered by the middle of the 1990s.

COLUMBIA AREA CPE COMMITTEE

Prior to my move from the South Carolina State Hospital to the Hall Institute in 1966, I had started conducting CPE committee meetings with Burt Newman, Glenwood Morgan, Obert Kempson, and myself for the purpose of handling the State Hospital's programming matters. After the changes occurred, we continued our regular committee work together. Since a CPE program was sought for the Hall Institute, it became helpful for us to remain engaged as a group in mutual planning and discussion.

This particular committee eventually became the forerunner to an informal Columbia area CPE supervisors' group. This constellation would convene for more than thirty years every other week in collegiality and planning. When Lin Barnett of the South Carolina Baptist Hospital began his CPE program in 1967, he indicated interest in joining the group in order to be a part of the colleagueship. It was Barnett's outreach that was a catalyst for these corporate interests. Adlai Lucas of the state's correctional system also soon joined these activities. Austin Shell, professor of pastoral care at the local Lutheran Theological Southern Seminary, became an early addition to the endeavors.

For several years the committee members cooperatively sponsored clinical pastoral orientation programs for community pastors. By 1968 we had named our gathering the "Columbia Area CPE Committee" and commonly called it CACPEC. The membership grew as other CPE programs were birthed in Columbia and additional supervisors arrived.

Various presentations about the CPE process were made by the supervisors or invited guests at the ninety-minute meetings. Other activities included conferences and workshops sponsored for all of the Columbia area CPE students, dialogues with the faculty of the Lutheran Seminary in Columbia, the making available of evaluation committees for students, and other various events.

At the end of every summer, the group traditionally has held a lakeside party. A total of thirty-two different CPE supervisors and twenty-eight supervisory students have been a part of CACPEC's experience since its beginnings. Several years ago, a written history of this group's journey—entitled *CACPEC: A History of Collegiality and Continuity*—was distributed to the Southeast Region of ACPE by its history committee.

In early 1998 the CACPEC members began intensive discussion related to the group's mission. Some former members had retired or moved, plus there were major changes taking place in the various CPE centers in the Columbia area. By the late summer, the group concluded some former directions. There then began a move toward the future with various hopes for transformation.

One of the most nurturing and beloved aspects of my overall CPE life has been that discovered from the resources of more than thirty years of this local collegiality.

A KANSAS CITY HAPPENING

What happened during the fall of 1967 was monumental in the history of clinical pastoral education: An assembling of the major and separate CPE organizations provided the birthing of the Association for Clinical Pastoral Education in Kansas City. The constituting groups of the Council for Clinical Training, the Institute of Pastoral Care, the Southern Baptist Association for Clinical Pastoral Education, and the Lutheran Advisory Council merged into one national body. During the ceremonies I could not help but recall my last visit in that part of the country six years earlier to visit Charles Hall, Tom Klink, and Joe Caldwell. Also entering my memory were the boundary turfs that I once witnessed between the Council and the Institute during that fascinating conference five years earlier on Cape Cod.

This outstanding culmination into ACPE was built on almost thirty years of rugged attempts at building standards, the struggles confronting the Committee of Twelve, and some earlier aborted federation efforts. Celebration rippled throughout the atmosphere in Kansas City. However, there was a lapse into drowsiness experienced by many at a lengthy banquet. Alas, the major benefactor of financially underwriting much of the merger process droned on into the night with a dissonant speech on the power of positive thinking. However, the merger became one of the most noticeable milestones in the history of the entire CPE movement. Charles Hall would be named as ACPE's executive director several months later, and he capably would hold that post for the next seventeen years.

THE BIRTH OF A NEW REGION

At the time of this above merger, the Council's previous Southeast Region was in a metamorphosis due to the advent of ACPE. Nine regions were newly delineated throughout the nation, and the five former organizations blended according to these regional boundaries. This meant that ACPE's newly created Southeast Region now embraced Alabama, Florida, Georgia, Mississippi, South Carolina, and Tennessee. As a new structural day appeared for clinical pastoral education, I nevertheless felt the loss of the earlier Council ties with the supervisors in Virginia, Maryland, Delaware, and the District of Columbia. I would miss being able to associate regionally with persons like Pat Prest, Dave Gregory, Keith Keidel, Bob Robey, and Ralph Carpenter.

A southeastern regional conference had been called in the spring prior to the national formation of ACPE in anticipation of the proposed regional structures resulting from the merger. This meeting was conducted at the Georgia Mental Health Institute in Atlanta. Obert Kempson was selected as the Region's first director, and he would be in that position for five years. Kempson also served as regional chairperson for three years. He was followed in that latter role by Professor John Gessell of the Sewanee Theological School.

Those early years brought a comfortable mix of former Southern Baptist and Council supervisors into regional life. Much of this was due to the previously developed interorganizational relationships that were forged at the Milledgeville State Hospital and the Georgia Association for Pastoral Care. Also, Kempson's skilled diplomacy, pluralism, and hospitable style assisted in this endeavor. I cherished the opportunity of becoming newly acquainted with other former Southern Baptist CPE supervisors such as Joe Abbott of Birmingham, Bill Mays of Nashville, and Roy Woodruff of Tuscaloosa.

One of the legendary gems of advice proffered by a seasoned CPE warrior to a younger one in the ranks was given at this time. It occurred when Jap Keith assumed the mantle as regional secretary. The elder Kempson is reported to have said, "Jap, if you work as their mule now, one day they may just make you into a racehorse."[5] For years there has existed some unclarity as to whether Keith actually was asked to work like a "mule" or as a "workhorse." Regardless, the prophesy came true. In 1984 Keith himself would become regional director in addition to being selected as president-elect of ACPE in the early eighties.

During the genesis years of the Region, the business meetings were characterized by process-oriented energies in deference to structural or organizational issues. This was due partly to most of the pastoral supervisors' experiential heritage. If Paul Tillich's polarity of "form and dynamics" in his *Systematic Theology* had been a gauge to assess the members' interest in the conduct of business sessions, the most obvious thrust would have assuredly knocked the top out of the dynamics column. The form dimension hardly was seen. I recall a regional meeting in Columbia during the very early 1970s wherein the attendees decided to retract the majority of the past year's business decisions. Later on, an organizational consultant would help pull us out of this experiential mire and aided us to sharpen up our more left-brained organizational tools.

New training centers began to sprout up throughout the Region. For example, while serving in 1969 through 1971 as chairperson of the regional certification and accreditation committee, I had the opportunity in site reviews to experience the thrilling development of CPE in added locales. Some of my visits with those centers and supervisors included Bob Lantz at the Memphis Institute of Medicine and Religion, Bob Morris and a Florida mental health center in Winter Haven, Ron Mudd and the Methodist Hospital in Jacksonville, Alabama's Bryce State Mental Hospital with Roy Woodruff, and Chappell Wilson at a state regional hospital in Augusta. The total number of accredited centers in 1971 in the Region was seventeen. Twelve years later, that number had risen to forty-five. The regional budget climbed from $1,600 to $43,000 in that same period.

I recall that, on the same day of a site visit with one hospital, its circulated staff newspaper announced triumphantly that its CPE program had received accreditation. These late-breaking tidings echoed through the setting even before the site review's closing session ended! Such was the eagerness of some centers to get on about the business of CPE.

The exciting activity in the Region and the Hall Institute touched my own personal history. Like the earlier adventures of a newly developed swimming team at Wofford, new CPE pathways—where there previously had been none—were being fashioned.

AN ANCIENT CERTIFICATION BOX

A vital feature in the early days of the Southeast Region resided in the activities of certification and accreditation. Due to the importance of these two functions in CPE, some specific attention is now drawn to them as a part of my storytelling.

These two areas of professional concern were contained for a long while in the same committee. This was so at both the regional and national levels. The group was better known as the "C and A Committee." The main focus of the committee's work tended to be on the more animated appearances of candidates seeking certification approval. The review of reports on hospital settings for accreditation purposes received scant attention—sometimes only as an afterthought in committee deliberation. The committee tended to place much confidence on the certified CPE supervisor's capacity to develop the hospital context for trustworthy accredited programming.

The experiential, or process, emphasis was very much alive in the arena of regional certification review with candidates. The positive side of this was that candidates were met directly and affectively. A negative dimension was that these interactions sometimes avoided the conceptual area.

When I became elected as chairperson of the Region's C and A committee, my inherited committee materials that were related to candidates and centers were in a small cardboard box. The former leader, Henry Close, handed over this Ivory Soap box container to me. By the time that I would finish my tenure three years later, this time span had required no more than an extra two feet for the additional sparse materials in the box. When Jap Keith became the new committee chairperson, I met him halfway between Columbia and Atlanta. He was presented with the ragged, little box. It were as if a precious "Ark of the Covenant" was being passed along to a new shepherd.

The heretofore unified branches of certification and accreditation would be divided in 1975 by the forming of two separate committees. By then the evolving statements of "certification is for *persons*" and "accreditation is for *centers*" finally had permeated the awareness of CPE participants. Contextual evaluation of hospitals and other sites now began to take on increasing importance. Chappell Wilson assumed the role of regional chairperson for the new certification committee, while Bob Morris did the same for the accreditation committee. At that point the dilapidated cardboard encasement had outlived its usefulness. A new age of classy filing cabinets had arrived on the scene—much before the spawning of computers.

BLESSING AND CERTIFICATION

The certification processes of those earlier years contained strong potentials in so-called metaphoric "mythic moments of connection" for candidates. I have described previously one such tie as discovered by me with Armen Jorjorian in my own travels down the certification highway.

Another example of this connective phenomenon in certification occurred much later at the 1981 ACPE annual meeting in Estes Park, Colorado. A newly certified supervisor, Urias Beverly, was celebrating with some friends over his recent victory of having achieved his full certification status. This husky African-American minister, who later became an ACPE president, was mentioning at a party how he had positively encountered the strength of a committee member in the personage of John Paolini of Spokane. He inferred joyously that such a struggling, creative process had made Paolini his *"father* in certification."

Upon overhearing this moment of a described blessing, I remembered that ten years earlier I had had the good fortune of serving on Paolini's national committee when he appeared for certification. I approached Beverly and said, "Then I must be your *grandpappy!"* We then hugged victoriously and celebrated our certification and interracial lineage. When Beverly and I have spied one another at various meetings, there will be invariably a happy embrace of exchanging a "Grandpappy" and a "Grandson" greeting.

A knock on my office door at the Hall Institute in South Carolina a couple of years after the Estes Park conference reflected the expanded continuance of this mythic and intergenerational saga. As I opened the door, a young and lanky African-American pastor on his way from Indiana to Florida stood there. He asked this Caucasian, "Are you 'Grandpappy?' If you are, your 'Grandson' told me to stop by and tell you hello." This vignette with its powerful certification opportunities for inclusiveness and mythos has touched my soul for years.

I fear that, should certification procedures—or any, for that matter—become too unnecessarily bland, the power of mythic connections regretfully can be lost. I realize that some of my current reflections may have a tinge of nostalgia in them, but I hold that these strong ties rest near the heart of our experience-based pastoral education efforts. The combination of such affective ties and today's commendable certification emphasis on pastoral theology and theory enables the heart and head to find an ongoing unity.

My hope is that pastoral certification can not only be a mechanism for examining overt competency in supervisory practice and pastoral theology skills but also a systemic process containing the *blessing* of one's hoped-for entry into the power-filled life of certified pastoral supervision. It is this experiential blessing process that stirs and confirms internal creativities. It aids one in becoming a supervisory artist rather than primarily relying on technical skills. The long-lasting effect of the blessing in certification is that it serves as a vivid reminder to connect others up to the passing along of one's care. Thus, it is rooted in the mythos of intergenerational review and life. In chapter 8, the section on "An Inquiry into Pastoral Supervision" explores more thoroughly an interrelationship between blessing and competency in supervision.

A FAMILY GROWS

As both the Hall Institute and ACPE's Southeast Region expanded, so did my family. Boyd, our first son, was born in 1969; Mason followed his brother four years later. In those days, it was not very customary to allow fathers in the hospital delivery room. This was quite unlike the Orangeburg bedroom of my own birth—even though my father never quite made entry into that space.

When a nurse led me into the early morning dimness of a room containing a bonded twosome, the air filled with bright epiphany as I witnessed the wonder of a newly arrived first-son finding comfort on his mother's breast. A second-born was so eager later to get into the world that Marilyn and I hardly made it to the hospital delivery room before he greeted us. Boyd's name was selected from Marilyn's last name, while Mason took the name of my maternal Papa—the beloved Cross Hill grandfather. Up until Boyd's birth, Marilyn worked with the South Carolina State Hospital's vocational rehabilitation service as an evaluator of patients for potential job placements.

With the decade of the 1960s arriving at its end, my CPE journey thus far had embraced in its total of ten years an intricate entwining of the personal with the vocational. Awaiting around the corner, the next era would present me with its unique promises and tumults.

Chapter 8

Stretching Times, 1970-1982

In the evolution of my life's story and its involvements with clinical pastoral education, this interval of the next dozen years at the Hall Institute contains several overlapping time phases. For instance, the early 1970s are characterized by a period of my exploring the strenuously enjoyable element of creativity in certain models of programming for pastoral education. The middle part of that decade is visited by waves that roiled mightily within the personal sea of a commonly called midlife transition. A third feature later emerges with its preparatory focus on my movement toward an interest in pastoral care's bridge with social justice.

Attention is now drawn to a description of these years—ones that stretched my growth and pastoral education perspectives.

WINDS OF DELIGHT IN PASTORAL LEARNING

In the early seventies, a major staffing accomplishment transpired for chaplaincy and CPE at the Hall Institute. An additional CPE supervisor's position was approved, and this financial support enabled further program development. Bill Crittenden filled this position for several years before moving to Missouri. Crittenden, who provided a capable transaction-analytical dimension to his pastoral supervision, was followed in 1974 by Roland Rainwater—whose CPE training had taken place with Armen Jorjorian and others in Houston.

Rainwater and I would be colleagues in various program arrangements for the next twenty years before his retirement. He has demonstrated over the years a vital CPE interest in the integration of ecology and theology. His valuing of Loren Eisley's book *The Immense Journey* and Richard Elliott's *Falling in Love with*

Mystery demonstrates a devotion to this area. A coterie of other Columbia area CPE supervisors appreciating eminently this ecological framework have been Riley Eubank, Joe Slade, Harold Yoder, and Gene Rollins.

Dale Owen, who later became a leader in North Atlanta's Tri-Hospital center, also functioned in this particular position at the Hall Institute for five years. I learned much from her regarding the holistic dimensions of the inward journey and its symbols of right brain richness.

The first part of the decade also ushered in for me some cherished opportunities related to the clinical education of clergy, seminary students, and other pastoral representatives. Muscles of creativity were exerted in these learning processes. Hence, some of the described educational events below contain a congruence with my own roots of personal pilgrimage. This fortunate phenomenon of integrating some of the personal with the vocational fortunately allowed me to know a pronounced measure of delight in clinical teaching and programming.

Hunkering Down and CPE

As an example, the initial incorporation of the *hunkering down* metaphor into my CPE supervision took place at this time. Until then, I had not given much thought to this particular symbol since the occasion when it earlier was handed down to me by my farming and bus-driving parishioner, Rhoadus Blakely.

The introduction of the term into my pastoral care lexicon happened within the context of a pastoral supervision conference with a clergyman. Harvey was discussing with me his disappointment and resentment over not being accepted yet by the members of an inpatient ward staff. He defended himself by telling me how hard he had labored to lay down his formal guidelines to these persons. He repeatedly had told them what precisely they could expect from his pastoral role.

It appeared to me that he was pushing the staff around in a lot of busyness and structured distance. Harvey had not yet taken the time to know the staff members as persons. Instead, he wanted automatic acceptance because he felt that a ministerial prerogative deserved such.

I told him, "It seems to me that you're trying to *hustle* these folks, Harvey, rather than first *hunkering down* with them." In this teachable moment, the term found seeming release from somewhere deep in my memory and inner regions. In retrieving the history further, I then shared with him the story of my having hunkered down with Rhoadus Blakely and his cohorts on a hot summer day more than ten years before in lower South Carolina. Wondering where such a highly "intellectual" account was heading, Harvey first looked at me skeptically with a wrinkled brow and puzzlement.

Recovering from his surprise, the student and I then considered the sustaining role of pastoral care in contrast to the other three functions of healing, guiding, and reconciling. I talked with Harvey about some theological issues related to the matter of grace as over against works. I suggested that, thus far, he seemed to be operating from a works-righteous style of ministry. He had not been available with the staff members to allow the grace of his listening, support, and nurture to be felt by them. In short, he had not hunkered down with them.

I encouraged him to go back to his assigned ward and start hunkering down attitudinally with those in his surroundings or else he likely never would be soundly accepted as their clinical pastor. He bravely went back. An early report was that he felt awkward, because this thing of slowing down was new for him. But a pastoral care ministry began to yield fruit as increasingly he centered in with intently listening to the varied conversations and stories that staff members and patients shared.

Just as in those Orangeburg days of watching the budding process take place in a garden or chicken yard, the marvel and joy of his pastoral growth had enriching meanings.

In more recent years, I have conceptualized a sabbath rhythm as having potential interaction with the hunkering theme. In other words, hunkering as a pulling away into retreat can provide a gathered, restful sense of renewal within the person. One then becomes better prepared to go out further into the world for the service of ministry on the social margins.

In CPE supervision I appreciate such polarities as the mentioned renewal/service theme. Examples of other polarity matters are those of containing/releasing, individuality/corporality, faith/doubt, and form/dynamics. Polarity work gives alternating attention to two seemingly opposite and tensive poles. Subsequent integration of the two takes place within the increasingly informed middle ground. Interest in the field of bioenergetics and Stanley Keleman's two books, *Living Your Dying* and *The Human Ground*, have assisted me in this focus of seeking connections between two dimensions.

Pastoral Care Conferences: Marney Moments and Others

A significant activity got underway at the Hall Institute in 1972 with the advent of an annual statewide pastoral care symposium. Although not fitting into the category of accredited CPE, the pastoral conferences brought information about pastoral care to a wide variety of pastors and others. These one-day continuing education events attracted an audience of approximately two hundred community pastors to hear nationally recognized leaders from the pastoral care and counseling fields. Wayne Oates was the symposium's inaugural speaker, and his topic was that of "Pastoral Care and Cultural Change." Other subsequent presenters for this annual occasion included Reuel Howe, Howard Clinebell, William Oglesby, Myron Madden, Seward Hiltner, Paul Pruyser, George Anderson, and Mansell Pattison.

Additional speakers for other kinds of conferences at the Hall Institute were Charles Gerkin, Carlyle Marney, Sam Keen, John I. Smith, Jap Keith, James Laney, a team from the Atlanta Psychiatric Clinic, and Clark Aist.

These symposia and other continuing education events with such prominent leaders not only were stimulating to plan but also they offered occasionally some unanticipated moments. Several of these surprising times are included in this section.

For example, there was a major conference planned in 1973 with the famed Carlyle Marney of Interpreters' House from the mountains of North Carolina. The announced topic—worked out carefully beforehand with this prophetic and sometimes offhanded orator—was to be that of "listening and pastoral care."

After I finished introducing him to the eager conferees, the eloquent and silver-maned speaker stood up and produced some shocking news to me just as I was preparing to sit down. "Summers," he quietly whispered in my ear, "I've decided just a moment ago, while you were talking, that I want to speak about Carl Jung and religion rather than on the listening thing." The renowned theologian and preacher quickly walked toward the speaker's rostrum. This exceptional person participated brilliantly with Jung and the audience for most of that day in his deep, melodious voice. As usual, his remarks were packed with power.

However, for months afterwards I had to contend with the ire of the United States military. Approval had been granted to some of its chaplains for attendance at the conference, and they were expected to increase their listening skills. The military folks did not know that they were going to spend the day with Carl Jung nor with a speaker who had this trapeze talent of switching things around in midair.

Another "Marney Moment" happened during a scheduled break a couple of years later at a conference that was held at the Hall Institute. We were both using a rest room facility and responding to the call of nature. In that typically rich and loud voice that was his, he bellowed, "Summers, since you're a chaplain in the mental health field and hanging around with all of these psychologists, I'm going to tell you about a good way to diagnose how well preachers have developed their own sense of authority." As others entered and exited the room, he continued on to my dismay, "If a preacher makes noise loudly and joyfully right in the middle of the commode, then he's got a strong claim on his power and authority. However, if it's done quietly around the edges, you better watch out for him! He doesn't think much of himself." However, I must admit that I have never added this homespun and bladder-oriented suggestion to my array of diagnostic interests!

With the passage of time, I have learned about other diversified Marney Moments known by a host of persons. Many were influenced by the rich presence of this refreshing—but unpredictable—theological giant from the North Carolina hills.

A further vignette related to these pastoral education conferences took place with Wayne Oates of Louisville. The prolific author was having a meal in my home and was relaxing before his next day's speaking engagement at our symposium. Also present were some CPE supervisors and students on the eve before this conference. Oates, several others, and myself were seated around a table discussing some weighty matter like cross-grained experiences in supervision or Erich Fromm's personality theory. My son Boyd, then ten years of age, joined us at the table and was listening to these complex discussions.

During a lull, Boyd said, "Dr. Oates, I want to ask you something. Don't you think it's about time that me and my daddy took turns in who's first going to read *Sports Illustrated*? I know he's got the money to order it every year, but now I'm old enough to take my turn at getting hold of it first when it comes in the mail. Don't you think so?"

Oates laughed protractedly and showed enthusiasm in seeing this youngster express his personal claim and use of consultation. He used this conversation as an illustration in his pastoral care presentation at the symposium the next day. On many occasions thereafter, Oates inquired about my son and whether he was still fond of *Sports Illustrated*. In October of 1999, this eminent pastoral leader died in Louisville.

Incidentally, in the midforties it was Oates's strong leadership in the Louisville area that brought a Southern Baptist emphasis to the forefront in the clinical pastoral movement. He had been ironically denied certification earlier as a CPE supervisor by the Council for Clinical Training. Along with the assisting efforts of Richard Young in Winston-Salem and John Price and Myron Madden in New Orleans, Oates became a central trailblazer in the South. In a previous CPE day, there had existed the two unjoined elements of Boisen's focus on a study of theological dynamics and Russell Dicks's stronger preference for concrete verbatims in pastoral care. These two strands became synthesized in Oates's integrated writings. Hence, it remained for his literature and that of Seward Hiltner and Carroll Wise to pull together more profoundly the dimensions of reflective dynamics and illustrative pastoral care.

I appreciated thoroughly the aforementioned continuing education conferences at the Hall Institute not only because of the qualitative work provided by the speakers but also many of these interpreters of pastoral care had a personalized flair about themselves. In my earlier growing up years around Orangeburg and Cross Hill, I had relished the opportunity of encountering many colorful and strong characters in my southern culture. The likes of Oglesby, Oates, Madden, Keen, Marney, and Pattison definitely were additions to that preceding cast.

CPE and the Playground

The early 1970s also represented a time when I would begin a dozen years of providing therapy with families and their preadolescent children in the Hall Institute's child psychiatry outpatient service. During these years I led a therapy group for the parents. Also, I trained child psychiatry residents as group leaders with me in this activity. Harry Stack Sullivan's writings about the personality development era of preadolescence became a key resource. Sullivan intimates that it is in this particular period where a young person learns how to develop competency in interpersonal relationships through chumships and how both to give and receive mutual care. Freud's stress on latency development and Richard Gardner's work on storytelling became assisting literary aids in our endeavors.

Simultaneous to our parents' group, a group with the children was conducted by another therapist—accompanied by a child psychiatric trainee. A CPE student was regularly commissioned as a time-out coordinator for the children's group. The student's role was that of meeting with those children whose unruliness or lack of boundaries in the group on a given day forced them to be extracted from the group. When a child calmed down sufficiently, the pastoral student would permit entry back into the children's group. This activity was fertile ground for a pastoral student's learning more about preadolescence and boundaries.

The combined team of all these therapists met weekly for collaboration and supervision. Home visits sometimes were made with the families in addition to participation with them in such activities as bar mitzvahs and other celebrations.

This particular involvement with family systems—laden with their preadolescent issues—aided me in the forming of an assessment perspective about some dimensions of group life in the CPE process with pastoral students. This has been especially so in the opportunity of leading those CPE seminars that include an interpersonal relationship nature. I have often referred to this consideration as a "playground methodology" in evaluating the functioning of student members in the training group.

For instance, I attempt as a pastoral supervisor to be aware of what preadolescent residuals or unresolvements might be displayed by a student in her/his initial entry into the CPE group environment. Thus, arrival into such group life can be symbolically akin to that person's entering, for the first time, a figurative playground containing an awesome amount of uncertain peer interactions.

In other words, does this ingression for the CPE student propel him/her into a strong trend of timidity, boastfulness, domination, withdrawal, fright, or any other personality feature often perceived in preadolescent play and peership strivings? Much personal and pastoral learning can occur in group life by dealing with some of these unique interactions. Also, the playground perspective has aided me in targeting more accurately my pastoral supervision approach with certain students.

The metaphor of the playground in CPE contains personal meanings for me due to my own Orangeburg preteen days of variously playing ball games with peers, jumping into a cold river in the winter with them, seeking moments of solitude, or engaging in swampy mud fights.

An example of these so-called playground issues in CPE life can be seen in the apparent learning struggles of Cliff in the initial phases of his program. He had carried into his early thirties a very bossy trait. In the first several CPE weeks, he attempted diligently to control his five other student peers. Yet, he remained at arms length in his issuance of veiled condescending comments. In physical appearance, hardly a hair was combed out of place; his shoes were impeccably shined.

During these opening weeks, Cliff would bristle occasionally when any of his fellow students would express strong disagreement with each other in the context of seminar concerns. Upon being invited for dialogue, he usually offered instead a ready-made answer. At times it appeared that some of his peers were ready to walk away from him. In short, he stood outside of his potential learning space as if he had never in his prior years negotiated successfully interactive territory with peers. Instead, he stood outside of the playground's gate, so to speak, and directed negative judgments to those scurrying around inside with their various forms of interaction.

Behind any frightened part of us, there naturally rests reasons. Early years, for instance, had molded such a walled-off personal stance in Cliff. When he was eight years old, the loss of his father— through desertion from the family—had resulted in Cliff's being cast by a beleagured mother into a premature role as the family protector. He inherited this position because he was the oldest sibling of the four children. Burdened with shocking grief and anger, he forced himself to choke back his hurts and get on about the task of holding things together for his beset family tribe. His adopted philosophy was that there should be no time for play, only work. His later ministerial life had now nearly burned him out.

His grip on others was heavy and remained so until he faced this appearance of an ominous CPE arena where mutual give-and-take in the learning process was a prime value. Only that which he could control felt like a safe place to be; anything else had kinship to a symbolic recapitulation into the unknown and getting hurt again. As with most overcontrolling persons, his exterior looked impenetrable while an interior heart felt scared.

Would he enter through the gate into his playground of learning? Would he back away from this crucial developmental task of his and glance at it only from a distance—if at all? Those became the central questions that I entertained as I experienced his and the group's quandary.

The good news to report is that, in the course of time, Cliff's heart won out considerably over the vexation of his extreme historical loss. In a supervision conference, I once told him that I knew he was walking a difficult road, but I felt that he had it in him to find some strength. (Fosdick and McDill had done the same for me.) Thanks also to his courage plus the persistent support and realistic confrontation of his peers, he could not dam up any further some of the loneliness that he had been shouldering in his pastoral learning quest. Cliff slowly let the drawbridge down on the moat that had cut through much of his life with others. He had made quite an internal journey to transport that eight-year-old kid part of himself into the sunlight of a new playground for learning.

I first saw it when I observed him test out carefully some new waters by his offering a moment of warm support. This gesture was shown to a peer in that student's travails over a difficult pastoral care situation with a patient.

Furthermore, I knew that something was stirring in Cliff's pilgrimage when I noticed several days later that his shoes looked somewhat scuffed rather than exuding their usual luster. In my imagination, I wondered if he had been out on some dusty playground somewhere—or certainly was looking for one to enter.

CPE Goes to College

A further feature of my CPE story in this time period of the 1970s was the initiation of a full-time month's undergraduate training program at the Hall Institute for preministerial and premedical college students. Our pastoral education department collaborated with Wofford College in mutually shaping the clinical program. The period at the training center usually accommodated six students, and it was constructed along the lines of a miniscaled CPE model with clinical assignments, seminars, individual supervision conferences, lectures, readings, the writing of verbatims, and other features. This clinical academic program had its annual activity for the twenty-eighth time in January of 1999.

The professor, with whom this "Theology and Therapy" course was fashioned, was Dr. Charles Barrett of the college's religion department. He was a college classmate of mine years ago, and I served then as his sportswriter during his editorship of the college newspaper.

Over the years I have met now and then former participants who have enjoyed a career in their chosen fields of medicine, ministry, or some other vocational endeavor. Some have indicated that their previous undergraduate clinical and reflective time of being in a helping role with patients was a critical turning point in their overall career decisions and directions. This type of undertaking has convinced me that CPE principles and methods have extreme relevancy for college students in their preprofessional preparation for entrance into the helping disciplines.

Story Day

Another curriculum addition in the '70s became that of explicating a story perspective in the CPE format. My affection for such a narrative emphasis had been derived from various sources. For one thing, chapter 1 refers to my having been planted in lower South Carolina's soil of storytelling. My upbringing there afforded me countless opportunities of sitting around listening to relatives and colorful characters spin their yarns and adventures. In a 1981 journal article, I described the activity of sharing stories in a group from a group development standpoint. It expedites the potential of a corporate belonging or identification for individuals. Earlier childhood transactions of telling and listening to stories in a close group association, similar to a family's, can become rekindled.[1]

In addition, I had started to perceive—by the middle seventies—appreciable pastoral supervision links between storytelling, the stories in the biblical literature, and the pastoral care act of listening to another's personal historical story. Furthermore, the power of an individual's own mythic story—a notion derived from my growing interest in Jungian thought—was assuming by then more significance for me.

Hence, I have offered for nearly twenty-five years a program event—named Story Day—with each of my supervised CPE groups. The structure calls for a day to be set apart in retreat fashion, and it usually has been held in my home. An originally written story of six or seven pages is written and shared by each student and myself. Many of these productions start off with a "once upon a time" beginning. One's story is not to be dissected nor subjected to deep analysis in the discussion phase. The students are encouraged primarily to listen and to be open inwardly to another's creative offering. At the latter part of the event, reflection is developed around narrative issues. Some of these include personal creativity, the appearance of mythic themes and symbols in the stories, biblical implications, theological themes, and the pastoral care acts of both listening and narrative preaching.

The combination of authoring stories in this above format and a general consideration of narrative theology has piqued my interest for years about the issue of one's developing a sense of personal authority. The word *author*, for instance, carries with it direct connotations in the act of "creating" something. Throughout one's life an individual has the awesome challenge of authoritatively creating the chapters, as it were, in the progression of one's life.

These life-cycle blocks of experience are formed through an exposure to the daunting maze of choices, persons, struggles, passions, and hopes that enter one's walk through life. The shaping of a particular chapter's major thematic characteristic is more than likely perceived in personal remembrance. Thus, the shaping of a personal era's key theme is more strongly accomplished as a person looks over a shoulder at the past as over against a knowing in the immediacy of the present. For instance, it would take twenty years before I defined the "participant/observer" theme as a major motif from my early days.

The matter of personal authority takes on increased importance
for the person when some searching or perplexing life-questions
are entertained. Who is the major author in determining my pilgrimage? Is my script for living these years controlled predomi-
nantly by earlier parental injunctions, a partner, or some set of
external doctrines? What accommodations do I make beneficially
in response to those persons who are very important and dear to
me in life? What is the experience with my God in all of this?

The wrestling for personal authority, needless to say, is no easy
matter. It takes a lifetime. It is a formidable task amidst the multi-
plicity of relationships and happenings in our lives. Yet, within
these ambiguities we are obliged to risk taking a conscious ownership in authoring our daily pages with integrity. From beginning
to end, such a "created life-narrative" might well be the most precious gift offered back to a Creator—whose historical Creativity
has been storied by humankind since an early dawning of time.

Country Stores

Another program activity in this decade was the inauguration of
an extended CPE unit. This part-time structure for community
pastors was added to the other already existing full-time formats:
a summer program for seminary students, the residency year for
clergy, supervisory education, and the undergraduate thrust. This
additional program was called "Pilgrimage CPE." Years before, I
had become more familiar with the religious metaphor *pilgrimage*
in the pastoral care field from Lewis Sherrill's classic book *Struggle
of the Soul.* The congregational pastors enrolled in the program literally traveled and made a pilgrimage to Columbia from different
parts of the state on a one-day-a-week basis for nine months.

Along with the bulk of its clinical time spent at the Hall Institute in visiting inpatients and also some accountable time spent in
pastoral care with congregational members, the training group
spent an additional day together in each participant's local context.
During this site visit, the hosting student would introduce the fellow group members to various features in this particular parish.
The orientation allowed the group to gain more familiarity with the
total ministry context of this peer.

As an example, one such CPE pastor in a rural setting invited the group to sit around a stove with him on an early spring day in a country store. In this hunkering down mode, we met some of his church members and other persons from the little community as they entered the store. They had come there to buy groceries or to pick up their mail. Some would come over and sit down by the stove with our CPE group. Later that day a church member feted the group with a barbequed chicken lunch near a river. (Indeed, it was the Edisto River.) I was impressed that this kind of contextual emphasis within the student's own everyday environment allowed for a more total perspective on his natural gifts and unique style of offering ministry. Our group learning that day took place where the pastor actually lived out his ministry.

Such accompaniment in seeking these local flavors in education has enlivened my pastoral supervision. It very well could have some tie to those early days when my grandfather—Papa—cherished my going with him in his Model-A Ford during his tours of the countryside and stops at old stores.

Fishing and Arm Wrestling

It was during this period when I also began inviting some of the CPE groups to go fishing with me in a family pond down in Orangeburg County. I would ask my father to go with us, because he loved fishing just as much as his gardening.

Following an afternoon of pursuing bream and bass, we all would join my mother at the Orangeburg home for a delightful meal of barbeque. These celebrating occasions allowed the students to experience my own lower South Carolina heritage and family. I have pondered that, if part of my pastoral opportunity in relationally oriented supervision is that of getting to know the student's personal history, then she/he also should have access to some of mine. Due to such a fishing trip and also my occasional references to a historical grounding in such ecological treasures as rivers and frogs, a student from New Zealand once pegged me as being a "Tom Sawyer of CPE."

A more active and versatile pastoral supervision became included for me in the several or more years that I occasionally would invite a student to do some moderate and playful arm wrestling with me in the peer group context. More often than not, this periodic engagement would be in response to a student's ascertained growing edge in personal and pastoral authority development—especially if a student were suffering from the "grasshopper syndrome" (see chapter 6).

This activity did not focus on whom might be victor as it did on a mutuality in arm wrestling. There invariably would be an instant when both of the participants' locked arms would become impassed in a brief, but dynamic, moment of an equalized and trembling tension. Themes related to authority, theology, power, and Bible stories usually ensued from the experiential demonstration of our having wrestled as partners at this symbolic Jabbok Brook (Gen. 32: 22-32 NIV). After a while it became necessary to delete this experience-based approach due to some tendinitis showing up in my shoulders.

I remain grateful for these above seven programs or perspectives that have their origins for me from the early 1970s. Listening to a student's creative tale in Story Day, as well as huddling with CPE learners and some church members around a rural stove, serve to remind me of the rich gifts that reside in a person-centered form of pastoral education. These moments have brought a sense of delight to my educational process.

LEADERSHIP OF VERDERY

During this time Gus Verdery began a productive stint as director of the Southeast Region of ACPE in 1971. As mentioned he had begun his chaplaincy service at Georgia Baptist Hospital in Atlanta at the same time that I had made my 1956 transition from Wofford College to the seminary at Emory University. Verdery became the Region's second regional director by following Obert Kempson's five-year tenure. He built solidly on Kempson's firm foundation.

The soft-spoken leader's steady persistence, gentle wisdom, and cordial availability enabled regional members to feel at home. His wife Eleanor was a consistent presence in her gracious attention given both to persons and various administrative matters.

I recall both of them showing a 1983 enthusiasm in their preparations for moving to Switzerland. Verdery departed from his regional role and thus began teaching in a Swiss seminary. There soon would be shock waves felt throughout CPE life, however, when the news of his overseas death was learned a year later.

Kempson and I drove over from Columbia to Decatur, Georgia, for the supportive funeral. Jap Keith, who began his function as regional director that year, was the main preacher for this time of mourning Verdery's death and the celebrating of his life. I will long remember Keith's weaving of down-reaching pastoral care and theological remarks around the symbol of Verdery's classy signature: E. Augustus Verdery. On that day and for many thereafter, I would be thankful for the twenty years that I had known this highly respected man and Southern Baptist figure. When I had gone to Milledgeville young in CPE life, it was Verdery who offered much quiet encouragement and interest in me.

THE HUMAN POTENTIAL MOVEMENT

In the early 1970s, I began seeking in various parts of the country learning opportunities in group workshops and conferences that were related to group systems, gestalt, and human relations training. Group emphases and the loosely organized human potential movement had started to make a societal impact from the early 1960s through the 1970s. Initial contributions from such theorists as Abraham Maslow, Carl Rogers, and Fritz Perls aided in the momentum of this human enrichment emphasis.

Especially did a two-week program with the National Training Laboratory Institute (NTL) at Bethel, Maine, give me a 1972 experiential opportunity to study change in personal and organizational life. NTL was founded following World War II and was influenced inititially by the insights of Kurt Lewin's social theory.

One of the highlights of the overall NTL format in my particular Bethel program was that every afternoon all six of our individual training groups gathered together for several hours in the arena of a campus gymnasium. The only guidance given by the staff in this program segment was that of our total assemblage being encouraged "to develop and study a sense of community." That is all that was said to the seventy of us participants. From the ingredients of this chaos, unique organizational forms and structures eventually emerged from the disjointedness and confusion on the gym floor. These two weeks of activity represented cherished preparation for my later attempts in professionally attempting to respond during times of organizational unclarity and change.

Scott Peck states in his book *The Different Drum* some small-group learnings from that same 1972 NTL program. As the tune "First Time Ever I Saw Your Face" raged on the nation's airwaves, I made some first-time discoveries about large-group process in Maine.

Examples of my other training enrollments included the Gestalt Institute of Cleveland, the American Group Psychotherapy Association, and NTL sensory awareness workshops. Some workshop leaders who meant much to me at this time were Lucia Cobb, Sherman Kingsbury, Wesley Jackson, and Alexander Lowen.

However, some of my most profound learning from such events occurred in the group offerings of Joyce and John Weir. Under the auspices of NTL, these two pioneers in the human growth movement provided an active ten-day module. The schedule integrated very energetically the issues of perception, dream work, Jungian mythology, and body movement. Much of their work was conceptualized as having self-differentiation characteristics, and forty participants were enrolled normally for their training workshops.

I was with them on two occasions for this learning format at retreat centers in the Napa Valley of California and near Chicago. Some of my CPE interest has drawn considerably from my time with the Weirs. For instance, much of my pastoral appreciation for symbolization, the inner mythic story, and the phenomenon of both expressive and contained energy has some origins from my work with them. The Weirs' early methodology is described in a chapter from Jane Howard's book of the 1970s, *Please Touch.*

The influence of my participation in some of these above learning events broadened my horizons as related to the CPE effort of focusing on overall personal and pastoral formation with students. This also was a time in my life when I was somewhat infatuated with personal growth and the era's strong theme of "finding oneself."

DAYS OF SOCIAL PROTEST

This early phase of the decade saw ferment brewing in 1971 at the national ACPE conference in San Francisco. Several years earlier the nation's soul had been ripped apart with the assassinations of

Martin Luther King, Jr. and Robert Kennedy. Some college students' growing disenchantment with the government's continuing policies on Vietnam led to a demonstration near the conference hotel. A few CPE supervisors felt that not enough outreach was being made by ACPE to the protesters. Because of their concern, some asserted that they desired to relinquish their CPE credentials. This conference happened to be the second consecutive annual conference in which ACPE and the seven-year-old American Association of Pastoral Counselors met together.

Social protest was present also that same year when Jap Keith and I were rooming together in Washington, D.C., for the annual convention of the Association of Mental Health Clergy. From the hotel window, we could hear sirens in the streets and see trails of smoke scattered in certain parts of the city. Outcries were being made against the war in Vietnam. At this time I remembered my having seen the gradual increase of South Vietnam officers twelve years earlier at Fort Benning.

Little did I know that, in listening to the shrill human cry and ear-splitting sirens erupting from those Washington streets, my pastoral care interest later would lead me to some street journeys.

AN INQUIRY INTO PASTORAL SUPERVISION: COMPETENCY, ENCOUNTER, AND BLESSING

It was during this decade that I began to sense a considerable interest in studying several key themes in my pastoral supervision process. The emergent areas consisted of issues that dealt with competency, encounter, and blessing. These salient thrusts have since remained in my thinking throughout the rest of my supervising ministry. In this section I pause to examine these several matters and their relevancy to pastoral supervision.

Competency

In respect to evaluating a student's pastoral competency, I had put previously a major emphasis on evaluating how that person's care might become overtly demonstrated through the performance of

ministry acts. Evaluation of explicit pastoral care, needless to say,
is an essential dimension in assisting with a person's pastoral
development.

However, I added corresponding attention to my inquiry about
the area of assessment when I began to entertain more thoroughly
the nature of the *internal* push behind the *outward* pastoral performance. Thus, a regard for external skills took on new light for me
as I valued the key developmental role that such a competency
drive plays in the individual's life. For instance, Mark Rouch's
Competent Ministry reminded me that an internal striving for external mastery and capability is just as powerful within us as are the
sexual and hunger drives.

As an example, a forward-moving persistence can be seen early
in a child's attempts to learn how to walk or to conquer the awkward use of utensils for eating food. This native energy for developing capabilities throughout life is a force that provides the foundation from which a young person is propelled toward an ongoing
satisfaction of finding a place in the world as a social being. Any
surrounding comments of anger, anxiety, or ridicule in response to
these strenuous efforts invariably result in an activation of a frustrating shame within the individual's inner realms and interpersonal worlds. Support, celebration, realistic guidance, and accompaniment instead represent some of the supporting gifts that nurture this innate propulsion toward social performance.

In contrast, shaming is an enemy to this competency drive. The
theologian Paul Tillich alerts us to the tenacious grip of shame by
indicating its attacks on one's very sense of being, reality, or existence as a person. As a higher level of personality growth, guilt is
a response to what one might feel in having violated someone else.
Shame, however, is a feeling that is more primitive and contains
deleterious effects on one's own internal security and worth as a
human creature. The competency drive, which is enlivened by the
external accompaniment of support, is threaded throughout the
course of our adult lives.

The CPE student is in a pastoral care learning situation wherein an effort is made to integrate one's own personhood more
deeply into the performance of pastoral care activity. It is one thing
to show an effectuality in concretely building a chair; it is quite
another for a student to use a subjective self in integrating a personal and intuitive pilgrimage into pastoral care acts.   Hence,

throughout this personally oriented educational experience, the student's competency drive becomes *ambivalently* a moving force. Relative to the continuing presence of these internal competency struggles, pastoral supervisory interactions become governed, therefore, by their being intended for and targeted to the positive dimensions of the student's gradual momentum for *leaning* into her/his growth. The pastoral supervisor attempts to become sensitive in trying to determine to what degree there might reside toxic elements in a given supervisory input.

This sensitivity has utmost importance in the warding off of a catering to the student's sense of shame—especially in moments of supervisory frustration or exasperation. Examples of a collusion between negative supervisory comments and shame are represented in such shame-inducing illustrations as these following magnified exasperations: (1) "Well, you've messed up again." (2) "Caring for others seems beyond you." (3) "I'm tired of trying to get this point across to you."

Instead, more nurturing ways to indicate a valuing of the drive for gaining pastoral care capabilities can be seen in the following corresponding statements: (1) "There are moments when you must feel that nothing goes right for you." (2) "I sense that caring for others is not easy for you at times." (3) "We've been working at this matter for a long while. Why don't we take a breather and get back to it later."

Cliff—the student previously described from the perspective of a playground evaluative method—battled mightily with his internal competency strivings. It brought him face-to-face with a neglected part of himself; that is, needing a more mutual involvement with peers. Fright pulled ambivalently at him in his resistance; competency's strong salvation pushed him forward. I breathed a sigh of relief at this birth and had thankfulness that the trickster—shame—had not stood as a barrier in his gateway to a broader life with other people.

Encounter

Consideration about the nature of encounter also began to be informative to my offering of pastoral supervision within the CPE framework. The word *encounter* literally means "in/against." In general parlance, the word has taken on mistakenly a negative, conflictual ring.

However, Thomas Malone posits that the in/against notion connotes a warm image. It conjures up tones of educational exploration. Hence, the encountering discussion, says Malone, actually becomes a personal meeting.[2]

In this sense, an encounter with a student in an individual conference or in a seminar implies that the supervisor seeks to be "in" relationship with the student. From the connective resources of this interpersonal trust, the two have a greater possibility to push "against" the edges of their interactions and discussions with each other. This engagement time has a minimal cultural and a maximal personal emphasis. For a dialogue to maximize the cultural, the result likely would be that of an overly polite environment. The learning would become intellectual without much heart and soul, thus not pastoral.

Furthermore, if the "in" quality is absent from pastoral supervision, the "against" pole can be experienced by the student as promoting a hostile and intrusive context. Such aggressiveness, not rooted in relational trust, can attack the inward competency drive and promote shame. On the other hand, should the "against" availability of pushing growing edges not be present, the learning atmosphere, as already suggested, can drift into a friendly enmeshment between the parties. For example, I pushed against Harvey in mentioning his controlling pastoral behavior on his assigned ward. At the same time, I supported his efforts to learn more about hunkering down with the staff and patients.

The ideal of the pastoral supervisory encounter, therefore, is that of creating a trustworthy learning climate in which an honestly and personally *felt* review is experienced by both the student and the supervisor. Hence, the appropriate "in" and "against" qualities can provide the affective juices to a positive supervisory encounter.

Blessing

As a third dynamic seen in my pastoral supervisory inquiry of the 1970s, the theme of blessing is often seen as a transacted educational experience between the supervisor and student. Being the imperfect interpersonal world that it is, we carry with us from our

Charles Hall presents his executive director's report in 1968 to ACPE's executive committee (left to right): Os Anderson, Edward Thornton, and John I. Smith, the first ACPE president. (ACPER)

Carlyle Marney (left) and I talk during a break at a 1973 pastoral care continuing education event held at the Hall Institute. It was the same conference in which the legendary minister changed the main topic immediately before speaking.

Wayne Oates, one of the most recognized leaders in the history of the clinical pastoral movement, led some pastoral education conferences at the Hall Institute.

► Knox Kreutzer (left) and Wayne Oates years ago share a banquet laugh. Kreutzer served on the first regional certification committee with which I met in 1962. (ACPER)

The delightful Bill Oglesby—ACPE's president-elect in 1975—ventures to Lake Tahoe, Nevada, to break bread with the regional members at the Pacific Region's annual meeting. (ACPER)

Reuel Howe, whose interest in the clinical pastoral field stretched back to the 1930s, was renowned for key linkages made between seminaries and CPE programs. Howe was a featured leader for some clergy programs at the Hall Institute in the 1970s.

Gus Verdery (left), who served more than a dozen years as the regional director for ACPE's Southeast Region, stands with Per Naydal of Norway at the 1975 International Conference on Pastoral Care in Switzerland. (ACPER)

Bill Phillips, a fellow sports trivia buff for years, is shown with his wife Nan.

Jap Keith (left) and Charles Hall confer at the first meeting of ACPE's newly created national accreditation committee in 1975. (ACPER)

In 1976 some Summers men don hats in preparation for a fishing trip to a pond near Orangeburg. My sons Mason and Boyd are on the first row, and my father stands to my left.

Mason (left) and Boyd enjoy kittens in 1978 at their maternal grandmother's farm near Trio, South Carolina.

I have wanted for years to wear again this 1976 polyester leisure suit, but it is nowhere to be found.

Boyd (left) and Mason bring back sombreros from their 1979 visit with their Uncle Carroll and his family in Laredo, Texas.

Boyd, my mother-in-law Mary Lee Boyd, Mason, and Marilyn are ready to attend a wedding in 1979.

Len Cedarleaf, a popular 1978-1979 ACPE president from the Pacific Region, emphasized collegial pastoral care among the CPE supervisors. (ACPER)

Tim Little is shown in the late 1970s. In our many travels together, we once knew a cold snowstorm in Kansas City.

My mother and father in 1980.

Urias Beverly—ACPE's president in the middle 1990s—and I have appreciated since the early 1980s a unique greeting that has its roots to intergenerational ties in certification.

A 1983 service is held in the Chapel of Hope on the campus of the South Carolina State Hospital to celebrate the inauguration of the Academy for Pastoral Education in the South Carolina Department of Mental Health. (SCDMH)

The Chapel of Hope, which has housed the Academy for Pastoral Education, was built in 1965 from the bricks once included in the high wall that surrounded the State Hospital campus. (SCDMH)

◀*Urias Beverly (left) talks with Duane Parker at a conference during the era when Parker was serving in his significant role as ACPE executive director for more than ten years.*

▶ *A seminar is being conducted by Joe Slade (at end of table to the left) and me (in middle of far right side of table) with some CPE students of the Academy for Pastoral Education in 1984. (SCDMH)*

CPE supervisors of the Academy's upper-state Piedmont Area CPE program in the middle 1980s: Will Manley (left) and Fred Reid (right). The Harris Psychiatric Hospital director shown is James Anderson. (SCDMH)

Howard Clinebell (facing the camera), who spoke on "Pastoral Care in the Nuclear Age," talks with some attendees during a break at a 1985 statewide convocation sponsored by the Academy for Pastoral Education. (SCDMH)

The summer of 1985 saw nearly thirty-five CPE persons—seminary students, yearlong residency students, supervisory students, and faculty members—participating in the Midlands Area program of the Academy. (SCDMH)

pasts the mixtures of blessing and pain. Affirmative care likely has been received in past years from some people significant to our lives. These nurturing memories dwell in us as places of hallowed grace. On the other hand, there are perplexing gaps and vacuums that yet yearn in the present for the balm of a confirming care.

Naturally, students bring these combined elements into the supervisory setting. The need for seeking further or, for some students, a more initial blessing becomes heightened due to the perceived role of power attached to the supervisor. Further, a learner's competency energies long for an available confirmation of one's growing niche in the pastoral care world. In this vital transacting role, the pastoral supervisor is understood as the main designated bearer of affirmation in the educational venture.

A student's hunger to find blessing sometimes gets disguised in various distorted ways. For example, there may be observed a frantic work ethic in a person's attempt to gain superior approval, even if exhaustion sets in. Elevated anger, as another illustration, is exerted as a maneuver in trying to manipulate forcefully a moment of attentive concern from the provisions of the supervisory agent. Another signalled plea for approval often lurks behind someone's overly pleasing mask or persona. A further exaggerated sign that might be present in the need for confirmation is that noticed in a more dependent indication for blessing: the personal style of one's persistently lingering and waiting for an authority figure to take external action on one's behalf.

As Myron Madden infers in his book *The Power to Bless*, there is no way of escaping from such above distresses and traps—entanglements that serve to impose an isolation from one's deeper self—except from some point *outside* the self. Hence, the CPE supervisor represents a very important outward healing resource in the educational process. Madden asserts: "Just as one life comes from another, so blessing comes from another."[3] Similarly, the Silver Fox transmitted such to me in a football yesteryear.

In the context of depth listening and the encountering climate set in the supervising relationship, it is hoped that the student begins to sense a trustful connection with the supervisor. This becomes a safe territory in which the student's own growing power, uniqueness, skills, and worth become mutually valued by both. The acknowledgement becomes more a silent matter of the heart and an intuitive sensing rather than something visibly attained.

Hence, this supervising midwifery offers an empowering presence to the student's growth directions both as a person and pastoral care-provider. The quality of the latter is highly dependent on the positive development of the former. In this subtle blessing process, some of the previous untended gaps find possibilities of revision and redemption.

The blessing process in supervision assumes no cheap-grace characteristic by prematurely letting the student bypass the encountered edges of the learning process nor does it keep the student shackled in a dependent relationship. The Genesis philosophy of "bless me and let me go" (Gen. 32: 20-30 NIV) is a freeing theme in the supervisory relationship. Thus, the "blessed pastoral student" ideally is one who can depart from the learning venture and become a more equipped blesser of others. From a Judeo-Christian standpoint, it is not a blessing unless it has the potential of being handed down to the generations. In never subsiding, this human need for affirmation stays with us from birth to death.

These interrelated supervision motifs of competency, encounter, and blessing provided fertile ground for my explorations during this second decade of my CPE life.

THE INTRAPERSONAL AND DOCTOR OF MINISTRY STUDIES

As the middle phase of the 1970s appeared, I entered into a four-year doctor of ministry degree program at the local Lutheran Theological Southern Seminary. I developed a research project with the title of "Clinical Pastoral Education and Its Intrapersonal Dimensions." Some of this particular interest had grown from my involvement with various features in the human potential movement. My educational design was constructed basically around perceptual theory, that is, one's unique viewing of the world as based on the individual's inward process of handling sensory data.

A focus on this inward-growth characteristic had had an explicit CPE alignment to one of the four certification criteria utilized jointly by the Institute of Pastoral Care and the Council for Clinical Training in the first part of the 1960s. In addition to the intrapersonal, the other three general evaluation areas in assessing candidates for CPE supervision back then were the interpersonal, theoretical, and integrative.

The intrapersonal theme was very congruent with my growing interest in studying inner connections between persons. James Hillman, a Jungian theologian/psychologist, describes this inward phenomenon in the following manner:

> The human connection is an extraverted encounter to be sure, and the communication between people unites through interchange, interview, interpersonal relations. But there is as well the intrapersonal relation, the vertical connection downward within each individual ... The inner connection is the contact two can have with each other from within, from below; for I am connected to this moment just now as it is I am also connected to you. The ground of being in the depths is not just my own personal ground; it is the universal support of each, to which each finds access through an inner connection.[4]

A main emphasis of my doctoral project included the impact that such internal perceptions as self-regard, body image, and an inner-directedness might have upon the CPE student's outward pastoral care functioning. These overt ministry areas included visitation with patients, preaching, offering prayer, and teaching. This interest of such interrelationship was derived partly from my aforementioned considerations about the competency drive. The assessment of the students' inner perceptive process was accomplished through the administering of evaluation instruments five times a year for two consecutive yearlong student residency groups.

One aspect of my research data interestingly revealed that there was an unsettling phase of inward development for the CPE students consistently showing up near the midway point of their training year. The features of this inner unclarity suggested the occurrence of a midstream inner transition for the students. Both the search for new symbols and the startling meridian awareness that their life-cycle of learning in the CPE program was now halfway completed contributed plausibly to this transitional anxiety. I began conceptualizing this particular time phase as being the "topsy-turvy drama" in the CPE process.

I gained permission, incidentally, from the seminary's supervising committee for me to evaluate some of the project's overall learning goals partly from the perspective of a concurrent dream journal that I was maintaining. The use of the dream material was intended to relate an aspect of my own intrapersonal life to the project.

An example of such a dream occurred less than a year prior to my graduation from the program. This nocturnal experience came soon after I had completed successfully my qualifying examination. In the dream I had been on a long, tiresome walk through a dark forest. After a time the dream portrayed my approaching a huge medieval castle that was located on the outskirts of the forest. I stood outside of its gates, and I became surrounded by an unruly and disorganized crowd. I knew that I wanted to enter the castle, because I was assured that there was a priceless gift in there for me to discover. My older son Boyd suddenly emerged from the mob, came over to me, and held my hand. The dream concluded with my feeling hopeful of making my way into the castle.

At the next meeting of the seminary's committee, I shared this dream. We discussed its meanings in reference to their potential relationship to several of the project's learning goals. For instance, the inner journey through the forest felt connected to the outer completion of the qualifying examination. The castle may have represented the presence of the seminary. Also, my son's appearance suggested the availability of not only family nurture but also a fuller integration of my own earlier boyhood fascination for adventuresome learning.

My participation in the degree program with this particular area proved to be of immense assistance in my exploring more thoroughly the inner dimension of the CPE learning process.

MIDLIFE AND EXILE

In 1975 the Association for Clinical Pastoral Education celebrated the fiftieth birthday of the CPE movement in Minneapolis. I was entering personally—in my fortieth year—a time that brought midlife wrestling. Indeed, it contained its topsy-turvy proportions.

This phase of several or more years held both exciting and precarious features. It was invigorating in the sense of my grasping newly found internal resources and passions. It was shaky in that it was difficult to synthesize these into my everyday roots. I pushed my strivings for individualism very strongly and sometimes too strenuously. Any stored-up rebelliousness seemed to cascade like an avalanche through my life's terrain.

As already indicated, I was pursuing ardently around this time my growth gains in workshops and other contexts. I was somewhat smitten with this process. In a theological sense, one might say that I became more familiar with idolatry. In these middle years, my soul's journey seemed to move into a life-cycle rhythm that tingled with a fervent hunger for new life. Were leftover breezes of spring wafting through my days?

An extreme emphasis on this inner journey and its relationship to ministry was described by me in a 1977 article. In that writing I attempted to stress the point that one's inner territory is *the base point* and foundation out of which one's personhood and pastoral practice are extended to others in relationship ministry.[5] (Even with the merits in this perspective, I now view some reductionistic limitations in such an emphatic notion—especially with relevance to a social justice form of ministry.)

Armed in a protective stance with a "right" to an enlivened finding of myself, I blindly resisted accommodations. For awhile I eagerly sought horizon's dreams and subsequently stumbled. And, in so doing, I ran headlong into the sin of my own quiet pride. My sight of what was at stake and that surrounding me grew limited. My marriage became severely strained, and I plummeted into a time of raw separation from Marilyn.

Gradually the dark months of an exilic period—where a soul walks into "the valley of the shadow of death" (Ps. 23: 4 NIV)—moved us fortunately into the beginnings of risking a renewed marriage relationship. It were as if my impassioned energies had coaxed me into a far country. Themes of shadows and innocence collided. Luckily, my weather-beaten soul led me back to a homeland. It would be there where my redeemed hopes would be devoted—rather than to any here-and-now loyalty. Marilyn's and my hearts learned slowly how to commence toward a new pathway. Amidst brokenness, we found each other again. As a steady help, we had visits with Rives Chalmers in Atlanta. During a part of my forties, I felt as if I had been on a tumultuous voyage of searching.

As a reminder about the depths that relationships can encounter, an unforgettable dream occurred for me during this rigorous time. The opening scene displayed a comfortable ride that Marilyn and I were taking in a small boat on a placid lake. All of a sudden, the craft sharply swerved. We toppled out into the water and were plunged far down into its almost limitless reaches. Separately, our feet hit bottom and sprang us upwards—squirming toward a hoped-for surface. In the dark waters, we surprisingly found each other for an embrace. While holding on, we proceeded together to make an ascent. The dream concluded before any destination was discovered; but, in awaking, I felt in my heart that we were jointly on our way—going somewhere.

Once again, healing waters had poured themselves into my life's story. Their amniotic release had long ago ushered me into the world in a little back bedroom. Buoyant currents once snugly cradled me in the arms of the flowing Edisto. Rippling swimming lanes had excitedly provided a watery joy for Wofford years. Salty tears finally found an imprisoned release in the warm harbor of an Emory group. Their restorative mysteries had now appeared again—this time in a dreamed drama filled with the promises of depths.

At that time in my life, my experiencing of displacement and the eventual semblances of some prospective new directions seemed similar to the ragged phases that Walter Brueggemann describes in his biblical model of orientation, disorientation, and new orientation.[6]

Also known in these years was a rugged sifting through of some critical human developmental polarities that ricocheted seemingly throughout the caverns of my soul. Some of this exploration contained the poles of youthfulness/oldness, ending/creating, feminine principles/masculine principles, and attaching/separating. Many of these energies—yearning for an ongoing blending—would accompany me in my voyage to future years.

REUEL HOWE AND JOHN PATTON

Simultaneous to my navigation through these rocky and promising shoals in this part of my life, I assumed the role as chairperson of the ACPE's Southeast Region. Ron Mudd of Jacksonville had been my predecessor, and Boyd McLocklin of Athens would follow me. I had served as program coordinator of the Region's annual conference for a two-year period prior to becoming the regional chairperson. The program for the 1978 meeting in Atlanta had particular significance for me in several ways.

First, our program planning group shaped the conference's major theme to be that of "A Journey toward Community." My interest in a large-scaled group process had some roots in systemic learnings that were gained from the NTL experience in Maine six years earlier. Our regional business meetings had been often fraught with some unclarity due to the preponderance of information in so many reports. Therefore, the attendees at the Atlanta meeting were divided up into designated "tribal units." We suggested that each of these smaller groups give more thorough and independent study to one or two specific agenda items. Each group then brought its recommendations back to the total body. The approach played havoc with *Robert's Rules of Order*, but it seemed to open up more in-depth discussion and ownership about business matters.

Secondly, that year's program featured a presentation pertaining to the nature of community-building by Reuel Howe. He had moved recently to Jekyll Island, Georgia, in hopes of establishing a clergy training institute there similar to his long-established one in Michigan. This noted author had been a key pastoral educator as early as the 1930s. In those earlier days, he was a leading pioneer in the bridging of CPE in hospitals and other sites with the seminary curriculum. Howe accomplished this integration as a professor both at the Philadelphia Divinity School and later at Virginia Theological Seminary. Unfortunately, his stay during the 1970s in Georgia was brief. He died not too many years later back in Michigan.

I had appreciated my previous time spent with Howe in such activitites as the pastoral care symposium that he had led at the Hall Institute in 1973. This Episcopal priest also facilitated for the Hall Institute a workshop for clergy and their spouses two years later at Seabrook Island on the coast of South Carolina.

Howe once told me that, when he was in grammar school, he was very shy and awkward in social relationships. In addition, he had seen himself as a slow learner. His creativity only began to blossom, he said, after a fifth-grade teacher patiently offered him ongoing affirmation. Apparently, his competency drive discovered a blessing. He mentioned that he often wondered what would have happened to him had it not been for that relationally oriented teacher. I suspect that many CPE students also could testify similarly about the received gifts from such inclined CPE supervisors. Two of Howe's books, *The Miracle of Dialogue* and *Man's Need and*

God's Action, remain particularly as valuable classics in the pastoral field.

Another long-lived remembrance from the 1978 meeting was that of a keenly felt moment of personal support that was offered by John Patton. Knowing that I yet was walking on a painful road in my middle years, Patton came up to me and simply said, "Tom, the main reason that I came to this meeting was to see you and to let you know that I care." His undramatic—but deeply touching—outreach came from an appreciated history that stretched back to our younger Georgia Association for Pastoral Care days. Many pastors probably can recall those hospital emergency room moments or in other times of distress when, in being present with a parishioner at a point of crisis, a brief and unadorned word of care lasts a lifetime for the one in pain. That has been the effect of Patton's nurturing comment for me.

PASTORAL CARE WITHIN
THE CPE COMMUNITY

As described above from the late seventies, such a warm gesture from Patton serves as an illustration related to the tradition of pastoral care offered within the CPE community. Perhaps the reader can dramatically recall a propitious time, when floundering in the middle of some crisis, the phone rings or a letter is received from a colleague. The salve of comfort touches the soul when an acquaintance lets it be known that care is felt.

Object-relations theory speaks to this important matter of there existing such a "holding environment" so that trust and care can become nurturing threads for the human growth process to take place beneficially. Donna Upchurch, a marriage and family therapist, points out that there was a time when personality development theory tended to be slanted heavily in terms of the male experience—equating the masculine values of separation, differentiation, and autonomy with maturity. Only in the late 1970s did the literature, Upchurch writes, begin to describe the female experience with its emphases of attachment, interdependence, relationship, and attention to context.[7]

The reality of such relational connections, in contrast to an independency, has tremendous importance for the creation of care in the collegial holding environment. It is ironic to note that, since the early CPE eras were very male-dominated years, the values instead were directed more toward masculine autonomy and independence. As a colleague offering support, Patton's comment to me represented a warm moment in which the trends of attachment and relationship were paramount.

This section now explores additional persons and features concerning pastoral care within the CPE community

Len Cedarleaf

One of the most notable ACPE conference presentations in my memory was that made nationally by Len Cedarleaf in the early 1970s. This major leader from the Pacific Region tendered a paper that dealt with the pastoral care of the CPE supervisor and others in the CPE network. The Sacramento minister constructed his remarks from the warp and woof of his own recent personal encounter with the depths of emotional and depressive suffering. Cedarleaf recounted the special nurture that he had received from some fellow CPE supervisors during his brokenness. This tall man of good cheer was known for a later ACPE presidency as well as his famous skills in playing poker. One of his main legacies was that of his continually raising within the clinical pastoral organizations a need for mutual care to be shared among the members.

Watching Paint Dry

Joe Slade of Columbia is an example of another CPE figure who has shown committed care to colleagues throughout his career. For nearly thirty years, I have known his special touch of care as expressed in hearty laughs, our trips together to Atlantic marshlands, supportive warmth, and poignant irreverent reflections about life's ironies and mysteries. In all of these years, this earthy man has shaken his head in disbelief over my love for the game of baseball. He has occasionally muttered, "Watching baseball is like sitting around and watching paint dry." In the past twenty years, Slade has hosted jovially and gracefully an annual end-of-the-summer party at his lakeside home for the Columbia area CPE supervisors and supervisory students.

Chappell-Grams

In terms of relational nurture, I have been further grateful for the many "Chappell-Grams" sent to me over the years. These hardly readable, handwritten epistles of five or six lines each have shown up unexpectedly in the mail. They have emanated from the weary pen of Chappell Wilson. He has been a cherished vocational friend since our days from the early 1960s in Milledgeville. I began to discover years ago that many other CPE supervisors across the country were receiving such similar, inexhaustible scribblings from him.

Filled with various trivial tidbits, there is lodged consistently in his information some singular kernel of critical importance that the tall, slow-moving Georgian desires to convey. For instance, in one missal of several years ago, he thus began: "I picked up a book called *Deep Enough for Ivory Bills* and it talks about woodpeckers and the swamps of the Pee Dee River. You'd like it." After several more scratched sentences, he concluded: "By the way, I'm moving to Boston for the summer to conduct a CPE program. And how about that article I sent you about Coach Frank McGuire? It reminded me of our basketball days in Milledgeville."

Two hours after reading the Chappell-Gram, the insight suddenly struck me right in the middle of a seminar that I was conducting: The guy is telling me that he is making a move to Boston! A student happened to ask me why I was smiling so as we were reviewing his verbatim report. Contacts like these by Wilson represent an interpersonal mortar that has aided in holding the organizational bricks together for many supervisors and others in the CPE movement.

Who Was That Leadoff Batter?

An example of playful care that I have known with some colleagues is that of the shared penchant held for insignificant sports information. For years this bridge of mutual interest, for instance, has existed between Bill Phillips and myself. Phillips is a retired CPE supervisor and pastoral psychotherapist now living in Jekyll Island, Georgia. Years ago I would be jolted out of a prolonged sleep in early morning hours by his long-distance telephone calls with this kind of earthshaking question: "Who won the NFL rushing title in 1959?" Or during a lull in some meeting, a note would be passed to me with such a query from Phillips: "Who was pitching the night that Joe DiMaggio's fifty-six game hitting streak was broken in 1941?" A Georgia applicant to the CPE program at the Hall Institute once opened up the committee interview with a question directed to me, "Bill Phillips asked me to ask you, 'Who beat Joe Louis—and in what year—to take the heavyweight boxing crown?' "

In more recent years, Dick Stewart of the United Methodist Section of Chaplains and I also have entertained some tough questions related to sports history. He almost stumped me once with the interrogation: "Who was the leadoff batter for the Boston Braves in 1948?" (Eddie Mirmow, my sports mentor, would have loved that question.) Such moments—built around a common interest—profoundly represent for me the vocational potentials that are in play and comradeship.

Stories Shared by ACPE Leaders

The 1979 regional meeting in Orlando provided a panel that consisted of ACPE's executive director and its president, Charles Hall and Len Cedarleaf. They had been invited to talk about their personal and professional stories as related to CPE. It was a dynamic experience for the regional audience to hear the movement's two most prominent leaders at that time indicate their own pilgrimages. I had often wondered if the much earlier CPE founders and pioneers were so trapped in their primacy needs, turfs, and competive struggles that they may have missed out on this more intimate form of sharing. In Orlando there was a mutual sense of care known—both by the presenters and the conferees.

For several or more years following the Orlando meeting, Cedarleaf and I had correspondence and conversation related to our common interest in the relationship between collegial care and personal storytelling. He had been influenced by such writers as James McLendon (*Biography as Theology*) and John Shea. In one of his letters to me, he preferred to call what he was formulating in this area of interest an "autobiographic theology." Although Cedarleaf was known widely in CPE circles for his versatile off-the-cuff narrative capacities, he told me that the caring reception received in Orlando was the initial arena that had propelled his story focus toward its theological considerations.

Needless to say, one of the good fortunes cherished by many in the CPE movement has been the presence of care as expressed in various forms in this collegial community of learning.

SOCIAL JUSTICE AND PASTORAL CARE

As the decade of the 1970s concluded, the rhythm of my pastoral care interest began to embrace more strongly its links with social structures. There grew a stirring in me for a vaster interaction between the inner life and that of social concerns. Slowly but surely, I began to consider more actively some social matters that tended to structurally lodge prejudice and hurt for individuals. After all, the Christian faith sprang from Jesus' modeling of ministry on the oppressive social margins. In commenting on this dire importance of the intermeshed relationship between the individual and society, Mary Catherine Bateson remarks: "It is not the individual organism that survives but the organism in the environment that gives it life."[8]

Impacting me particularly at this time were concerns involving the social plight of the severely mentally ill, the oppression of racial injustice, and nuclear disarmament. For instance, the simmering of my historical devotion to Louise Spann opened up for me a greater awareness about racial inequities in the culture. The next chapter describes more fully my growing perspectives and actions taken regarding these and some other social matters.

It is interesting to note that, in any CPE exploration of the bridged theme between pastoral care and social justice, a worthy consideration is that of Anton Boisen's use of sociology in his work. However, his interest in the crushing effects of alienation is more strongly remembered in the CPE tradition for the *psychological* processes found in such aloneness and isolation within the person. But Boisen's view on alienation was not restricted to just the inner person. He also placed his disciplined searchlight of inquiry on the social arena. His book *Religion in Crisis and Custom: A Sociological and Psychological Study* was published nine years after his memorable *The Exploration of the Inner World*.

In *Religion in Crisis and Custom*, he makes the case that alienation—whether it be in an individual or a social group—moves invariably toward the direction of disorganization. In his early ministry, Boisen utilized social surveying methods in evaluating parish life. Thus, his more total theological perspective is highly influenced by a blend of psychology and *sociology*. In its various eras of development, the CPE movement however has shown a much stronger devotion to the former than to the latter.

Furthermore, a discussion about social justice and pastoral care has formidable implications for pastoral care's historical function of reconciliation. William Clebsch's and Charles Jaekle's *Pastoral Care in Historical Perspective* delineates three other defined pastoral care functions: healing, sustaining, and guiding.

For example, healing—seen as a restoration in wholeness for a person beyond one's previous condition—is exemplified in my growth experience with the therapy group at Emory. Sustaining, which nurtures trust and comfort by a sense of presence, can be seen in the model of hunkering down with others. Guiding offers the function of assisting a person to move in some appropriate course of action or decision. I attempted, for instance, to provide Harvey some pastoral supervisory guidance in suggesting that he go back to his assigned ward and get to know more closely the staff personnel.

As the fourth historical function of pastoral care, reconciling focuses instead on broken relationships. Persons hunger for a unity in response to any such big-banged splintering of elements. Reconciliation has been often viewed as the restoring of relationship between person-to-person or person-to-God. However, a social justice concern broadens the scope by affirming the emphasis of bringing *groups* of persons into a social harmony with each other. The next chapter fleshes out this matter of social justice's reconciling strength in pastoral care. One such description there is the role of public marches as a reconciling agent amidst social divisiveness and brokenness.

THE DIALOGUE BETWEEN FLUIDITY AND CONTINUITY

My search through the complexities of my early forties already had begun to stimulate a stronger reach for more integration with the continuities of my own family heritage, community, and society. Furthermore, some consultation with Rives Chalmers in Atlanta assisted me in wading through some of these yearnings and struggles.

Some books on adult development such as Levinson's *The Seasons of a Man's Life* also aided me. My book's first chapter, "Embraced by a Family and a River," deals with a description of my kinship system and some of its anecdotal history. A part of this material grew pointedly from this later quest of my wanting to know more about my own historical roots. Anyway, an old saying once heard also speaks to this search: "South Carolinians are always trying to find their cousins!"

In balancing the competing—but also complementary—dimensions of social living and the personal inner life, I discovered once some pivotal reading in William Kilpatrick's book *Identity and Intimacy.* Through evaluating philosophies and methods dealing with self-actualization, the author uses a counterpoint discussion in the area of personality development—a contrast between Carl Rogers's theme of "fluidity" with that of Erik Erikson's "continuity."

Kilpatrick's thesis is that, in the long run, more sturdy commitments are built through the continuing ebb-and-flow of family and community interdependencies. On the other hand, the promotion of a fluidity in an overly emphatic autonomous self erodes self-identity, bonded connections, and intricate intimacies with significant persons. Other insightful literature along this same vein are *Seduction of the Spirit* by Harvey Cox and *Psychology as Religion* by Paul Vitz. Material from these two books exhibits some qualitative work in correlating theology with both the assets and liabilities of the personal growth movements—thrusts that were so strongly present in the culture during the 1960s and 1970s and having a strong influence on the CPE enterprise.

SPECIAL STUDY

Existing in the national background during the late seventies and early eighties was the work of a Special Study Committee that was authorized by the Association for Clinical Pastoral Education. Its formidable task was that of setting forth proposals that dealt with ACPE's future directions in mission, organizational structure, finance, and other areas. This important effort purposed to equip the organization in facing the challenges of the 1980s and beyond.

The report produced some controversial issues. One recommendation boldly intended to unify the whole pastoral care field.

Some persons questioned whether there was a theme of arrogance seen in such a move. There also was postured an added membership level through the recommendation of a new clinical member status. Some perceived that such a category held a heavier revenue-producing interest in contrast to a professional one. Development of both a more efficient governance and the promotion of a new direction in the certification system was expounded in the study's report.

I was distressed about a proposal that might have allowed ACPE in due time to certify pastoral practitioners. This potential action of expansionism would have damaged considerably the certifying functions of ACPE's sister cognate organizations. For instance, intrusion would have been felt in the Association of Mental Health Clergy's certification of its mental health chaplains. At that time, I happened to be functioning as chairperson of the mental health clergy's certification commission.

I recall that heated discussions related to the Special Study took place in the ACPE House of Delegates' sessions at three successive annual conferences. From 1979 to 1981, these meetings were conducted in Washington, New Orleans, and Estes Park. In New Orleans the Southeast Region's delegation voted to delay any vote on the report. By showing such caution, the regional delegates strongly desired much more time for continued, intensive review of these perceived uncertain matters. By a narrow vote of the regions, it was decided to proceed and make some decisions on the proposals. I remember one of the Southeast Region's representatives grumbling, "Let a camel stick a nose in the tent; and before you know it, the whole camel is living with you." In the long run, however, some of the features derived from the adopted proposals proved helpful in ACPE's move toward the future. Thank goodness, the issue pertaining to the certification of pastoral practitioners by ACPE did not see the light of day.

LONG YEARS OF SERVICE

The retirement of Obert Kempson from South Carolina's state mental health agency also took place during this time. After forty-seven years of service, he entered into another ten years of employment in staff development with a nearby Lutheran-sponsored retirement center. More than a dozen years later, he and his wife Rachel moved into a cottage at this same retirement center near Columbia.

But before he took his leave from the Department of Mental Health, the chaplains sponsored a statewide colloquium in his honor with the featured title of "New Images of Pastoral Care." Invited speakers were Charles Hall, John Patton, Clark Aist, and John Claypool. Their papers, plus an essay ("A Giant from Little Mountain") that I prepared on his personal and professional life, were published in a 1984 edition of the *Cura Animarum* journal.

The river of life—containing the events of the 1970s to the early 1980s—had given me the opportunity in those years to traverse some strong currents. Arriving now at a far riverbank, I apparently was poised to risk a more strengthened walk into some oppressed social areas. We will now take a look at where I went and how I got there.

Chapter 9

---◈◈◈---

Keller Revisited: Interest in the Streets, 1982-1999

From my late forties into my current midsixties, my vocational journey has included a fuller exploration of the societal features in pastoral care. As this final chapter looks at those discoveries, my search possesses kinship to a historical rootage.

For instance, in the early dawning of Hebrew religious care for persons, there was a mixture of diverse emphases present. Two of these included the wisdom (individual personal guidance) and the prophetic (social concerns) traditions. Over the course of Judeo-Christian time, the former trend gained an ascendancy while the latter somewhat faded. The focus of care on the individual became more highlighted and enlivened by the functions of guiding, healing, sustaining, and reconciling. (See Charles Gerkin's literature.)

The two pastoral care matters—the individual person and the social context—have been seen again as tensions in various historical epochs. As an example, the early part of the 1900s saw not only a gulf between the two in the United States but also the simultaneous presence of both the Emmanuel movement (a psychotherapy healing ministry) and the Social Gospel movement (the addressing of social ills). One became heavily identified with psychology; the other, with sociology.

Although both of these initiatives had begun to lose some strength by the time that CPE was created by Boisen and others, the CPE movement eventually became more influenced by psychology and a one-to-one psychotherapy paradigm. Intervening decades have brought a larger social consciousness from such issues as the Vietnam War and the liberation movements to the CPE table. However, the separation that took place between individualistic care and societal care at the turn of the twentieth century still erodes a more holistic and integrated pastoral care as the twenty-first century gets underway.

It is paradoxical that such a split even exists at a time when the heavy waves of many critical social matters currently pound the beaches of pastoral care. The 1982-1999 years represent my attempts in learning how to walk on this shoreline.

NEW CPE DIRECTIONS

The early 1980s brought forth new structural changes for clinical pastoral education in the South Carolina Department of Mental Health. The developments, which leaned toward a strong community emphasis, are examined in this section. This was a time when transition rippled throughout the context of clinical ministry and education.

Budget Woes

Budget crises and other larger systemic factors not only promoted a major shift for CPE in the Department of Mental Health but also they sensitized my concerns for a broader networking. It was announced that, due to some financial retrenching in state funding patterns, the support for the Hall Institute's CPE program would need to be reduced by nearly half of its size. Such action would have resulted ultimately in either drying up or crippling the effectiveness of the program. The reduction also would assuredly have a domino effect on other accredited CPE efforts in the state mental health agency. With the loss of prospective pastoral students, this would erode both the pastoral education heritage and diminish its provisions of pastoral care resources for the patients.

Thus, there was initiated a statewide and national letter-writing campaign. Concerned pastors, former students, and pastoral care leaders were requested to express their apprehension about the funding reduction. A substantial response of more than one hundred letters was rallied. The State Legislature decided eventually to reinstate funds for the CPE program by the summer of 1982. In those early stages of the eighties, this overwhelming and generous support demonstrated by the state and national pastoral care community contributed greatly to the ongoing continuance of CPE's future mental health ministry in South Carolina.

The budgetary concern was present at the same time that other issues were being tossed about in the state's mental health agency. One was represented in a trend toward program consolidation. Another was reflected in a commitment for transformation into a community-based system of mental health care. As the overall mental health delivery system began to move into a noticeable shifting, I recalled those learning moments from ten years before when we National Training Laboratory participants were requested to create a new system inside a Maine gymnasium.

Birth of the Academy

A request was made by the mental health administration for the construction of a proposed plan to unify all of the previously accredited CPE programs in the state agency. Four of them had been in the Columbia area: Hall Institute, South Carolina State Hospital, Morris Alcohol and Drug Treatment Center, and Columbia Area Mental Health Center. There were two additional centers in the upper part of the state: Greenville Mental Health Center and the mental health center in Anderson.

The adopted plan for combining these centers—resulting from a year's preliminary work—called for singularly accredited programs by the Association for Clinical Pastoral Education in these two regions. The name chosen for this organizational umbrella in the Department of Mental Health was the Academy for Pastoral Education. The Columbia centers were consolidated into the Academy's Midlands Area Program, while the two CPE supervisors in the upper part of the state were employed into a Piedmont Area Program focus at the new Harris Psychiatric Hospital in Anderson. The merged faculty of CPE supervisors for the Academy's program in the Midlands initially included Joe Slade, Riley Eubank, Hayden Howell, Dale Owen, Roland Rainwater, Jerry Alexander, and myself. Will Manley and Fred Reid combined into a a CPE staff for the Piedmont area.

I became appointed at the outset of the planning as director of the Academy. In addition I also was selected as pastoral consultant for the Department of Mental Health. Office space in the chapel on the campus of the State Hospital was designated as the administering focus for this new operation. After seventeen years of being involved satisfyingly with the Hall Institute, I packed up and trav-

eled again more than four hundred yards back to the Chapel of
Hope. I was now forty-nine years old.

Christa Syrett, who had been the chaplaincy secretary at the
Hall Institute for two prior years, was appointed the administrative assistant and registrar for the Academy. This loyal and talent-
ed staff person had a major role for years in the ongoing mainte-
nance of the Academy's administrative programming prior to her
departure from the Department of Mental Health in early 1998. I
would sorely miss our working relationship. Her concern for persons on the margins was always an inspiration for me. She had
entered the United States from Bavaria at age nine—not knowing
then the first word of English.

A worship service of celebration was conducted for the purpose of announcing the opening of the Academy in November
1983. Jap Keith, who represented ACPE's Southeast Region, participated in the program. The ceremonial service was initiated
with a processional of mental health leaders, religious representatives, and CPE folks trailing behind colorful banners. Mansell Pattison, the head of the psychiatry department at the Medical College
of Georgia, was a featured speaker following the celebration event.

Moving into the Community

Program interests for the Academy began to point outwardly to the
community. For more than thirty-five years, the major CPE
emphasis in the Department of Mental Health had been mainly on
the clinical pastoral needs within hospital walls. The exception to
this was the pastoral training in the several previously accredited
community mental health centers and also in the extended pilgrimage programs with parish pastors.

As the state mental health system began taking some initial
steps in the early 1980s toward becoming more community-orient-
ed in the treatment and care of the severely mentally ill, the Academy's Midlands unit moved boldly to distribute more than sixty percent of the CPE residency students' clinical time into community
sites. These locations included boarding homes, day psychosocial
centers, a soup kitchen, shelters, a center for homeless mentally ill,
outreach activities, and a variety of other community programs.

The deinstitutionalization process had already rapidly begun removing many patients from the South Carolina mental hospitals. Hence, the Academy's philosophy became that of attempting to follow pastorally the patients where they actually were located—whether that was in the hospitals or beyond those walls. Jerry Alexander, who was a member of the Academy's faculty and chaplain at the Columbia Area Mental Health Center, championed much of this innovative effort. Although a heavy number of CPE faculty positions have been lost due to financial attrition since the founding of the Academy, the program has maintained steadfastly this concerted emphasis on the community training experience. This has been supremely so in the yearlong residency assignments.

In the beginning stages of this approach, one advanced yearlong student group was presented with the task of moving completely into the community. Their learning process was to be found in the construction of program links between pastoral care and boarding homes, mental hospitals, congregations, and other community sites. There were few existing models throughout the country for them to follow. Due to their pioneering labors in the community, various collaborative programs began to take shape as a result of their work. For example, one student formed an orientation program of pastoral care for congregational members in preparation for their volunteer visitations into a mental hospital. Another built a project related to a church's concern for discharged patients residing in isolated boarding homes.

Much of their pastoral supervision was offered from a community-systems approach. I once described these students to the state mental health director as being "pastoral-nauts," since they were branching out into the reaches of the unknown. Two of the pastoral residents, James Rawlings and David Johnson, are now CPE supervisors respectively at Carraway Methodist Hospital in Alabama and Cabell Huntington Hospital in West Virginia.

Due to their previous community mental health center backgrounds, Will Manley and Fred Reid of the Piedmont program in the Academy incorporated also a strong community emphasis of CPE at the acute care hospital in the Upper State. Their purview included a catchment area of more than twenty counties. Hence, one hallmark of the Piedmont's programming became the cultivation of numerous parish pastors in the CPE outreach. In developing projects while participating in CPE, some of these clergy built some congregational support systems for the patients.

Convocations

As the Academy furthered its CPE development during this genesis period of the early 1980s, it also began sponsoring periodic statewide pastoral care convocations. The first such continuing education program for community pastors and mental health workers was held in conjunction with the Academy's opening celebration. The animated and rich skills of Mansell Pattison were apparent in his presentation dealing with community support programs in response to severely mentally ill persons. Many persons throughout the nation were saddened six years later to learn about Pattison's death due to a critical auto accident that left this creative psychiatrist comatose for a couple of years. His classic book *Pastor and Parish—A Systems Approach* remains as a valuable contribution to systemic thought in ministry.

Further convocations featured these following persons and their emphases: Howard Clinebell and his concern about pastoral care in the nuclear age; James Cone's look at ministry from the Black perspective and his book *For My People;* Robert Anderson's interests in congregational programming with discharged mental patients; William Oglesby's consideration of social justice and the mental illnesses; and James Forbes's special homiletical skills concerning the theme of reconciliation and mental illness. Most of these programs resulted from the Academy's coalition-building with various advocacy and community organizations for program sponsorships.

A NATION TAKES A MORE SERIOUS LOOK AT THE BRAIN

The early eighties ushered into national consciousness an alarm about the biological and social plight of severely mentally ill persons. A family movement of great power was a driving force behind much of this momentum. Even though I had been involved with mental health ministry for more than twenty years, startling new insights began to be added to my perspectives.

Finding New Teachers

This was an era when glaring societal needs of mentally ill persons were becoming more obvious throughout the nation. Because of deinstitutionalization, hospitals had been emptying patients from these timeworn warehouses into many unprepared communities for more than two decades. It often was said that many of the discharged patients were going from "back wards to back alleys." The United States at that time was spending more on dental gum research than had been spent previously on brain research. Compounding this enormous tragedy, mentally ill persons comprised more than thirty percent of total American homelessness.

I was able fortunately to be in collaborative contact with various South Carolina advocacy groups that were beginning to strengthen in the state. These organizations included the state Alliance for the Mentally Ill, the Mental Health Association, and SHARE (a statewide consumer group). Some of the family members and former patients from these groups became literally my new teachers in the area of the mental illnesses. The anguish of their personal stories aided in my perceiving, as never before, the horrible welter of social justice matters and public neglect that surrounded the area of mental illness.

Earlier teachings regarding Freudian psychoanalysis began to assume a smaller relevance as neurobiological insights steadily shed light on such severe mental illness as schizophrenia, bipolar disorder, and major depression. Research breakthroughs in biochemistry and neurology began to be increasingly reported. Families and consumer advocates held that these brain disorders should be seen with equal regard as other bodily illnesses, such as kidney or heart disease.

The decade of the nineties later would become hailed as the "decade of the brain." A massive study of the body's main, three-pound organ and its central importance to severe mental illness began to be made. Brain studies using computerized tomography revealed groundbreaking understandings. Also the gaining of greater knowledge about brain sites and the complex role of neurotransmitters (chemical substances which convey messages between nerve cells) opened up a wealth of new knowledge about the various mental illnesses. As a precipitating influence, the strong factor of stress was highlighted.

This long-neglected research would not have occurred so impactfully had it not been for the push by the families in the National Alliance for the Mentally Ill and the consumer movement. No longer could the notion of "faulty parenting" be labeled so stereotypically and generally as the major causation of a severe mental illness. In addition, critical needs became strongly apparent for comprehensive construction of psychosocial networks of care in uncultivated communities throughout the states. The term *mental illness* will increasingly fade; something akin to *biological brain disorders* has emerged.

The background of my involvement with the aforementioned advocacy groups prepared me for my speaking engagements related to the subject of pastoral and congregational care for mentally ill persons and their families. For the next fifteen or more years, I would have opportunities to address these concerns in such locations as Saint Louis, Dallas, Nashville, Atlanta, Oklahoma City, Greensboro, Sacramento, San Francisco, and other venues.

A Theology in the Trenches

As increased knowledge grew about the workings of the brain and their intricate relationship to the severe mental illnesses, this information influenced my CPE supervision as done in the public mental health system. For instance, take Gloria—whose graduate degree in counseling and religious education had been acquired in the middle part of the 1960s. Her academic and practical work were impacted by the prevailing nondirective counseling methods of that day. This approach in investigating a person's inner meanings fostered the client's moving toward insight more solely through these intrapsychic processes.

In that era prior to the later brain research findings, there also was some credence given to a view of mental illness that gave little attention to discrete diagnosis. Instead, this perspective substituted an ideal of diagnosis and treatment that saw *all* disturbed states as but stages in a single, reversible process. Furthermore, the academic curriculum in preparing mental health professionals included little emphasis on the care and treatment of severely mentally ill persons. More focus was placed on the existential angst of human relations in the problems of everyday living. In short, there was little room in the academic and psychotherapy training inn to house the particularities of the seriously mentally ill.

After having had a couple of decades of being influenced by these above counseling perspectives, Gloria entered our CPE program. In being assigned as a student chaplain to a community day center, she naturally met a large number of persons with such severe mental illnesses as schizophrenia and bipolar disorder. Her initial attempts at pastoral care with them were flavored heavily with a nondirective approach. She had hopes that they would gain some dramatic psychological insights. Buttressed by a "triumphal theology" that sought notable internal change in persons, she was plunged into frustration. She had not seen results from her counseling labors of trying to effect marked change or cure. In our pastoral supervision conferences, I suggested that she consider the more beneficial contributions from her overall pastoral care role rather than a nondirective counseling one. We talked about the external support needs of mentally ill persons and the strong impact that the sustaining pastoral symbol brings to the caring process. However, I reminded her that there was much from Carl Rogers's client-centered and nondirective philosophy that can be helpful in pastoral care with mentally ill persons, namely, the attitudes of empathy, depth listening, congruence, and unconditional positive regard.

Gloria began to have her eyes gradually opened to the special neurological obstacles which many mentally ill persons face. For instance, she discovered that persons struggling with organic and biochemical disconnections were more in need of a trusting interpersonal atmosphere in contrast to being moved back into a perplexing internality of emotions through nondirective means. In order to assist in her growing understandings, she took advantage of reading updated literature, for instance, Nancy Andreasen's *The Broken Brain*.

Her listening skills became increasingly honed with the day center's abundancy of general pastoral care opportunities. Gloria's heart danced with some folks whose eyes brightened as they shared with her some newly found accomplishment in their daily lives. She celebrated with a person's grasped competency of being able to stay seated with others during the entirety of a meal; she walked with others going through various regrets. Bridges were built by her for some persons to move into the naturalness of supportive parish life with a nearby community congregation. Gloria learned that the refreshing trips of accompaniment with the center's members to the zoo or to a community festival were just as powerful moments as those in overt spiritual discussion. She marched with many—carrying a banner—in an annual statewide awareness-raising event that called public attention to the critical social needs of mentally ill persons.

In the middle of these learning experiences, she and I once referred to this general, everyday, sustaining mode of pastoral care at this site as carrying out a "theology in the trenches."

The Boisen-Cabot Disagreement

It is interesting to speculate on how different the history of the clinical pastoral education movement might have been had Richard Cabot and Anton Boisen been privy to this late twentieth century brain research. Because of their strong and reductionistic disagreement over the organic versus the psychological and theological issues pertaining to the causes of mental illness, these variances were a part of the complex reasons that led toward the rupturing of the CPE movement in its early stages.

Since they did not have access to a broader picture of mental illness in those days of the 1920s and 1930s, they had little latitude for a more definitive discussion of their viewpoints. As in most impasses, a strict either/or position taken by both parties usually pushes participating discussants into separate corners. This is exactly where Cabot and Boisen found themselves—as did also Carroll Wise later with Cabot. Boisen may have perceived Cabot's strong organic ideas as being a threat to his religious view that mental illness can be nature's attempt to heal and transform inner chaos. On the other hand, Cabot's scientific impulses probably led him to feel that Boisen's perspective had some naivete gathered about it.

The split in the CPE movement undoubtedly would have occurred anyhow due to the antagonism between Helen Flanders Dunbar and Philip Guiles. However, the Boisen-Cabot disagreement added another dose of heavy fuel to the fire.

I find it interesting to consider that, in his correspondence with me during recovery from the strains of my shattered experience in the late 1950s, Harry Emerson Fosdick once offered the suggestion that consultation with a neurologist be sought—even though at the time I did not. His reminder about this resource in one's mental and spiritual anguish was interestingly present even amidst his several decades of experiencing previous fascination with the then strong emergence of psychological theory in the mental health field.

However, as suggested in this section, it would take until almost the late 1980s until fuller information concerning the major importance in the workings of the brain would come before the public eye. Today a more integrated view about the treatment of severe mental illness appreciates the combining of elements: the biological, the psychological, and the social. The spiritual component is being increasingly recognized by the mental health field also as an indispensable feature in this emerging holistic approach.

THE THREAD OF SOCIAL CARE

As intimated, the appearance of the early 1980s represented a time when my increased concern over the social plight of marginalized persons would more overtly evolve. This section takes a look at this public interest. Also a noting about CPE's earlier history with social care is offered.

Leaning toward the Streets

As described in chapter 1, by this time my concern had grown about the spiraling escalation of nuclear weapons in our nation. I was particularly bothered about the potential toxic effects on my boyhood river home—the Edisto. Some conjecture began to be expressed in the media that a nearby weapons plant—the Savannah River Site—could represent a seepage danger to her and some other rivers. Furthermore, it made little sense that the cost of one slaughterous nuclear missile from a Trident II submarine amounted to twenty million dollars, while only twenty dollars of research money were being allocated federally per victim of the dreadful mental illness onslaught of schizophrenia.

Public hearings related to nuclear weapons issues and the Savannah River Site began in the state. I availed myself of various opportunities around Columbia to offer public testimony in some of these meetings. More often than not, I included in my comments some references to the Edisto River and the vulnerability of other rivers to potential radioactive spoilage. Added also were references to the disparity in the huge funding that our government was providing for nuclear arsenals in contrast to the attention needed for major social ills. Often mentioned was the social neglect of the mentally ill.

My first participation in a public protest march took place during this time. A local peace resource center was sponsoring a six-mile march through the streets of Columbia in an attempt to bring attention to the stockpiling of nuclear weapons. I felt awkward in the first stages of the march, but I soon began to feel that I was in the right place. It was my love for the Edisto that had brought me out more publicly. Apparently many of my energies about the two social matters related to the plight of mentally ill persons and that of ecological justice for the environment had begun to be woven together toward a greater public focus. My life with Louise Spann also had prepared me for this.

My empowered feelings for marching seemed in resonance with a Chinese saying: "The longest journey begins with a single step." It was beginning to dawn on me at this stage of my vocational life that I had started embracing in my pastoral care purview not only CPE seminar rooms, my office, and hospital wards but also now the streets. Earlier daring in Edisto swamps or college trips perhaps had ripened into pastoral social action.

The Verbatim Report as a Bridge to Social Justice

In evaluating with students their pastoral care activity, my former use of the written verbatim report became expanded by my adding a focus on social justice features. I became interested in how students might learn to reflect on the relationship of the patient's unique individual predicament with that of the negative influences brought from the wider social world.

As an illustration, Agnes once brought into our supervision conference a written verbatim report that pertained to an elderly female patient. This African-American woman, knowing economic throes, had endured long years of neglect by her family and community; she became destined to live out her days in a state facility. In discussing the social concerns of the patient, Agnes immediately remarked on the most observable factors in the patient's ward environment. Such matters as how this woman interacted with the other patients were most definitely an aspect of her social situation.

However, I encouraged Agnes to considerably open up the whole realm of social concerns by speculating on how the larger systemic issues in society may have showered negative effects on this elderly person's existence. Professional journals and other surveyed materials were sought by Agnes for the purpose of developing pertinent issues and questions related to social justice matters. She soon delineated such questions as: How much money do state citizens pay for recreation purposes in comparison to tax dollars devoted to the constructing of an adequate mental health delivery system for indigent persons? Does an elderly minority person receive less adequate health care than that provided to others?

One of the strengths of the CPE supervision encounter has been traditionally that of its utilizing the concrete pastoral care relationship between a student and a patient—such as that between Agnes and this elderly woman—as a central hub for reflective learning. Some of the conjunctive educational resources in this supervisory exploration of pastoral care have included the wealth from psychological theory, theology, educational theory, personality development, or the student's knowledge of his/her own personal growing edges. As well, another crucial avenue for supervisory reflection is that one traveled by Agnes in her searching out the plausible societal dimensions that have a seeming intersection with this patient's life. Such an inquiry can aid in forging an educational bridge between a verbatim's examination of pastoral care and its broader reach into a more comprehensive world. This approach implies that a moment of pastoral care anywhere with another person can never be separated from larger factors in the total society.

William Keller and CPE

An impetus toward social issues is not something new for clinical pastoral education. As a matter of fact, chapter 1 reveals that, located solidly in the early origins of the CPE tradition, there rest the training emphases of Cincinnati's William Keller. A historian indicates that Keller—a socially minded physician—had interest in introducing theological students to critical social needs in the early 1920s. His programmatic format of social ministry preceded by a couple of years Boisen's first clinical training undertaking in a hospital. Keller's activities later were bolstered by the pastoral and theological supervisory additions of an eventual leading author in the field of ethics—Joseph Fletcher.[1] The preponderance of CPE's historic momentum has made alignment, however, with the *health care* tradition as over against Keller's early *social care* direction.

For a substantial period of time, the Southeast Region of ACPE included accredited structures primarily for social ministry as seen in Palmer Temple's program with the homeless at St. Luke's Episcopal Church in Atlanta and also with Peter Thomas's involvement with inner-city ministry in Birmingham. Another notable example of CPE's integration of social justice principles and methods was contained in the street and protest ministry of Dave Duncombe in San Francisco. But I suggest that we in CPE have not generally addressed very well an explicit program concern for social justice.

I attempted to raise this historical issue through the following portions of a parable that was published in the *Underground Report:* (The parentheses are added.)

> Legend has it that a young warrior, named Rellek (Keller spelled backwards), ran throughout the Land (theological education) urging that the trails (CPE programs) be kept lit for those persons who had no Voice (the socially disenfranchised). He yearned for words of strength to arise from them. He wanted them to hold berries (food) and to find a secure place of rest (shelter). Those Tending the Light (CPE programmers) drifted back to the assurance of the caves (hospitals).[2]

A Network in Social Responsibility

However, in 1984 the clinical pastoral movement was gifted with a specific accentuation on the area of pastoral care and social justice. Following the ACPE convention in Chicago, Howard Clinebell and John Thomas convened a meeting of representatives from the various pastoral care, counseling, and education groups. Its purpose was to develop a national network devoted to social and environmental justice. Ed Dystra and I represented the Association of Mental Health Clergy along with approximately ten other attendees from the various groups. Mike Ebersole and Thomas were the ACPE delegates. Clinebell's organizing investment had arisen from his leadership in this area with the American Association of Pastoral Counselors. The newly formed network was known as the Pastoral Care Network for Social Responsibility (PCNSR) and became open to all members of the various organizations in the clinical pastoral movement.

In serving on its board for more than seven years, this activity profoundly attracted me. It became a place where common interests were discovered around the matters of pastoral care, social justice, and pastoral psychology. The board experience and later continued membership in the network have struck me as being similar to the action/reflection model that is so apparent in CPE. A person therein has access to a group of peers for the sharing of information, papers, the receiving of feedback, and celebrating over one's learning and ministry activities. I found comparably in the network a mutual interest for the expanding of individual case studies into larger social systems where institutional or structured social oppression might reside.

It was largely within the PCNSR that I began to share with my peers the beginning stages of my interest in the connections of pastoral care with some of the goals of public marches. Such marching activity is described later in this chapter. But first, a distraught interlude is now recounted.

MORE STORM CLOUDS

A dark night of the soul appeared for me personally as the early 1980s were concluding. A ragged excursion began for awhile through the anxious depths of what best could be described as panic reactions.

There was a combination of crises stirring both within me and around me at this time. On the one hand, our family had gone through the crushing loss of my much loved mother-in-law due to her sudden death. Mary Lee Boyd, who reared eight children and two stepchildren in a farming setting, was one of life's precious jewels. Imbued with the gift of innate nurturance and understanding for others, she possessed a sparkling, natural personality. She also quietly touched the lives of all in her midst, regardless of who they

were. Following Marilyn's and my sharing the news with her about
our decision to marry in 1962, she wrote me a tender letter indicating that she loved me even before she knew that Marilyn and I
"were really noticing each other (that much!)." She will remain for-
ever as one of the most significant persons in my life.

In addition, the previously described attempt in garnering leg-
islative support for the clinical pastoral education program—in the
face of its prospective reduction at the Hall Institute—perhaps
played its part in sustaining some neglected stress in my life.

Similar to a lightning bolt blasting down from clear skies, a
frightening grip of utter helplessness suddenly struck me as I was
driving a car one day with Marilyn and our two young sons. We
happened to be traveling across a high bridge. My heart abruptly
on this occasion raced rapidly out of control on the span. I feared
that I might pass out before getting to the other side. I had driven
ironically across bridges countless times.

But on this day, fearful attacks of dread—without warning—
moved in on me. I became alarmed for the safety of all in the car. I
felt as if I were losing control of my mind. Breathing a sigh of relief
in reaching the end of the bridge, I continued with our family's
journey back to Columbia. However, deep down within me, I
knew that some unknown terror had stormed quickly into my life.

Further events of trepidation were not uncommon for future
months. Approaching other bridges—or even elevated locations—
represented awesome tasks. The anxiety, too, rippled out into
some social areas. For instance, speaking engagements now
unpredictably contained fearful times in my preparation and in the
anticipatory fear of facing an audience. There also were irregular
moments of my not knowing whether I could remain seated
through the entirety of a meeting.

Even though such perilous days were akin to an undertow
pulling mightily against a sense of hope, I longed for resources on
which I might cling and grow toward balance. I consulted some
with Rives Chalmers in Atlanta. On one occasion, he gave me a
professional article concerning the various biochemical and neurological implications of stress and anxiety. Although the bulk of my
own psychotherapy in the past was focused on the more phenom-
enonological and experience-based features in my life's pilgrimage, this added biological perspective further broadened my view
on the unique bodily patterns in my current travails.

I certainly had placed earlier much intellectual and theoretical value on the biological in my training and studies. But now, I was being affectively—gut wrenchingly so—involved with it. I began searching the literature for materials related to stress and its physical activation of adrenaline in the body. I also reviewed a couple of past events—long forgotten—from my high school days that seemingly contained some constricting elements slightly in resemblance to that known on the bridge. One involved a church setting; the other, a baseball practice.

This venture of considering pointedly the physiology of the brain and its relationship to the mind and spirit was remarkably new for me. It probably had more to do than anything else in getting me prepared not only to deal with my personal predicament but also with the field of burgeoning biological research pertaining to brain functioning. Especially helpful during this vulnerable time were some workshops on the nature of stress and also the positive effects of meditation practices. Robert Handly's book *Anxiety and Panic Attacks* and Shirley Swede's and Seymour Jaffee's *The Panic Attack Recovery Book* were like manna from heaven. I also consulted some with a Columbia psychologist, Dr. Karen Drummond.

A day would come when I went back to the once imposing bridge; I drove back and forth over it several times. When I first met with success on the other side, a loud "Yes!" arose from my soul, and I thanked God that these particular storm clouds had passed. My beleagured and persistent competency drive had redeemingly pulled me through the darkness. This time, a "Bridge over Troubled Waters" held me securely.

The expedition in this bewildering territory produced elements of personal and vocational promise. For one thing, a greater appreciation for the theme of wounded healing's relationship to suffering became more enlivened for me. These difficult times served to increase my social advocacy efforts even more for other brothers and sisters besieged with various ills.

Also the necessity of my reaching desperately inward to grasp more fully the sustenance of cognitive and meditative resources has aided in offering a more centered balance to my outward social justice pursuits. For instance, contemplation and active justice-ministry are no longer separate measures for me, but rather they are pieces of the same cloth. The sabbath rhythm of providing quiet renewal—then followed by active social service—informs this unity.

Furthermore, my travel through this time of unpredictable anxiety reaffirmed for me—once again—Anton Boisen's belief about a key aspect in the nature of acute upheavals in our lives. Such disruptions, he inferred, can represent a personality's attempts at further reorganization and growth. Added to Boisen's values would now be my greater appreciation for the physiological influence of stress and its results of overly activated adrenaline on the oneness of body, mind, and spirit. Similar to the volcanic days of my early twenties in seminary, I—now in my late forties—had been impelled to search again strenuously through some dangers and challenges for the continuance of my ongoing growth journey.

My alarming sojourn through this time of intermittent apprehension was somewhat contained and made only a small intrusion in my ongoing work and with other persons.

ACPE TRANSITIONS

Sharp transitional times also were occurring in this period within the life of the Association for Clinical Pastoral Education. This was principally so at the occasion of the 1983 national conference in Portland, Maine. For instance, some results from the aforementioned Special Study were being integrated into organizational structures. Also, Charles Hall* was moving toward retirement from his long and outstanding executive director's work of seventeen years. Many considered the consistency of his handling details and his accessibility to members to have been among his many fine qualities. The decision of moving ACPE's office from New York to Atlanta represented an additional major theme at the Maine conference.

Whether or not these above factors had any effect on the degree of alertness for the General Assembly at this conference, I do remember that there seemed to be a strong lethargy in us as our assembly discussed and voted on the far-reaching certification proposals brought in by the certification leaders. In my opinion we

---

*As this book went to press in January 2000, the sad news was received about his death.

did not go strongly enough to the mat to wrestle through some historically key issues. From that day onward and for quite awhile, an underlying question about certification was bandied about in ACPE circles: Has the process of reviewing certification candidates become too distantly objective? (I can only guess what Armen Jorjorian's response to that question would have been.) Likewise, some critics have held a strong reservation about ACPE's accreditation standards possessing an obedience to considerable federal government alignment.

PUBLIC MARCHES AND SOCIAL MINISTRY

Previously in this chapter, I mentioned my initial action of joining a public march by referring to a Columbia-based action concerning nuclear disarmament. Since that time I have either organized or been related to a number of other public marching events. In a biblical sense, I perceive that a march can carry with it vivid symbolic overtones of the exodus theme. The Old Testament drama is re-enacted by a corporate effort to rise up, as it were, from the shackles of severe oppression and to signal a promising call for liberation from our social wildernesses.

These public events have been attempts to garner attention toward some glaring social or environmental ill in hopes that greater social healing and reconciliation might result. Herein, healing and reconciliation are expanded from the person-to-person plane to the social criticality of the group-to-group relationship. My involvement in some of these activities is described below.

A Peace Train Is Coming

My investment in the protesting of the nuclear armament build-up continued as the 1980s progressed. For instance, I availed myself of the opportunity in 1987 to join a national protest action concerning this heavy escalation. I made such a trip on a "Peace Train" that was mobilized by a planning group in the Northeast. It meandered its way down the eastern coast and picked up some passengers as it passed through Columbia. I boarded it there, and our railway community arrived at its destination near Cape Canaveral in Florida.

After that event on the Cape, I endeavored to reflect on the experience through the following material in the newsletter of the Pastoral Care Network for Social Responsibility:

> I felt a mixture of fright and inspiration on a balmy January 17 in Florida as our immense crowd of more than 5,000 persons marched away from a rally site. The multitudes moved toward the gates of the Cape Canaveral Air Station to engage in nonviolent protest of the first test flight of the Trident II nuclear missile program.
>
> *Frightened* that the development of such an ultimate first-strike weapon represents a new effort to militarize the oceans! Frightened that only one submarine, containing its awesome Trident II nuclear payload, could have the potential to obliterate 408 Russian cities or military targets! Frightened about a spiraling nuclear insanity that results in the allowance of over $20 million to be spent for the fashioning of one slaughterous missile—those same dollars would be enough to eradicate this year's budget deficits anticipated for my native state's (South Carolina) life-nurturing program of health care for the poor!
>
> *Inspired* by the mobilized outpouring of individuals from all reaches of the nation to form a mile-long throng of pilgrim thousands corporately embodying an emphatic NO to nuclear lethality! Inspired by the vibrant striding of young children and the elderly who were among the Canaveral procession! Inspired by the existence of shared hopes and energetic efforts of a Pastoral Care Network for Social Responsibility!
>
> I much later stepped from a northbound Peace Train onto Carolina soil. The twinkling stars in that darkened night—yet preserved from toxic clouds of any nuclear winter—served for me as sprightly reminders of a passionate Grace pulsating on our creaturely behalf throughout the mysterious heavens.
>
> Little was I to know in the quietness of that evening that the next weekend would bring forth another stirring event of *fright* and *inspiration*. A massive human caravan would then gather again to make its way toward a town square in Forsyth County, Georgia, in order to pronounce a resounding invocation against the devastating human missiles of racial injustice.[3]

Take Me to the River

Two years later I formed a thirty-five mile "Walk for Peace" to be accomplished in two days during Holy Week. Three CPE supervisors participated with me in this activity: Chappell Wilson, Gene Rollins, and Don Prince (New Zealand). The walk was an attempt to raise funds for the travel expenses of a pastoral representative from a Developing Nation. Funding was accumulated so that this person might be able to attend the historic international pastoral care conference on justice-based peacemaking. The meeting was conducted that year behind the Iron Curtain in the former Czechoslovakia, and the Pastoral Care Network for Social Responsibility was one of its sponsors.

Our very small-scaled march began not too far from Columbia and concluded at the borders of the Savannah River Site. As mentioned, this setting was one of the major nuclear weapons plants in the United States. The walking activity through horrid spring storm conditions began with the symbolic depositing of some leaves in the early headwaters of the Edisto River stream. Its origins gradually become fifty miles downstream the larger Edisto. The march eventually concluded with the sprinkling of cornmeal upon the bordered grounds of the weapons plant. One of the marchers had a Native American heritage, and this ceremony was another symbolic custom directed toward a blessing of the earth and water.

I was fortunate to be in attendance at the European conference later that spring to make a presentation on the program. It was heartwarming to be in the company of the international delegate for whom the travel funds were raised.

Stamping Out Stigma

A public march that has aided in developing greater public sensitivity for the needs of severely mentally ill persons in South Carolina is that of the Mental Illness Awareness Walk. The mobilized statewide rally is an annual event that has been conducted since 1988. I originated the model through the early building of a steering committee and a coalition consisting of advocacy groups and professional associations. I remained as chairperson for this march for six years.

Participants in the awareness activity are drawn from a wide variety of sources including high schools, colleges, religious congregations, family groups, a military base, industry and business, consumer groups, and others. The crowd estimates for this time of consciousness-raising has reached on occasion several thousand participants.

In addition to its purpose of heightening awareness about the critical social support needs of mentally ill persons, the public event also attempts to reduce stigma that yet might be attached to

a mental illness. The format of the event usually begins with a celebration rally and speeches on the grounds of the South Carolina
State Hospital and is followed by a two-mile march through the
downtown streets of Columbia. The route nears the proximity of
the State Capitol; and on some occasions, the opening phases of the
event have begun there. Usually the march proceeds back to the
hospital grounds where prevailing are several hours of entertain-
ment, talks, festivity, and exhibits.

It was during one of these early march events that my ideas
about advocacy for the socially marginalized became more greatly
enlarged. My former perception of advocacy (Latin, *vox*, "voice")
was that of primarily speaking out *for* someone or a group whose
voice had been oppressively silenced.

Added meanings to this interpretation occurred for me due to
the courage I once witnessed at a rally in one of these marches. I
had known of a woman who spent some lengthy time in one of the
desolate back areas of a public mental hospital. She became discharged and fortunately found some places of strong community
support. A passion began to develop within her to try making
some changes in the public mental health delivery system. It was
an awe-inspiring moment to stand alongside her on the steps of the
State Capitol as she found shaky and forceful words in speaking to
several thousand citizens. She told her powerful story and found
a vital voice in doing so.

I now find a central task in pastoral advocacy, regardless of the
oppressive issue, to be that of aiding another person to *find* her/his
voice and for that mighty story to be told. For example, that is why
it is so important for religious congregations to invite panels of
socially oppressed persons to share their compelling stories of having encountered the first-hand effects of prejudice. Social stigma
lessens when a story is told from a suffering heart. In other words,
the issue needs a face—and a voice.

Gay Rights

Another focused march that possesses importance in terms of its
pastoral implications for social and individual care is that which
features involvement with the needs of gay and lesbian persons in
South Carolina. The kindling of an interest in this religious advo-

cacy rested in my having been invited almost a decade ago to conduct a funeral for a gay man whose death was due to AIDS. Both his family and his church had sadly rejected him because of his sexual orientation. Participation with this agonizing situation was a stirring and eye-opening experience for me. That year I decided to participate in the annual Gay and Lesbian Pride March in Columbia for the purpose of not only indicating my support but also out of a desire to learn more about the degrading effects of such vitriolic social prejudice shown to homosexual persons.

The next year I organized a contingent of more than thirty clergy, laypersons, and colleagues for the purpose of participating in the Pride March. I also began to develop some written materials concerning a critical need for the religious support of gay and lesbian persons. Further, some newspaper interviews were published. I shall always hold special appreciation for the balanced awareness shown by a bishop in my having pushed such a hot social button. In negative response to my advocacy in this area, there was generated some outcry related to the continuance of my identification as an ordained United Methodist clergyman. This bishop invariably answered to such pressure by including a statement concerning my pastoral obligation to minister to *all* persons.

Since the early 1990s, our group has marched behind a sign that is inscribed with "South Carolina Clergy and Friends Supporting Rights of Gays and Lesbians." The effort is made to show a religious solidarity with gay and lesbian persons as they yet face some severe social vilification in this Bible Belt section of our nation.

This particular outreach has brought forth some other opportunities of demonstrating support. For instance, in April 1998 the "Clergy and Friends" contingent sponsored a one-meal fast in which all South Carolinians were invited to participate. Citizens were asked to engage in prayerful reflection and to ponder over the hopes and struggles of homosexual persons in our state. Other activities have included speaking engagements, vigils, panel participation in community forums and other venues, and public testimony with State Legislature committees.

I was dismayed over my United Methodist denomination's 1998 judicial ruling that restricts its clergy from participating in same-sex commitment ceremonies. This decision impedes a dialogical honesty that can be found in the church's quadrilateral heritage—rich with its historical elements of reason, experience, tradition, and a biblical perspective. A legal halt to such ceremonial ministry drives a committed relationship between homosexual persons further into the lonely shadows—rather than ushering a beholden love into the full celebrative light of a public religious blessing.

The tragic and ancient theological split between body ("bad") and spirit ("good") is still alive. I believe that this wall still resides in those religious systems that show doctrinal oppression toward homosexual persons. Due to a lack of realizing more fully the nature of sexual orientation, such religious systemic stances still image homosexual persons from a reductionistic genital perspective rather than from a more holistic *relational* one. A nonrelational view could represent a form of theological pornography.

In an early 1999 appearance before a committee in the South Carolina State Senate—considering a proposed bill on hate-crime legislation—I attempted to convey this same above concern about reductionism in my following testimony:

> Negative condemnation displayed to homosexual persons fails to contain an appreciation of the heart-hunger for companionship and relationship that all human beings have. Sexual activity is only one aspect of that overall striving for human relationship. A very special hurt that the homosexual person is forced to endure is that he or she often is not viewed from this *relational* perspective. Instead the homosexual person is judged in a reduced fashion for her or his sexual activity. Left out of this attitudinal equation is the underlying heart-hunger for an enduring partnership with a companion. Sadly, many persons in society still possess a stereotypical view of homosexual relationships only in terms of genital sexual functioning rather than the broader soulful human need for companionable relationship.[4]

It is ironic to note that, in the Christian tradition's historical claim on its "care of souls," the gay person's more total love for a soul-mate has been profoundly discounted. Until such pervasive rejection finds redemption, the religious hostility shown over the ages to the homosexual community will remain as an inhumane blemish on Christianity's institutional striving to impart care and grace to all persons.

Walking for Louise Span

Further, I have had the opportunity to participate in public marches concerning racial insensitivity. For instance, mention has been made about the march in Forsyth County in Georgia a dozen years ago. I was present with Fred Reese—a ministerial colleague from South Carolina—in order to join in on the protest of negative activity that was inspired by the Ku Klux Klan.

In recent years there have been some marches in South Carolina with a focus being directed to such social issues as the continuance of flying the Confederate flag atop the State Capitol, the burning of Black churches, and the attempt to diminish affirmative action. When I have participated in such marches and issues that are related to racial injustice, I have carried Louise Spann in my heart. With the innate brightness that she had in her mind and soul, it is no telling how far she could have gone along life's highway had it not been for the structural social evils that held back her race. Some of those chains, though disguised, still rattle in our society. The sight of some historical symbols, such as flags, break open the wounds of slavery for many African-American persons. Souls writhe tortuously in agony and anger over the memory of a beloved ancestry brutally ripped away from a hearthed homeland and dispatched in horrible passage to foreign shores.

These various public marching experiences, such as the above five illustrations, have been enlightening for me. From their resources, I have formed some ideas about marching's contributions to pastoral psychology. I was invited in 1994 to present a paper dealing with this subject at a theory-building conference. The meeting in Italy was sponsored by the International Pastoral Care Network for Social Responsibility. My presentation intended to show that a public march could be viewed symbolically as a collective "societal white blood cell or antibody" that—in being alarmed—takes action against a "pathogenic" social injustice. The injustice is potentially injurious to the "health" of the communal body. A march does not wildly chase after some tilted windmill. Rather, it zeroes in, like a laser light, on a social infection. As well, my paper attempted to point out that pastoral participation in an intentional march stretches the contextual paradigm of pastoral care all the way from the counseling or supervision office to the streets.[5]

In some of these strenuous street scenes, there may be encountered some opposing reactions from the sidewalks or in other
places. This has been true occasionally in regards to the religious
support group's involvement with South Carolina's Gay and and
Lesbian Pride March. In the face of contrary response, I feel that
the pastoral care principles of rapport and regard for each person's
basic worth—including the perceived oppressor—are helpful
guides in addressing the heat of conflict. If such regard is not striv-
en for, then both sides—including mine—become oppressors of
each other.

An interest in that intersection where the traffic of pastoral care
and social justice merges can find some educational explication in
clinical pastoral curriculum endeavors. The materials of such
authors as Gordon Allport, Harvey Cox, Walter Brueggemann,
Howard Clinebell, Walter Wink, and Stewart Govig offer much
background assistance to such integration.

ASSOCIATION OF
MENTAL HEALTH CLERGY

As my own history with clinical pastoral education began to move
into the middle part of the 1980s, I concurrently assumed a 1985-
1986 presidency with the Association of Mental Health Clergy
(AMHC)—an organization that I had been closely involved with
for years. As president I announced my interest theme to be that of
"congregational care for the seriously mentally ill."

A Besieged Poster

Initially named the Association of Mental Hospital Chaplains,
AMHC began to be formed in the 1940s in order to provide professional support for the nation's mental hospital chaplains. This was
during an era when the large state mental hospitals were scattered
heavily throughout the nation, and their chaplains sensed a need
for supportive collegiality.

Its organizational birth was due to the leadership efforts of
Obert Kempson and Ernest Bruder. The new association initiated
a tradition of holding its annual convention at the same location as

did the American Psychiatric Association (APA). This action fostered a long-standing relationship between the two groups. In the midseventies, AMHC hired George Doebler of Tennessee as its first part-time executive director. His excellent leadership for the next twenty years would steer the professional interfaith group through many changing times.

A memorable and naive attempt at marketing took place in my very early entry into AMHC. It was in 1966 that the president Doug Turley asked me to produce a chaplaincy display for the annual convention and to have it placed in the psychiatric association's exhibit hall in Atlantic City, New Jersey. It was the same arena where the annual Miss America Contest is held. Not ever having attended one of these national psychiatric conferences, I had no idea that the array of displays by pharmaceutical companies and other groups would be as dazzling and expensive as they were.

Not having this knowledge about the quality expected for a display, I went about my task by merely preparing a small poster. I secured one of my CPE students to take a few photographs of a posed chaplain in such depicted ministry acts as visiting a patient, conducting a worship service, and attendance at a treatment team meeting.

As I arrived at the spacious convention hall, I was startled by the glitter of all the professionally made booths, exhibits, and displays. I hastily stuck my little poster on a wall in its assigned out-of-the-way location with the assistance of an adhesion that resembled a wad of bubble gum. During the days of the AMHC conference, I would go back sometimes to this extravagant setting to sheepishly stick the poster back on the wall had it fallen to the floor—an action that it often took. Nevertheless, this "sophisticated" networking strategy paid off. An occasional psychiatrist would wander by while I attended to the bruised poster and talk with me very briefly about religion and psychiatry.

A Snowstorm in Kansas City

One of my dearest AMHC memories rests in an act of nature that caught Tim Little of Sacramento and myself in its web. When he had previously lived in Atlanta, we often traveled together in doing the work of the organization. As he slipped into complete sightlessness, this prodigious man's formidable mind became even more prominent in the mastery of bylaws and other materials. Incidentally, one of Little's earliest mentors was the same Joe Woodson as described in chapter 5's sketch of my stay on Cape Cod.

During winter conditions I always preferred to have much heat in the hotel rooms where Little and I stayed. He liked the room to be eternally cold; and, with my being the southerner that I am, anything below sixty degrees represents a warning that an arctic freeze is on the way. Once in Kansas City, we were staying in a seminary dormitory one wintry night. I got up in the still of nighttime and quietly pulled the window down. Sometime during those nocturnal hours when I was fast asleep, he silently threw this window near my bed wide open. Later in the night, a snowstorm struck the region and snow eventually piled into our room while we slumbered. I have not thawed out to this day! Upon greeting one another now, quick comments like "Have you thrown any snowballs lately?" will emerge.

Words Can Kill

Through my AMHC activity, I was grateful for the opportunity to continue the religion-psychiatry dialogue with the American Psychiatric Association. Some meaningful discussions were now held—twenty years after the casual conversations near my Atlantic City poster. This came about due to my membership for six years on the APA's Committee on the Chronically Mentally Ill. Interaction with such noted psychiatrists as Walter Menninger, John Talbott, and David Cutler enabled me to strengthen my understandings about the dire societal and prejudicial burdens that our nation was placing yet upon the severely mentally ill.

It was during my preparations on the subject of social stigma for a committee-sponsored symposium in San Francisco that I came across the potent research work of Gordon Allport in his book *The Nature of Prejudice.* His model impressed me in terms of its contributions in considering how the nation's mentally ill and some other groups have been historical recipients of stigma. Sticks and stones can break our bones, and words also hurt us. Actually, Allport surmises, they have the potential to kill us. Words have lethal consequences and can have a direct relationship to the social build-up of stigma. As an illustration, Allport describes a five-staged schema that shows a social progression that begins with verbal disparagement. This initial phase encompasses an early, incubating level and moves subsequently to a fifth and lethal condition.

Allport's first social level of *antilocution* ("speaking against") shows how jokes, slurs, or other negative verbals spoken about a group of persons can set in motion a progressively dehumanizing process. For instance, such slurs as "faggot," "queer," or "pervert" become early weapons in the social draining of human qualities from homosexual persons. In this ridicule, they are seen less as persons and more as despicable objects of derision. In regards to mentally ill persons, words like "psycho," "crazy," or "nut" lead toward the same social results. These disparagements loosen the social soil and make it more permissible for prejudice then to more easily sprout and move toward a more heightened successive stage.

Hence, the first phase of verbal derision (antiocution) allows a second stage to then more extremely appear—that of social avoidance. The further advanced phases sequentially follow: *discrimination* (both social and legal), *physical attack*, and ultimately *extermination*. It is no small wonder, for instance, that the human soul of any homosexual person shakes in indescribable fear, anger, and terror on hearing a spoken slur. Such a word-weapon contains potentially the seeds of physical attack or even murder.

In 1999 the United States saw a tragic massacre take place in the horrible deaths of high school students and a teacher in Littleton, Colorado. Intermingled in that catastrophe were such separating and divisive verbals as "jocks" and "Goths."

In social living, words indeed can result in death. From the perspective of a justice-based ministry and its relationship to the importance of words, I have utilized the insights from Allport's model quite often in talks and seminars.

CONTEMPLATION AND SOCIAL ACTION

The middle to late 1980s fostered in me a greater interest in considering the relationship of personal contemplation with social care pursuits. I began to view contemplation as the inner process of my searching for a centeredness of soul. Breathing exercises, prayer, guided meditation, visualization, and quiet renewing times—inter-

ests sought during the earlier winds of panic—became valuable
assistances. Contemplation further includes an openness to considering the mystery of awe and wonder in one's life. My boyhood
pensiveness, no doubt, helped to prepare this contemplative pathway.

As previously mentioned, the dimensions of the inner life and
the outward expression of social action are sought ideally as an
integrated whole. Sometimes such unity is not easily balanced. We
run into much clutter—both from within and without—in our
daily living. However, a frenzied attempt to rectify social ills can
lead toward some blind and frantic activism. It fosters a form of
works righteousness. On the other hand, I have found that an
exaggerated life of inner journeying—void of much connection to
accountability or social care—can promote an encapsulated sense
of self-protection.

For its vocational contributions to my endeavor of seeking a
stronger bridge between the inner life and social justice, I have
been blessed by the programs of such places as the Kirkridge Center. It is an ecumenical retreat and learning context in the Pocono
Mountains of Pennsylvania. Periodic pilgrimages to this place of
serenity and power have allowed me to engage the gifts of many
skilled persons, namely, Morton Kelsey, Walter Wink, Parker
Palmer, and Robert Raines. These and others have facilitated many
clergy, laypersons, and therapists in exploring the vital blending of
spirituality and societal areas.

My attempt to integrate more closely the poles of the personal
and the social at this part of the 1980s led me to explore assumptions
and methods from the lives of Mahatma Ghandi and Martin Luther
King, Jr. I began to look more specifically for their theological
reflections on public marches and a concurrent relatedness to inner
spirituality. Informing to my pursuit have been Judith Brown's
Ghandi: Prisoner of Hope and King's own *Stride Towards Freedom*.

Incidentally, during this same time in the middle part of the
1980s, I keenly appreciated the leadership of and working relationship with Dr. Joseph Bevilacqua—the director of the South Carolina Department of Mental Health. A commitment to social care
pervaded much of his vision and work in ten years of leadership.
His community-based energies in making the state agency more
heavily influenced by consumers and their families represented a
major part of an exciting era.

TIMES OF GRIEF AND THE
ADDITION OF A WAND

It was during this same approximate 1985-1990 season that some poignant moments emerged concerning the regional and national life of CPE. Folded into the mixture of this period were the elements of grief, celebration, the discovery of a ritual, and utter shock.

Stirring Moments in the Region

There was an empathic time, for instance, at the 1985 national ACPE conference in San Diego. Upon completing his second and final presidential address to the conventioneers, Jap Keith was called back immediately to Georgia to be at the bedside of his much loved and dying father. From our Milledgeville days together and beyond, I recalled hearing Keith talk about fond memories of assisting his father with a grocery store business in a small Georgia town.

In strong contrast to this loss, the Southeast Region had delightful feelings stirred when it was visited by one of the nation's most outstanding homileticians. Professor Fred Craddock, the winsome storytelling teacher, spun his special brand of magic at an annual meeting in Athens, Georgia. Those in attendance almost could taste his rural parishioner's homemade biscuits that were described in one of his marvelous presentations.

Grieving moments surfaced again in the Region by 1990. The tragic suicidal death of Charlie Newman, the chief chaplain of the South Carolina State Hospital and a member of the Academy for Pastoral Education's faculty, painfully affected the lives of many persons. Feeling disheartened in the aftermath of the horror, I met at Hickory Knob State Park with the Region's executive committee to share this loss.

Following the evening session and feeling totally exhausted, I occupied a room with Jap Keith. In continuing to talk about my bewilderment with him further into the night, he recalls my falling off to sleep. He later told me that I stopped almost in the middle of a sentence and did not awaken until the next morning. That time of care and rest with regional colleagues became the initial stage of my beginning to deal more closely with my shock and grief.

The Wand and Cane

The next year brought a major shift within the organizational life of ACPE at its national conference in Breckenridge, Colorado. Adopted was a new form of governance with the strong focus of power resting within a board. This move represented a more narrowed authority and a more defined accountability in contrast to a populist general assembly model. The latter had been ACPE's previous governmental hallmark.

Some CPE supervisors, for instance, Len Cedarleaf, had strong feelings and serious concern about the loss of the Assembly. There was a valuing of its having acted in an open public context in the past with a published agenda. I regretted the loss of the Assembly, but the increasing growth of ACPE probably has necessitated some manner of streamlining the decision-making process.

However, there was always something rather appealing about the vigorous, colorful, and sometimes ostentatious way that some members of the former General Assembly would go about their deliberations. This provided an interactive mythos and energy about the atmosphere of organizational life that might be difficult to ever duplicate.

A much highlighted moment took place at the Breckenridge meeting when the president-elect of ACPE—Kathy Turner—received an important symbol from Jo Clare Wilson. Turner was offered a magic wand rather than Anton Boisen's old wooden walking cane—the same one he often used to drive home some teaching point or observation. The latter emblem of leadership had been given ritualistically to former elected presidents—all of whom previously had been males. The presence of ACPE's first female president-elect represented a powerful and long overdue event. Wilson herself would assume the presidency in the late 1990s.

Disbelief in Georgia

A jolting event for those in clinical pastoral education to absorb was an unbelievable budgetary decision made by the State of Georgia in 1991. In a sudden maneuver, abolished were almost all of the state chaplaincy positions throughout its large state government. Putting an immediate stop to nearly thirty years of profound clinical ministry and CPE in that prominent state was unimaginable.

Pictured are three of the Academy's supervisory CPE students in the middle 1980s (from left to right): Gene Rollins, David Johnson, and Jim Rawlings. They later would become certified CPE supervisors. (SCDMH)

George Doebler (left), part-time executive director for the Association of Mental Health Clergy for more than twenty years, and I at the 1989 annual convention of AMHC in Chicago.

Chappell Wilson (right) and I take a break at a country store during the thirty-five- mile Walk for Peace conducted in a two-day rainstorm in 1989. The fund-raising march originated near Columbia and concluded at the borders of the Savannah River Site—a nuclear weapons plant.

Bill Oglesby (left) pauses with Christa Syrett (Academy registrar) and me following his Academy-sponsored convocation presentation on "Pastoral Care and Social Justice" in 1989. (SCDMH)

I embrace my father in his favorite chair. This picture was taken a couple of years before his 1992 death.

Eddie Mirmow, my Orangeburg sports mentor, played golf almost into his ninetieth year.

In contrast to receiving the traditional Boisen Cane as an ACPE president-elect, Kathy Turner (left) is presented instead with the Magic Wand from Jo Clare Wilson in 1991. Turner became ACPE's first female president.

The CPE faculty of the Midlands Area Program of the Academy in 1993 (left to right): Mary Rae Waller, Joe Slade, Jerry Alexander, Christa Syrett (registrar), me, and Roland Rainwater.

I am shown with Antonia and her family near Matagalpa, Nicaragua, in 1994.

Marilyn (fourth from left) with her nine sisters and brothers in 1994 (from left to right): Sam Cottingham, Margaret Smith, Mitchell Cottingham, J. D. Cottingham, Juanita Gordon, Wallace Cottingham, Elton Cottingham, Doris Lee McCants, and Walter Cottingham.

◀ *Two of my brothers-in-law, Sam Cottingham (front) and Heyward McCants (rear), are cooking chicken for a family gathering at the Trio farm.*

▶ *Mason (left) and I visit with Louise Spann in 1994.*

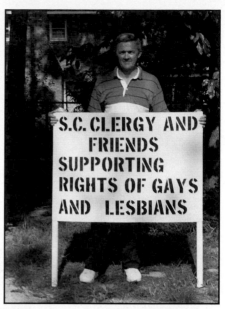

At the age of eighty-nine, my mother was a marcher in the annual two-and-a-half-mile Mental Illness Awareness Walk held in Columbia.

Since the early part of the 1990s, I have been involved with a clergy and laity advocacy group in South Carolina attempting to demonstrate religious solidarity and support for homosexual persons. The group also marches each year in the state's Gay and Lesbian Pride March.

The supervisors of CPE in the Columbia area meet at Joe Slade's lakeside home for their annual tradition of an end-of-the-summer party. This event has been held at Slade's home for the last twenty-five years.

Joe Slade, who has worked as a CPE supervisor in both the state departments of mental health and corrections in South Carolina since 1970, has been long cherished by many for his supportive pastoral care of CPE supervisors and other persons.

Following the celebration of the Fiftieth Anniversary of CPE in the South Carolina Department of Mental Health on 16 August 1996, Jap Keith (far right) and I meet with Obert Kempson at his home to present him with a commemorative plaque.

A panel is convened at the 1997 ACPE annual convention in Orlando to address the area of "stories in CPE." I am telling my story about hunkering down, Rhoadus Blakely, and pastoral care. The other panelists (left to right): Bill Russell, Max McGuire, Jap Keith, and Jo Clare Wilson.

▶ *Psychotherapy colleagues in Columbia have met regularly in a longtime relationship to discuss "thumb-things," especially the art and science of supervision. Seated (left to right): Donna Upchurch, Leah Lake, and Lucy Gordon; standing, Owen Tucker and me. Absent, Howard Waddell.*

▲ *My brother Carroll (right) and I in 1998.*

▶ *Carroll is a civic leader in Texas and also loves the outdoors and his ranch.*

► I hunker down for one last time with some Academy CPE students and staff on my final day of employment with the South Carolina Department of Mental Health in 1999. Hunkering down (left to right): Elnetha Pickett-Martin, me, and Gail Holness; standing, Billy Wilson, Julie Carone, Charles Robinson, Mary Rae Waller, Ann Wallace, and Alice Haynes. Absent, Ted Jefferson. Above us is a portrait of Elias Hort—the first chaplain of the South Carolina State Hospital in the 1840s.

◄ Marilyn and I with our two sons and their wives in August 1999 (standing): Mason and Anne Culvern Summers, and Boyd and Janet Edwards Summers.

► My CPE story concludes on this little screened porch—a hallowed space where my father and I often watched Orangeburg sunsets in late afternoons.

For example, it was appalling to realize that the wondrous CPE and full-time chaplaincy days of Milledgeville would remain only as a fond memory.

Throughout its existence the CPE format at the Milledgeville hospital—by then named the Central State Hospital—offered a significant place for numerous CPE supervisors and supervisory students. Many were launched into outstanding careers throughout the Southeast and other parts of the country. In addition to those mentioned in earlier chapters, others included Kempton Haynes, Jack Gleason, Don Cabiness, George Colgin, Robert Powell, Russell Davis, James Hardie, Ron Wilkins, Charlie Newman, and Jonathan Waddell.

Not that what happened in Georgia will become a forerunner to what might take place in most state or federally supported CPE programs throughout the nation, it did serve shockingly however to remind those in CPE that governmental health care budgets likely would continue going through crisis and shrinkage for years to come.

A RETURN TO CHICKENS

As the nineties progressed, one of the strongest learning experiences in my life was discovered in the hillsides of Central America in 1994. At that time I was selected as a delegate by Witness for Peace (WFP) for participation in its short-term program of dialogue and religious support in El Salvador and Nicaragua. I was in my fifty-ninth year.

WFP, which began more than a dozen years ago, originally offered protective accompaniment to Nicaraguan peasants as they tried to avoid the terrors of war being waged in their country. The program currently seeks to expand awareness of Central America's issues through such activitites as interviewing with political and religious leaders, tours, and a submersion into the culture.

The major part of my experience took place in the countryside where our delegation stayed in repatriated and resettled villages. I resided with a seven-member Nicaraguan family unit in a two-room hut and slept on its dirt floor. The family, which had no men in it, had an annual income of no more than four hundred dollars. Antonia was the maternal leader of this brood. She would awaken its courageous members early each morning to start making tortillas so that they might be bartered during the day for some food and other necessities. A teen-aged daughter would walk a seven-mile round trip by roadsides and through fields twice a week so that scraps of wood and twigs could be gathered for cooking purposes.

Each night the family would tie one of its two thin chickens—a layer and a fryer—by a leg to a table near my sleeping bag. This was done in order to prevent the laying hen from being stolen by outside thieves. While there I could not help but reflect on the circular nature of life. I marvelled at how the mystery of my life's journey had taken me from my boyhood in a chicken yard behind a little house in South Carolina and brought me again to a chicken—this time, in the socially devastated mountains of Central America.

In returning from Central America in 1994, I sketched part of my experience in El Salvador with the following published reflections:

> As a full moon scattered its silvery brightness on the countryside village in El Salvador during this past New Year's Eve, my experience there provided me with added meanings to the biblical declaration that indeed the light shines in the darkness (Jn. 1: 5 NIV).
>
> A courageous Jesuit priest—just recently ending a twenty-eight-day fast partly to bring attention to injustices apparent in the administering of national election procedures—conducted an inspiring Mass that night under a large shed for those in the resettled mountain village.
>
> For more than a dozen years, Salvadoran days and nights had been filled with terror. More than 75,000 persons were killed—many as a result of a systematic military policy. Just four years ago, six of the priest's beloved Jesuit colleagues were murdered in one cataclysmic moment due to their solidarity efforts with social liberation.
>
> The peace accords of 1992 were to signal an end to the atrocities, but even now the intimidating threat of death squads exists. (In the month prior to our Witness for Peace's arrival for a two-week stay, twenty opposition leaders had been assassinated in El Salvador.)
>
> Amidst the historical backdrop of such horrible cruelty, the priest's homiletical words—expressing a yearning for peace with justice and a hope for reconciliation and reconstruction—penetrated the darkness of the night air with the illuminating power of courage. His message was profoundly wrought from unimaginable human suffering.
>
> As I eventually returned to my own country, I have remained aware of carrying from the crucible of Central America the sustaining memory of a hopeful light weaving its way through the darkness of systemic evil.
>
> Such a poignant moment on a moonlit mountain enhances once again a perspective that a more total pastoral care is inextricably wedded to broader social issues.[6]

Since that memorable trip, I have retained my ties to WFP. I have appreciated the opportunities of letter-writing campaigns and other projects. (For example, WFP is devoted to closing the government-funded School of the Americas at Fort Benning. The unit has trained thousands of Latin American military graduates in terrorism. This has been used against people in their home countries, for instance, Nicaragua. Multitudes of persons have "disappeared." In late 1999 I returned to the fort for the third time in my life—this time, to stand with thousands at a main gate to protest the school's presence.)

A FIFTIETH ANNIVERSARY

Another memorable time from the decade of the nineties is that which was found in the celebration of the Fiftieth Anniversary of CPE in the South Carolina Department of Mental Health. This day of remembrance was held on 16 August 1996 in the Chapel of Hope on the campus of the South Carolina State Hospital. The featured speaker was Jap Keith; also in attendance was ACPE's executive director, Russell Davis.

The anniversary indicated that the six decades' combined summary of clinical pastoral education in the state's mental health agency had produced some strong results. In those 50 years, there had been a total of 22 CPE supervisors who had served as certified pastoral teachers. The programs had produced 1,209 CPE students (accumulating 2,152 quarters or units). If all of these CPE student hours were combined, they would unfold into the equivalent of 98 years of consecutive, around-the-clock hours of ministry with patients and reflective learning in seminars and conferences. On that day, I felt grateful to have experienced directly 33 of those 50 years.

Obert Kempson, the 1946 founder of the state agency's first CPE program, could not be present for the occasion due to health problems. Later in the day, Keith and I went to his house at the retirement center and presented our long-time vocational friend with a commemorative plaque. His wife Rachel also was present with us. Following this anniversary occasion, I wrote Keith:

> You and I have been colleagues and professional brothers for nearly forty years, and I want you to know how fortunate I am for that. You have graced our South Carolina programming with care and interest

over these years. You have been with us in energetic times of new beginnings; you have walked with us in some tragic and wrenching days; and
the other day, you offered affirmation to the CPE years gone by and
hopefully to those yet to come. Thanks for who you are and the strength
of your constancy in the devoted relational ministry you offer to those
around you.[7]

Soon thereafter, Keith moved from his twenty-five-year stay at
the Columbia Theological Seminary in Decatur, Georgia, to become
senior minister of the Decatur Presbyterian Church. He had
assumed the chairmanship of the seminary's pastoral care department when Tom McDill retired. Obert Kempson had mentioned to
me once that it was McDill who offered Kempson much support
and nurture when the early days of CPE in the southeastern section
of the nation were rather lonely ones. The reader also may recall
that McDill's supportive care in the early 1960s encouraged me to
remain in the CPE certification process.

The occasion of Keith's departure from the seminary represented a time when Ann Titshaw—his personable office assistant—
retired. For years many throughout ACPE's Southeast Region
were the beneficiaries of her efficient and hospitable style.

THE KEMPSON LEGACY

In less than a year after the Fiftieth Anniversary event, Kempson
passed away. Before his death, he and I would talk regularly by
phone and through visits. His statesmanship and the likelihood of
a historical connection are now described.

A Clinical Pastoral Statesman

I feel that this man will be long remembered in the CPE tradition
for his loyalty to organizations, his astute wisdom, and the pursuing of issues with the tenacity and curiosity of an English bulldog.
He gave much assertive service in the area of keeping alive the
structural life of various organizations. A large part of his legacy is
that of his being considered by many persons as one of the leading
"statesmen" in the overall history of the clinical pastoral movement. He had much political savvy in organizational life.

In my days of having been a CPE student under his pastoral supervision in the early 1960s, he was more like an "uncle" to me rather than a "father" in the learning process. Therein, he offered prods, support, suggestions, nudges, and ways of considering options. Kempson was a master at mixing the advisory flavors of consultation into his brand of supervision. He never intruded deeply into the student's personal issues.

I had the opportunity to visit with him shortly before his death. Although in a weakened condition, we were able to do some talking. For a moment I placed my hand on his arm and told him that he meant much to me. Through our mutual nods we acknowledged our care for each other. My soul remembered the many trips that we had taken together in attending meetings, the times of grief and celebration, and a longlasting interest in each other.

Before my leaving he said in a faint whisper, "Tom, go get that nurse over there and tell her I said to *immediately* come right on over here. I want to tell her to do some things." A warmth graced my heart, for I knew that a strong life force—so long characterized in his aggressive and sometimes feisty interactions with others— was still operative in this amazing man and unusually committed pastoral leader.

A most gratifying moment occurred for me in 1998 when the Southeast Region of ACPE awarded me the periodic J. Obert Kempson Distinguished Service Award. I later wrote his wife Rachel: "I know of no prouder day in my life than that of being given the award that bears his name."[8]

A Tie between Sullivan, Kempson, Boisen, and Bruder

There is a bit of plausible history that connects together Harry Stack Sullivan, Kempson, Boisen, and Ernest Bruder. Prior to his death, Kempson had bequeathed to me the 1936 book *The Exploration of the Inner World*—a classic that had been given to him personally by its author, Boisen. Some months following Kempson's death, I happened to be perusing the book for the first time. Noted was this inscription on the front page: "With pleasant memories of St. Elizabeths. Anton T. Boisen. 11 August 1947." Resting behind those words is a speculated scenario that may have some relevant meanings for clinical pastoral history. Its drama is described below.

Boisen's visit to the St. Elizabeths mental hospital in Washington would have coincided with the same interval that Kempson was located there in supervisory training with Bruder. In those middle 1940s, Boisen's program at Elgin State Hospital had begun to be severely distanced from the accreditation of the national Council for Clinical Training. Some historians might suggest that Boisen was being pushed aside. This was due to the developed variance between him and the CCT in training assumptions and methods. The Council designated him subsequently with a role as a traveling consultant. In this function he was asked to make visits to CPE supervisors in other programs.

Boisen made such a visit in the summer of 1947 to Bruder. This visitation fostered his "pleasant memories" held for Kempson. It is my understanding also that Bruder would utilize Boisen not only in consultation but also as a noted lecturer with the hospital staff during some of his various visits to Washington.

I find it further interesting to consider that, since it was the summer of 1947 when Bruder and Kempson first envisioned the organizing of an Association of Mental Hospital Chaplains, Boisen undoubtedly would have given attention and a blessing to Bruder's and Kempson's joint dream. More than ten years later, AMHC would originate its prestigious Anton T. Boisen Award that is still periodically presented to a clinical pastoral clergyperson for distinguished service.

A further dimension to entertain about such connections is the key role of Harry Stack Sullivan. Boisen's 1947 visit to Washington most definitely would have contained the shared interest that he and Bruder possessed for the interpersonally oriented psychiatric work of Sullivan. Sullivan earlier had worked as a young psychiarist at St. Elizabeths. Bruder studied later under Sullivan and others at the noteworthy Washington School of Psychiatry—an activity that would result in Bruder's receiving from the school the first certificate to be awarded to a minister in applied psychiatry.

Boisen also maintained over the years a significant professional relationship with Sullivan. Since Boisen carefully scrutinized his own inner world so diligently, this self-study was appealing to Sullivan's talent in the sensitive exploration of the inner dynamics within his own schizophrenic patients. Boisen and Sullivan kept considerable professional contact, and Sullivan once gave a favorable review of Boisen's *Exploration of the Inner World* in the *Journal of Psychiatry.*

The summer of 1947—the same season that my preteen baseball team won the Orangeburg City Playground championship—likely was a period seeing much creative energy flowing through a rhombus that connected together the likes of Kempson, Boisen, Bruder, and Sullivan's legacy.

MERGER NEAR A RIVER

In addition to a CPE anniversary in South Carolina and the passing away of a dear friend, the 1990s also brought forth the momentous marriage of two clinical pastoral organizations: the College of Chaplains and the Association of Mental Health Clergy. I had the opportunity to serve on the College-AMHC Transitional Task Force. This committee shaped the proposals for the eventual joining of these two national pastoral care groups. It was an exciting moment when the two bodies—with their long and rich histories—merged officially and became the Association of Professional Chaplains. This action took place in late April 1998 near the Columbia River at a conference site in Portland, Oregon. Luckily, it was warm weather; Tim Little had an itch to open many windows in our hotel room.

Displayed in the merger process was the skilled leadership of the two presidents, Dick Stewart (the College) and David Carl (AMHC). Their collegiality and intentionality in systemic negotiations provided a rich model for the whole clinical pastoral field to witness. Parenthetically, the opportunity of my working on this merger process also allowed Stewart and myself to engage in the golden moments of exchanging sports questions—our mutual enterprise described in chapter 8. Hardly a coffee break or any other interlude escaped such an earthshaking cross-examination as: "Who was the tailback that succeeded the All-American Doak Walker at SMU in the late 1940s?"

In addition to the many benefits of the merger, two traditions now became organizationally blended: the heritage from Russell

Dicks (general hospital ministry) and that from Anton Boisen (mental health ministry).

CHALLENGES IN CPE

As the decade of the 1990s fades, there are challenges facing CPE in its historical vitality. Several of these themes are explored in this section: cross-culturalism, postmodern implications, and CPE's situation in today's public mental health arena.

A Cross-Cultural World

In the estimation of many educators, the bridging of cultures will become increasingly one of the most critical issues to be faced in professional training programs. Needless to say, there is an escalation of contact between various cultures in today's shrinking world. In the pastoral realm, this factor will necessitate that one's pastoral care embrace a respect for and a knowledge about the abounding variety of religious faith traditions. As an example, competency for a pastoral care representative of the Christian faith in this broader involvement points to a greater preparation for pluralistic collaboration with other faith groups such as Muslims, Hindus, and Buddhists. CPE's principles and methods can thrive on a receptivity to the rich educational gifts brought to the learning process by students from a wide array of faiths and cultures. Pastoral care will need to value the diverse religious paths leading to unique understandings about God.

Particularly, a strong encouragement for ethnic pluralism is crucial. This is extremely important since the CPE movement originated from a heavy Eurocentric backdrop. This grounding contained a western dominance in Caucasian, masculine, Christian, hierarchical thought. In contrast, many of the nonwestern contributions to the movement are highly flavored by the affective learning and ministry features seen in the matters of celebration, myth, a oneness with the earth, and a strong valuing of maintaining connection with ancestry and relationships.

In the past dozen years, representatives from African countries have eminently blessed my cross-cultural experience in CPE. Among its students, the Academy for Pastoral Education's program was fortunate to have had some yearlong residency participants from Liberia, Ghana, Sudan, Tanzania, Nigeria, and South Africa. Examples have been numerous in which the richness of their training involvements have added fresh perspectives to the learning process.

For example, a student with a Tanzanian heritage once sketched the roots of his clinical pastoral care interest to village days where he tended loyally to his family's cattle herd. Each of the many cows was given a name by him. A view on covenantal theology later grew in him due to this profound relatedness to his fellow creatures and the earth.

Another CPE student, dressed in his colorful Nigerian ceremonial regalia, helped to coordinate a program of African drum beating for a large audience of adolescent patients and staff members. A very reclusive youth in the gathering was touched by the ministry from the rhythmic nature of the pounding. He arose from his usual territory of isolation. Like a modern-day Lazarus, he went to the stage and danced to the heartfelt cadence of such pulsating grace.

A further illustration of understanding about diversity was seen in a unifying group ritual as provided by a student from Ghana. The event occurred within the format of a Story Day in my home (see chapter 8). Prior to sharing his written story, he explained to the group that, before anyone tells a story in his homeland, the designated tribal storyteller is obliged to engage everyone present in the setting with a preliminary and individualized ritual. Through the words of his native tongue and an embrace, the student went to each person and brought the individual into a sense of corporate belongingness with all in the room before he verbally presented his story.

Students from Africa also have taught me much about the scars still carried from the past eras of western colonialism in their countries. Any form of subtle superiority or insensitivity shown in supervisory critique, especially as offered by White persons, can be scorching symbols and reminders of an earlier exploitation by the western world.

Cross-culturalism has further spawned some noteworthy concepts that are quite transferable into general pastoral care practice. David Augsburger's *Pastoral Counseling Across Cultures* has helped considerably in blazing such trails. His remarkable perspective on the issue of "interpathy" (a state of creating a "feeling between" cultures) implies that the main task of a pastoral care-provider, in talking with someone from a different culture, is that of assuming an attitude of being a "visitor" engaged with the other person's unique background. One then becomes more like a tourist in a new learning experience about a person whose roots might be radically different from his/hers. The interpathic relationship is this positive regard felt between the cultural differences. Hence, the pastoral care-provider becomes a simultaneous learner in this caring situation.

Likewise, in the early stages of pastoral supervision with *anyone*—regardless of the culture—the supervisor is a visiting tourist in that person's landscape and background. This phase allows for a deeper supervisory sensing of the student's uniqueness to develop. Without such interpathy, the supervisor likely will be left supervising his/her own uninformed surface expectations or distorted "diagnoses" made about the student.

Postmodern Issues and CPE

As the curtain has dropped on the twentieth century, the CPE initiative is faced with the implications of these commonly known postmodern times. Some social analysts are indicating that a general loneliness, anonymity, and disconnectedness from community has resulted from the amorphous sweep of modern technology through our lives. Another growing postmodern feature is that of the individual's tendency to deconstruct a multitude of social meanings. Skepticism has replaced any certainty; thus, many social propostions no longer get transferred very clearly. Change and relativity are becoming the norms in this general deconstruction. Hence, some of this poses a great threat to the past glue that has held a common life together.

Therefore, in looking at these times from the lens of postmodernism, no longer can a pastoral care-provider perform as a Lone Ranger in attempting to meet today's serious human need for a rootage in community. There is sensed a transitioning taking place in pastoral care's once pronounced reliance on a one-to-one form of care. Hence, the psychotherapeutic paradigm—so long a prevailing influence on general pastoral care and also on CPE—may not offer in this individualism the necessary ingredients for a communalism of care. Today's needs may be aching for an undergirding of greater networked nurture. Charles Gerkin's recent *An Intro-*

duction to Pastoral Care provides penetrating insights into the receding of this individualistic paradigm in pastoral work.

Further, some leaders in the marriage and family therapy field are demonstrating a contemporary interest in bringing a broader community dimension into the therapeutic process. This emphasis is a counter to the accented individualism of the past several decades. Such therapeutic expansion provides a model in which the method promotes the client's consistent moral assessment of how her/his situation or behavior affects close relations and the community. William Doherty is a leader in this growing area.

Postmodern concerns regarding community-building create a need for CPE to consider much more thoroughly such potentializing educational dimensions as the congregational context, the pastoral leadership of groups, collaborative networking skills, and the development of pastoral competencies in mobilizing systems of care for persons. Undoubtedly, the tightrope to walk in such systemic efforts will be the balancing of sensitive care for the individual's inner soul life as it relates to the fibers of any corporality.

The Plight of CPE in Today's Mental Health Context

The past ten years or so have fostered a pronounced awareness about the vulnerability of clinical pastoral education in the public mental health setting. A welter of major changes and upheavals is currently found there.

Most of the state mental hospitals in the nation have undergone heavy dismantling. In terms of Boisen's signal contributions to the whole clinical pastoral momentum, it is ironic to remember that CPE had its birth in a public mental hospital in Massachusetts. Now that the focus is on the care and treatment of mentally ill persons within community settings, it is increasingly problematic to consider that CPE never made, in the first place, much headway into the nation's community mental health centers. This generally unsuccessful attempt resulted from case-management priorities and the now current restraints of financial reimbursement. Also, the hiring and retention of CPE supervisors in state and federal positions, whether in hospitals or the community, have been enormously difficult because of low salary conditions.

As the public mental health delivery systems across the land have been involved with cataclysmic change, the once strong CPE presence in mental hospitals has dimmed almost into oblivion. The trends of managed care, privatization, attrition for existing positions, and a general diminishing of public funding for clinical education in governmental systems have served as further contributing factors to this decline. The total number of ACPE accredited centers yet remaining in a defined mental health context now amount to only *six* percent compared to the other types of CPE training programs throughout the United States.

Further, it is alarming to recognize that the percentage of correctional or penal settings for CPE is decimated even more drastically than that in public mental health. It is bewildering to note that two of the nation's most glaring social ills are those related to the astounding increase of locking up persons in jails and to the historical public neglect of the seriously mentally ill. Should CPE continue to be lost from these two critical contexts, the CPE-informed ministries to those particular living human documents therein sadly may cease to be. This startling phenomenon shows that CPE has not been able to align itself well to the Keller tradition of providing social care.

It is also grievous to know that these two crucial issues—jails and mental illness—have currently merged into a serious national concern. There has been a lack of proper reponse by the community to the numbers of mentally ill persons needing public services. Hence, the jails of this country have become the dumping ground for many severely mentally ill persons. Their symptoms of mental illness often do not receive adequate treatment in such incarcerated settings—but rather punishment. Some critics feel that mental illness has now taken on the added feature of criminalization. Sadly, there are now 283,000 mentally ill persons in jails—more persons than there are in psychiatric hospitals!

The sufferers of a mental illness have known historically a great woundedness not only from the damage caused by their illnesses but also from a lack of public resourcing. I feel that any further dimming of CPE's public mental health light across the land can serve only to add to the perpetuation of that darkness.

In my opinion, these above issues of cross-culturalism, postmodern times, and CPE's relatedness to the public mental health situation are some of today's strongest challenges.

As early 1999 arrived, I undertook entry into another challenging river. After thirty-six years of full-time state public mental health service, I retired from the South Carolina Department of Mental Health. This transition time of my life is commented upon more fully in the book's conclusion.

The writer of Ecclesiastes mentions that everything in the human pilgrimage has its own "season" (Eccl. 3:1-9 NIV). Most certainly, the harvesting from the 1982-1999 years brought a stronger sense of Keller's historical social care interest into my fuller awareness and pastoral life-cycle.

The winds from bygone years had their strong hand in preparing me for this particular concern. Unquestionably, some of them were in the following facilitating forces: responsiveness by my mother and father to the suffering of others, a cherished African-American woman forced to sit in a movie balcony, the courage of a swimming team, a forgotten woman on a back ward peering at me and her secluded world with fire in her eyes, the story of Anton Boisen holding on to life and creativity, and Tom McDill letting me know in an impressionable conversation that he felt I could make it as a CPE supervisor.

Their footprints and those of many others have been evident in my attempt to join my pastoral care perspective with its march toward the territory of social justice implications.

Conclusion

---◄◊◊►---

A Story Birthed on a Porch

It has been the intent of my book to show an *integrated* crisscrossing of my own personal journey with that of CPE's evolving history. As the chronicling of this tour through those years moves toward an ending, there are some pertinent areas that are mentioned in conclusion. These focal points deal with some general reflections, a reference about my loved ones, my entrance into a current time of passage, and the likely influence of a porch on my vocational history.

REFLECTIONS

In looking back over the years of my clinical pastoral education life and at the current time, there are some considerations that grab my attention. These are devoted especially to provisions from younger years, gratitude for the elders, breathtaking changes, inclusivity, and the promises of a renewal/institutional polarity.

For one thing, I remain grateful for the early resources in my life—factors that have aided me tremendously in my clinical pastoral pathways. These include most basically my family members, Louise Spann, close relatives, friends, and the years spent in Orangeburg.

Most certainly those young developmental days of both tending to chickens and plunging into the Edisto River—even on freezing days—entwined themselves somehow into my practice of pastoral supervision. I am confident that such growing-up years help to shape a CPE participant's manner of responding later to the myriad moments of learning in the experience-based CPE process. The section of "Early Influences on CPE" in chapter 1 is an effort to explore some of these foundational roots from my boyhood days; for example, the phenomena of participant/observer and storytelling. It is as if these background threads from the budding of youthful life weave themselves in and out of my daily consciousness and help to form substantially who I am.

Furthermore, I was blessed in my early twenties by being provided with a listening heart from someone like Professor Floyd Feely during the hurricane season of my seminary turmoil. His pastoral care of me at that critical phase of my young adult life enabled that day's literature—the contributions of Anton Boisen, Seward Hiltner, David Roberts, Karl Menninger, and Paul Tillich— to inform me immensely during my quandary. Hence, it was through the gateways of my own hunger and wounded search that I entered the CPE field at a rather young pastoral age.

Secondly, there is thankfulness for those numerous leaders who preceded my entrance into the movement. They already were on CPE's stage and awaiting the arrival of participation with the oncoming drama of my generation. I have attempted to introduce many of these elders to the reader. I shall never forget the Kempsons, McDills, and others.

In the third place, I find myself astounded with the mind-boggling changes that have transpired from the time of my stepping into the CPE story in 1960 until the conclusion of the 1990s. During my interminable flight from South Carolina to meet with Charles Hall, Tom Klink, and Joe Caldwell in Kansas, I never could have entertained the idea that we of the cardboard boxes were only several decades away from a rapid computerized information highway with its e-mail and other technologies.

An appreciation is felt for some exciting changes of social liberation over these changing years. As an illustration, most of the pastoral care contact years ago between a chaplain and a person with a severe form of mental illness was a ministry to that individual on a desolate back ward in a massive state mental hospital. Because of active community support programs in some parts of the country and more efficient medications, today those same two persons amazingly might be found instead sitting around a conference table in planning advocacy activities with community leaders in a town.

Invigorating energies of diversity and inclusivity also have breathed new life and changes into the CPE field. Some of this opening-up process in the Association for Clinical Pastoral Education was influenced by the nearly thirty years of sensitivity shown in the consecutive executive directorships of Charles Hall and Duane Parker.

As seen in so much of my early CPE story, there was a deprivation of the diverse elements surrounding us CPE participants. Not until the middle of the 1970s was the first caucus of Women in CPE called forth at an annual ACPE conference. Inclusive progress has been reflected in the fact that, out of the last four elected ACPE presidents, two have been Caucasian females, one an African-American male, and one a Caucasian male. Prior to the early 1990s, I had known only Caucasian male presidents either in the Council for Clinical Training or ACPE. The celebration of inclusivity is seen in ACPE's selection of Teresa Snorton—an African-American woman—to lead its historical efforts into the twenty-first century as a new executive director.

Yet, an incongruity in this overall freeing process exists on some regional ACPE levels. Caucasian male domination still prevails there in terms of the numbers of certified CPE supervisors. Distance is yet to be traveled by the CPE field in its search for certified inclusivity; perhaps cross-culturalism's impact has not made its way heavily into the review system. For example, thirty percent of South Carolina's population is African American; the Southeast Region has only five percent of its supervisors as African American. Forty-nine percent of the total CPE students enrolled nationally are female, while in the Southeast Region only twenty-two percent of the CPE supervisors are female. The use of these figures is intended not to overemphasize one particular region but to illustrate the incongruous dilemma in CPE's search for a fuller diversity and inclusivity.

A fourth reflection is gathered around my hopes that, as ACPE has now progressed seemingly in its organizational development sequences from an early energized movement to that of an institution, it will be able to include a sense of renewal and heroism as the next years emerge. Some persons today strongly contend—rightly or not—that its undertaking has become too standardized. As far back as 1974, Wayne Oates predicted that the CPE movement would continue to have a vital and lasting impact unless it fell into a "methodological sterility."[1]

My guess is that much risking will be needed to keep a *passionate pastoral* search for learning alive in the oncoming years for this form of experienced-based education. If not, we could become mere custodians of a standardized structure. In this regard, ACPE might benefit greatly from an ongoing dialogue with the College of Pastoral Supervision and Psychotherapy and its interest in the "recovery of soul" for CPE learning.

Thus, there exists a need for us in the CPE field to be pastorally proactive in this very complex age of technology and reductionism. CPE persons are urged to keep telling, on the one hand, the stories of our CPE forebears to remind ourselves from whence we came. With the other, there is a need for stretching toward the future with a new mythos of bravery by creating newly hewn stories. Boisen, Dunbar, Keuther, Oates, and so many other early pioneers—in facing their challenges—have left a legacy of wondrous clinical pastoral stories and histories. A question today could well be asked: What will be the stories handed down by this current clinical pastoral generation to those yet to follow? Without such stories and energies, an organization likely will rely strongly on its formalized and power-oriented drives. Lost in such exteriority can be a sense of deeply cherishing an organization—and its historical journey—as a significant "home."

It is interesting to note that a former ACPE president—James Gebhart—established an ACPE "Reunion" in the fall of 1999 with the expressed purpose of telling such stories. I was among the fifty persons who went to Saint Louis from all parts of the nation for a time of momentous sharing. The atmosphere was akin to the movie *Field of Dreams:* If a context of cherishing is offered—indeed, "they will come." Risking the loss of energy, a CPE supervisor battling cancer traveled from Pennsylvania with his wife so that he could be once again with his vocational family. Another attendee, who was certified as a CPE supervisor by the Council for Clinical Training nearly fifty years ago, was able to spend only one night at the gathering. He primarily came so that he could engage in a long-standing game of cards with historical friends. As he prepared to travel back to the East Coast, he happily remarked to me: "The ritual was performed." In any family or organizational living, members can be potentially ushered into the benefits of a lively mythos—a soil that promotes the process of cherishing. Persons need only to claim therein those stories that are their birthright.

COMMENTS ABOUT DEAR ONES

As my CPE tale reaches its conclusion, I also share with the reader some updated information about my closest loved ones. They have been described previously in various parts of the material, and their positive influence on my life remains constant.

My father died more than seven years ago at the age of ninety-one in the old home's back bedroom in Orangeburg. It was the same room and bed in which I was born more than sixty-five years ago. That particular room space had served also as the valued location where he and I built the plans for our chicken enterprise. This hallowed parental room further offered another significant backdrop in my history. It was there where I had taken a deep gulp—in my junior year of college following the swimming season—to announce to my parents an interest in entering the Christian ministry.

My mother moved into an Orangeburg retirement center in 1995. It was the same Methodist nursing home context that I had worked in during the summer immediately following my college graduation. Until a stroke in 1997, she was walking a mile a day. Although now quite weakened, we still are able to reflect some on the mutual history of our lives, some humorous people and events known from past years, the life of her beloved husband and my father, and some Cross Hill days. Struggling in my early twenties for a greater grasp on an independence in our relationship, I have come since to realize over these past decades that she became—along the way—one of my dearest and most courageous friends. When she was eighty-nine years old, she came to Columbia and joined several thousand other persons in the annual two-mile Mental Illness Awareness Walk. In her ninety-fifth year, our family held a birthday party in her honor amidst forty of her close friends and relatives in Orangeburg. She arose to offer a brief remark of gratitude to this gathering. The remnants of elocution were still present.

Louise Spann passed away several years ago when she was ninety-two years old. I was invited by her family and church to speak at her funeral. I mentioned on that occasion that our two lives had now come full circle. "She was present in my home's back bedroom on the day of my birth to hold me," I said, "and now I have the privilege of being present at her death to 'hold' her with a farewell." During the last eight years of her life, she had to have both of her legs amputated due to a diabetic condition.

In once visiting with her in a nursing home, she said, "When I get there (pointing heavenward with a finger), I'll wait for you." I replied, "And if I get there before you, I'll wait for you." From then on, our visits concluded with our fingers pointed upward in this symbolic ritual of wholeness. My thoughts would drift back invariably to those bygone days when an upper movie balcony had separated us—but our hearts were never divided.

My brother Carroll and his family have remained in Laredo, Texas, since his 1958 wedding to Evelyn Bruni. He owns a cattle-food processing company. An avid hunter and fisherman, he is recognized also as a community leader, an honored rancher, and a devoted land conservationist. His family was touched by the hand of tragedy more than twenty years ago when a young teen-aged son, Carroll III, accidentally was killed.

Carroll has been there consistently for me in my own life. In my growing up, it was quite beneficial in many ways to be his younger brother. When I once was getting beat up in a fight during a grammar school recess, he ventured over from the nearby junior high school to yank the older opponent away from the battle. He yelled at him, "The only reason you're whipping my brother is that you're older than he is; and, anyway, he hasn't felt well today." (Of course, he was lying.) During my pain in the unsettledness of my early forties, he often made supportive phone calls from Texas.

Marilyn and I have celebrated now more than thirty-seven years of marriage. From the history of our marital journey, I have drawn my greatest anchoring, love, continuities, and growth. I receive also much learning from observing her strong giftedness in the area of developing networks of nurture with a variety of groups—her church committee work, a neighborhood association, her work setting, and various community projects. She possesses uncanny skills in keeping communication flowing between persons. We have experienced together the parenting of two adult sons, the loss of loved ones and friends to death, and the creative strenuousness of fashioning a lively interdependency out of our commonalitites and differences. We have lived now in our same Columbia house for more than thirty-three years.

The history of relatedness to the nine sisters and brothers of her primary family has provided vigorous occasions of large-scaled family reunions, dances, barbeques, and birthday parties. In times of grief and need, her family system gives to the ones in crisis a surrounding climate of care.

Our older son Boyd works with a computer systems company, while Mason has become a lawyer. Both became married within the last several years respectively to Janet Edwards and Anne Culvern. I felt honored in being invited to officiate at both of their weddings. I had the good fortune of weaving my spoken love for them and some nurturing memories of our historical relationships into the ceremonies.

PASSAGE INTO THE ELDER SEASON

I mentioned at the end of the last chapter that I retired from the South Carolina Department of Mental Health in early January 1999. Some grief naturally touched my heart, because I was letting go of an agency setting where meaningful relationships with patients, staff, and pastoral students were cherished for years. I feel fortunate to have had such a lengthy pastoral care and teaching role in this mental health "parish."

Some of my creative interests are invested in such activities as photography, reading about sports history (especially the 1945-1955 era), mountain hikes, a daily nap, dancing, movies, carving apple heads, watching Andy Griffith and Monty Python reruns, a regular walk, the surf at beaches, and writing human interest stories. Recently I have had some sportswriting published. One article was devoted to a morning spent with Doc Blanchard when I was eleven years old. He was the All-American football player of the famed Army teams of West Point in the middle of the 1940s. Another writing dealt with a a remembrance about an aged radio and listening to sports before the days of television.

Hardly a week goes by that I am not perusing timeworn sports magazines or game programs kept from the 1940s and 1950s. One of the greatest delights in my sports interest was that of having met with the legendary basketball coach, Frank McGuire, nearly fifteen years ago in South Carolina. He and I were able to talk at length about the olden days of New York City basketball. That was once his natural environment prior to his arrival in the South for a stellar coaching career. He seemed overjoyed to be talking with a southerner who, in not ever having seen a basketball game in New

York, could still dialogue eagerly with him about the earlier exploits of such Big Apple court stars as Sid Tannenbaum, Ed Roman, Harry Boycoff and Bob Zawoluk from the 1940s and 1950s. I am skeptical about today's heavy commercial emphasis in sports and more enamored with skillful, heartfelt competition for its own sake.

My work with various ministry and social matters in the community continues at this time of my life. Advocacy and planning efforts related to the causes of the gay and lesbian liberation movement, the psychosocial support needs of severely mentally ill persons, and the nuclear waste dilemma facing South Carolina—with its role as one of the nation's major dumping grounds—occupy a good bit of my time.

Long ago I began grasping the notion that, as I moved with an interest into any such area, I would attempt to assume a "learning project" attitude about the specific focus. This then allows me to move into the involvement not only as an active advocate but also as a primary learner. The persons more directly affected become my teachers and guides as I try to gain more knowledge about the issues. Hence, an expansion of knowledge and skills can result from such an experiential curriculum. I have found this to be true not only in the social justice domain but with any area of interest. Also, I have maintained for years a study of supervision with a small group of psychotherapy colleagues in Columbia.

At this particular juncture point in my vocational life, I cannot help but recall further words contained in Harry Emerson Fosdick's 1959 letter to me. He wrote:

> I like to think of you, not giving up the ministry, but going into it with an experience of God's saving help in difficulty, "strengthened with might by his Spirit in the inner man," to preach no mere hand-me-down gospel but a message based on first-hand knowledge and conviction. That can happen, my friend.[2]

I feel that what my corresponding supporter penned years ago represented profound guidance as I now look back over my shoulder at the contours of my pastoral pilgrimage thus far. I trust in the continuing presence of a thirst for more first-hand knowledge and experience.

I move into the future years not without some uncertainty. But I am aware of a fuller sense of awe and reflection. I bring a strengthened anticipation for what these upcoming times—brimming over with possible mysteries—might have in store for me in terms of choices, sorrows, values, new learnings, activities, and ponderings. In a conference at the Kirkridge Center several years ago, Robert Raines characterized these current chronological years of mine as being "the passage years into an elder season."

Earlier described in the rhythmic journey of my inner soul were such life-cycled developmental eras as "modifying" and "exile." It feels like I am now moving into the glimmers of another phase of the soul's journey. As I experience this passageway, I hold gratitude for the providence of care received from the CPE years and other places. Should I be so fortunate to reach an advanced age, it could prove interesting to see what descriptive term I might give—in looking back—to this entered phase of my life.

Taking these new steps seems akin to the reflections offered by John—the CPE student described in the book's preface. He had strolled away from my office as he completed his training program. In traveling toward the future of further learning in his life, he looked back at me and said, "Well, I think I've started opening up some old and new chapters in my own living human document." As well, my current times are beginning to turn simultaneously some old and new pages in my life's journey.

THE PORCH

With the curtain dropping on this particular chronicle, I desire to reveal to the reader at least two vivid discoveries while working on this writing activity. One deals with the renewed conviction that behind any CPE participant—or anyone for that matter—rests the unique and awesome features of a story. The second involves an hypothesis: The seeds for my written narrative began to be planted in the long, long ago rather than the project starting afresh just four years ago. Actually, this tale as related to CPE and the integration of my life's paths may have been greatly influenced by what occurred in the distant past on a porch. The scenario for such a happening is described below.

While I was growing up in the Orangeburg home, on various occasions my father would invite me to sit with him in late afternoons on the house's little screened side porch. There we would talk and sometimes watch in awe as the sun sank quietly in the western sky. We also liked to sit there and watch rainstorms at various times.

When his failing health prevented him years later from talking—and death slowly was approaching—we continued to sit on the porch during many of my visits. As we sat in silence, we again would witness the sun slowly vanish. The strong memories of my years with him would surface in my soul in that quietness. I would ponder within myself those days of his teaching me to swim the Edisto or his attentiveness to my teen-aged recounting of various athletic adventures. Especially remembered also were the five minutes or so of solemn stillness in the 1970s when our teary eyes once met mutually during the painful time of peril that midlife energies had brought to my marriage.

As Marilyn and I were preparing the old Orangeburg home place for closure—four years after his death and immediately following my mother's move into the retirement center—I came across a wrinkled 1919 letter in an old filing cabinet. It came at a time, too, when I had already begun some preparations for this writing project on *Hunkering Down*.

In the letter, my father had written to his own mother. It was composed soon after he had gone away to college. The year before, the tragic death in World War I and the influenza epidemic had swept away—within a brief span of four months—her beloved son (my uncle Tom) and her dear husband.

The consoling letter, which was filled with warm support, ended with my father expressing thanks to his brokenhearted mother for those many earlier times that their once intact family members had sat together late in the afternoons "to watch the calmness and beauty of sunsets." In reading those words, I trembled. I felt that I had just entered into one of the most sacred moments of my entire life. An intergenerational bond almost blew me away! A deep, warm silence remained with me for the rest of that day.

Wonder-filled similarities had previously been tasted at life's banquet table. For instance, the dim past had fed my young boyhood soul those sparkling shafts of sunlit wonder seen beneath Edisto's waters. A collegiate era was touched by a close Mystery in a moment of restless prayer. A gratitude—knowing no possible words for description—accompanied my two sons' birthed entries into this fascinating phenomenon that we call "life." Too, a peace-sprinkled California afternoon was known decades ago by watching the rhythmic splashing of a rolling surf—a unifying Monterrey moment following the days of traveling through dreams, Carl Jung, myths, and gestalt by way of Joyce and John Weir's amazing workshop talents. Indeed, wonder and awe are at our disposal for the feasting!

But on this special letter-finding day, I realized that my father had started early spreading at his familial table the bounty of his care. He had started putting on my plate years ago—young in my days—the transmission of a porch blessing. He had known such from his own early sunsets. In my later quest for further grace, my heart and wounds would lead me toward CPE's beckoning call for a pastoral life and teaching. Discovered on that affirming porch—where spiritual dreams arose—were the dwelling of similar elements as those later disclosed in a remarkable clinical pastoral movement.

One of the major benefactions from its treasure trove has been a priceless pastoral educational approach—one emphasizing the riches of relationship-building and a wounded form of healing. No wonder that creative and bruised Anton Boisen and the likes of Helen Flanders Dunbar, Seward Hiltner, Carroll Wise, and Len Cedarleaf were so devoted to this movement and fought so doggedly for its life and enhancement.

The crinkled letter, imbued with its awesome power, had nestled in a little house—an abode that was hunkered down not far from the flowing waters of the Edisto.

T. S. Eliot certainly must have known about such thirst as mine and other persons for this mysterious quality of continual learning when he wrote:

> We shall not cease from exploration
> And the end of all our exploring
> Will be to arrive where we started
> And know the place for the first time.[3]

Notes

CHAPTER 1: EMBRACED BY A FAMILY AND A RIVER, 1934-1952

1. Thomas Moore, *Care of the Soul: A Guide for Cultivating Depth and Sacredness in Everyday Life* (New York: HarperCollins Publishers, 1992), 29.

2. Seward Hiltner, "The Debt of Clinical Pastoral Education to Anton T. Boisen," *The Journal of Pastoral Care* 24, no. 3 (September 1966): 131.

3. Anton T. Boisen, "Period of Beginnings," *The Journal of Pastoral Care* 5, no. 1 (spring 1951): 14-15, quoted in Charles E. Hall, *Head and Heart: The Story of the Clinical Pastoral Education Movement* (Atlanta: Journal of Pastoral Care Publications, Inc., 1992), 7.

4. Edward E. Thornton, *Professional Education for Ministry: A History of Clinical Pastoral Education* (Nashville: Abingdon Press, 1970), 24-31.

5. Allison Stokes, *Ministry After Freud* (New York: The Pilgrim Press, 1985), 69-89.

6. Thornton, *Professional Education for Ministry: A History of Clinical Pastoral Education*, 52-77.

7. Ibid., 58.

8. Charles E. Hall, *Head and Heart: The Story of the Clinical Pastoral Education Movement*, 7.

9. Eudora Welty, "The Nation's Critics Bow Before the Small-Town Tales of a Masterly Southern Writer," *People Weekly*, 29 December 1980, 74.

10. Robert McAfee Brown, "Starting Over: New Beginning Points for Theology," *The Christian Century* 135 (14 May 1980): 547-48.

11. *The Orangeburg (S.C.) Times and Democrat*, 17 March 1952.

12. Thornton, 136-42.

CHAPTER 2: SWIMMING THROUGH COLLEGE, 1952-1956

1. Robert C. Powell, *Fifty Years of Learning through Supervised Encounter with Living Human Documents* (New York: Association for Clinical Pastoral Education, 1975), 20.

2. James B. Ashbrook, *In Human Presence—Hope* (Valley Forge, Pa.: Judson Press, 1971), 89.

3. Brian H. Childs, "A Twenty Year History and Twenty Years in the Making," (Southeast Region of the Association for Clinical Pastoral Education, 1987, photocopy), 20.

CHAPTER 3: PREPARED
BY A STORM, 1956-1960

1. Anton T. Boisen, *The Exploration of the Inner World: A Study of Mental Disorder and Religious Experience* (Chicago: Willet, Clark & Company, 1936), 54.
2. Fosdick to Summers, Boothbay Harbor, Maine, 18 June 1959.
3. Robert Moats Miller, *Harry Emerson Fosdick: Preacher, Pastor, Prophet* (New York: Oxford University Press, 1985), 256.

CHAPTER 4: A MODEL FROM
RHOADUS, 1960-1961

1. Thomas A Summers, *Riding to New Salem: A Short Story* (West Columbia, S.C.: Wentworth Printing Corporation, 1993), 7.
2. Feely to Summers, Atlanta, Ga., 7 December 1960.

CHAPTER 5: MY CPE
BEGINNINGS, 1960-1962

1. Alexander Jasnow, "Psychotherapy Redux," *Voices: The Art and Science of Psychotherapy* 31, no. 4 (winter 1995): 86.
2. Edward Shorter, preface to *A History of Psychiatry: From the Era of the Asylum to the Age of Prozac* (New York: John Wiley & Sons, Inc., 1997).
3. Edward E. Thornton, *Professional Education for Ministry: A History of Pastoral Education* (Nashville: Abingdon Press, 1970), 114.

CHAPTER 6:
MILLEDGEVILLE DAYS, 1962-1965

1. Allison Stokes, *Ministry After Freud* (New York: The Pilgrim Press, 1985), 44.
2. John L. Cedarleaf, "Anton Boisen — A Memoir," *Cura Anamarum* (1992 edition): 63-64.
3. Thomas A. Summers, "Pastoral Certification from a Developmental Perspective," *Journal of Supervision and Training in Ministry* 3 (1980): 73-85.
4. Armen D. Jorjorian, "The Meaning and Character of Supervisory Acts," *The Journal of Pastoral Care* 25, no. 3 (September 1971): 156.

CHAPTER 7: DAYBREAK AT A NEW INSTITUTE, 1965-1970

1. Daniel J. Levinson et al., *The Seasons of a Man's Life* (New York: Ballentine Books, 1978), 71-72.

2. Edward E. Thornton, *Professional Education for Ministry: A History of Clinical Pastoral Education* (Nashville: Abingdon Press, 1970), 76-83.

3. Carroll A. Wise, "Response to an Experience of Severe Stress in the Light of the Ideas of Anton T. Boisen," *AMHC Forum* 32, no. 1 (October 1979), 14.

4. Allison Stokes, *Ministry After Freud* (New York: The Pilgrim Press, 1985), 74-76.

5. Brian H. Childs, "A Twenty Year History and Twenty Years in the Making," (Southeast Region of the Association for Clinical Pastoral Education, 1987, photocopy), 16.

CHAPTER 8: STRETCHING TIMES, 1970-1982

1. Thomas A. Summers, "Story Day in CPE," *Journal of Supervision and Training in Ministry* 4 (1981): 43.

2. Thomas P. Malone, "Encountering and Groups," in *Encounter*, ed. Arthur Burton (San Francisco: Josey-Bass Publishers, Inc., 1969), 130.

3. Myron C. Madden, *The Power to Bless* (Nashville: Abingdon Press, 1970), 142.

4. James Hillman, *Insearch: Psychology and Religion* (New York: Charles Scribner's Sons, 1967), 37.

5. Thomas A. Summers, "The Use of One's Self in Ministry," *AMHC Forum* 29, no. 2 (January 1977): 105-09.

6. Walter Brueggemann, *The Message of the Psalms: A Theological Commentary* (Minneapolis: Augsburg Publishing House, 1984), 19-23.

7. Donna W. Upchurch, "Adult Development — An Oxymoron?" *The Palmetto Family* 12, no. 1 (spring 1994): 1.

8. Mary Catherine Bateson, *Peripheral Visions: Learning Along the Way* (New York: HarperCollins Publishers, 1994), 74.

CHAPTER 9: KELLER REVISITED, 1982-1999

1. Edward E. Thornton, *Professional Education for Ministry: A History of Clinical Pastoral Education* (Nashville: Abingdon Press, 1970), 41-46.

2. Thomas A. Summers, "A Parable: The Land of Long Ago and Its Light," *Underground Report*, no. 25 (1991): 1-4.

3. Thomas A. Summers, "Canaveral Reflections" (Pastoral Care Network for Social Responsibility Newsletter, summer 1987, photocopy).

4. Thomas A. Summers, *Public Testimony*, Subcommittee on Hate-Crime Legislation, South Carolina State Senate, 3 February 1999.

5. Thomas A. Summers, "Walking Toward Freedom: A Pastoral Perspective on the Relationship of Public Marches and Social Justice," in *Pastoral Theology's and Pastoral Psychology's Contributions to Helping Heal a Violent World*, ed. G. Michael Cordner (Surakarta, Indonesia: DABARA Publishers, 1996), 313-27.

6. Thomas A. Summers, "Salvadoran Light on New Year's Eve," (International Pastoral Care Network for Social Responsibility Newsletter, summer 1994, photocopy), 11.

7. Summers to Keith, Columbia, S.C., 21 August 1996.

8. Summers to Kempson, Columbia, S.C., 14 January 1999.

CONCLUSION:
A STORY BIRTHED ON A PORCH

1. Wayne E. Oates, *Life's Detours* (Nashville: The Upper Room, 1974), 57.

2. Fosdick to Summers, Boothbay Harbor, Maine, 18 June 1959.

3. T. S. Eliot, "Four Quartets," in *The Complete Poems and Plays, 1909-1950* (New York: Harcourt, Brace & World, 1962), 145.

Bibliography

BOOKS MENTIONED
IN *HUNKERING DOWN*

Allport, Gordon W. *The Nature of Prejudice*. New York: Addison-Wesley Publishing, Tenth Printing, 1987.

Andreasen, Nancy C. *The Broken Brain: The Biological Revolution in Psychiatry*. New York: Harper and Row, Publishers, 1984.

Arieti, Silvano. *Interpretation of Schizophrenia*. New York: Robert Brunner Publisher, 1955.

Augsburger, David W. *Pastoral Counseling Across Cultures*. Philadelphia: Westminster Press, 1986.

Boisen, Anton T. *Out of the Depths: An Autobiographical Study of Mental Disorder and Religious Experience*. New York: Harper & Brothers, 1960.

____. *Religion in Crisis and Custom: A Sociological and Psychological Study*. New York: Harper, 1945, 1955.

____. *The Exploration of the Inner World: A Study of Mental Disorder and Religious Experience*. New York: Willett, Clark & Company, 1936.

Brown, Judith M. *Ghandi: Prisoner of Hope*. New Haven, CT: Yale University Press, 1989.

Burton, Arthur, ed. *Twelve Therapists: How They Live and Actualize Themselves*. London: Josey-Bass Inc., Publishers, 1972.

Clebsch, William A. and Charles R. Jaekle. *Pastoral Care in Historical Perspective*. Englewood Cliffs, NJ: Prentice-Hall, 1964.

Clinebell, Howard. *Ecotherapy: Healing Ourselves, Healing the Earth*. Minneapolis: Fortress Press, 1996.

____. *Basic Types of Pastoral Counseling*. Nashville: Abingdon Press, 1966.

Cone, James H. *For My People: Black Theology and the Black Church*. Maryknoll, NY: Orbis Books, 1984.

Cox, Harvey. *The Seduction of the Spirit: The Use and Misuse of People's Religion*. New York: Simon and Schuster, 1973.

Eiseley, Loren. *The Immense Journey*. New York: Vintage Books, 1957.

Ekstein, Rudolf and Robert S. Wallerstein. *The Teaching and Learning of Psychotherapy*. New York: Basic Books, Inc., 1958.

Elliott, Richard F. *Falling in Love with Mystery: We Don't Have to Pretend Anymore*. Pittsburgh: Dorrance Publishing Co., Inc., 1998.

Fosdick, Harry Emerson. *The Living of These Days: An Autobiography*. New York: Harper & Brothers, 1956.

Fromm-Reichmann, Frieda. *Principles of Intensive Psychotherapy*. Chicago: The University of Chicago Press, 1950.

Gerkin, Charles V. *An Introduction to Pastoral Care.* Nashville: Abingdon Press, 1997.

_____. *The Living Human Document: Revisioning Pastoral Counseling in a Hermeneutical Mode.* Nashville: Abingdon Press, 1984.

Guntrip, Henry. *Psychotherapy and Religion.* New York: Harper & Brothers, 1957.

Hall, Charles E. *Head and Heart: The Story of the Clinical Pastoral Education Movement.* Kutztown, PA: Journal of Pastoral Care Publications, 1992.

Handly, Robert. *Anxiety & Panic Attacks: Their Cause and Cure.* New York: Ballantine Books, 1985.

Hiltner, Seward. *Pastoral Counseling,* Nashville: Abingdon Press, 1949.

Holifield, E. Brooks. *A History of Pastoral Care in America: From Salvation to Self-Realization.* Nashville: Abingdon Press, 1983.

Horney, Karen. *Neuroses and Human Growth.* New York: W.W. Norton & Company, Inc., 1950.

_____. *Our Inner Conflicts: A Constructive Theory of Neurosis.* New York: W.W. Norton & Company, Inc., 1945.

Howard, Jane. *Please Touch: A Guided Tour of the Human Potential Movement.* New York: McGraw-Hill Book Company, 1970.

Howe, Reuel L. *Man's Need and God's Action.* Greenwich, CT: The Seabury Press, 1953.

_____. *The Miracle of Dialogue.* New York: The Seabury Press, 1966.

James, William. *The Varieties of Religious Experience: A Study in Human Nature.* New York: Modern Library, 1902.

Keleman, Stanley. *Living Your Dying.* New York: Random House, Inc., 1974.

_____. *The Human Ground: Sexuality, Self and Survival.* Palo Alto, CA: Science and Behavior Books, 1975.

Kilpatrick, William. *Identity and Intimacy.* New York: Dell Publishing Co., Inc., 1975.

King, Martin Luther, Jr. *Stride Toward Freedom.* New York: Bantam Books, 1968.

Levinson, Daniel J. *The Seasons of a Man's Life.* New York: Random House, 1978.

Madden, Myron C. *The Power to Bless.* Nashville: Abingdon Press, 1970.

McLendon, James Wm., Jr. *Biography as Theology: How Life Stories Can Remake Today's Theology.* Nashville: Abingdon Press, 1974.

Michalson, Carl. *Faith for Personal Crises.* New York: Charles Scribner's Sons, 1958.

Moore, Thomas. *Care of the Soul: A Guide for Cultivating Depth and Sacredness in Everyday Life.* New York: HarperCollins Publishers, 1992.

Mullahy, Patrick, ed. *The Contributions of Harry Stack Sullivan: A Symposium on Interpersonal Theory in Psychiatry and Social Science.* New York: Science House, 1967.

Nouwen, Henri. *The Wounded Healer: Ministry in Contemporary Society.* Garden City, NY: Doubleday and Company, 1972.

Oates, Wayne E. *The Religious Dimensions of Personality.* New York: Association Press, 1957.

Oglesby, William B. *Biblical Themes for Pastoral Care.* Nashville: Abingdon Press, 1980.

Pattison, E. Mansell. *Pastor and Parish—A Systems Approach.* Philadelphia: Fortress Press, 1977.

Patton, John. *Pastoral Counseling: A Ministry of the Church.* Nashville: Abingdon Press, 1983.

Peck, M. Scott. *The Different Drum: Community-Making and Peace.* New York: Simon & Schuster, 1987.

Powell, Robert C. *Fifty Years of Learning: Through Supervised Encounter with Living Human Documents.* New York: The Association for Clinical Pastoral Education, 1975.

Roberts, David E. *Psychotherapy and a Christian View of Man.* New York: Charles Scribner's Sons, 1950.

Rogers, Carl R. *Client-Centered Therapy: Its Current Practice, Implications, and Theory.* New York: Houghton Mifflin Co., 1951.

Rouch, Mark A. *Competent Ministry: A Guide to Effective Continuing Education.* Nashville: Abingdon Press, 1974.

Sherrill, Lewis J. *The Struggle of the Soul.* New York: Macmillan Co., 1963.

Stokes, Allison. *Ministry After Freud.* New York: The Pilgrim Press, 1985.

Swede, Shirley and Seymore Sheppard Jaffe. *The Panic Attack Recovery Book.* New York: Nal Penguin Inc., 1987.

Thornton, Edward E. *Professional Education for Ministry: A History of Clinical Pastoral Education.* Nashville: Abingdon Press, 1970.

Tillich, Paul. *Systematic Theology.* 2 vols. Chicago: The University of Chicago Press, 1957.

Vitz, Paul C. *Psychology as Religion: The Cult of Self-Worship.* Grand Rapids, MI: William B. Eerdmans Publishing Co., 1977.

Williams, Daniel Day. *God's Grace and Man's Hope.* New York: Harper & Brothers, 1949.

Citation of Sources
for Photographs

———∽∞∽———

The following persons provided immeasurable help in securing photographs for the book: Joan Clemens, the Curator of the Archives and Manuscript Department at the Pitts Theology Library of Emory University in Atlanta; Tanya Elder, the Archivist of the Riverside Church Archives in New York City; and Milton Snyder with the Central State Hospital Museum in Milledgeville, Georgia. Appreciation also is felt for the services of Susan Craft of the South Carolina Department of Mental Health, Dean Livingston of *The Orangeburg (S.C.) Times and Democrat*, and Josephine Schrader with the Association of Professional Chaplains.

The acronyms, or codes, listed below represent the citation of the sources for many of the photographs that are used in *Hunkering Down*.

ACPER   Box 230, Association for Clinical Pastoral Education Records, RG 001, Archives and Manuscript Department, Pitts Theology Library, Emory University

ACPER - SRR   Box 5, Association for Clinical Pastoral Education— Southeast Region Records, RG 024, Archives and Manuscript Department, Pitts Theology Library, Emory University

APC   Association of Professional Chaplains

CSHM   Central State Hospital Museum

RCA   Copyright Robert Lawrence Pastner
Used by permission of the Riverside Church Archives, New York

SCDMH   South Carolina Department of Mental Health

WC   Wofford College

Index